ANOREXIA –

A STRANGER IN THE FAMILY

Katie Metcalfe

Published by Accent Press Ltd – 2006
ISBN 1905170351

Copyright © Katie Metcalfe 2006

The right of Katie Metcalfe to be identified as the author of this work has been asserted by her in accordance with the Copyright, Designs and Patents Act 1988.

Printed and bound in the UK by
Cox & Wyman, Reading

Cover Design by James Bridle

The publisher acknowledges the financial support
of the Welsh Books Council

Dedicated to my parents and inspiration in life and beyond, Julian Atterton.

Thanks to all my family. Without you the pen would have never touched paper for this book to happen.
Thank you Hazel and all at Accent Press for making the dream come alive.

Foreword

The reason I have written this book is to let other people know the truths about a possibly fatal disease. To help people discover what developing, living with and recovering from anorexia nervosa is really like. Most importantly, through my writing I aspire to guide people to understand how to deal with it.

The book is divided into three parts: the first part is my story, my battle, which I have tried to tell as truthfully as possible, even though aspects of my suffering are still very painful for me, even now.

The second part of the book is given over to my family – I wanted my loved ones to have an opportunity to express how they feel about my anorexia, which became an unwanted part of our family, and how they feel it has affected them as individuals and us all as a functioning family unit.

The third part of the book gives some helpful (I hope!) advice to people whose lives are being affected by this disease, this comes partly from my own experience and partly from my research.

My family, as well as many others who have suffered in similar ways, feel anorexia is a demon and that it is the voice of the demon that anorexics find themselves listening to.

I hope my story is helpful to you and will open new doorways in your mind about the real truth behind a disease that creates a stranger in the family.

Katie Metcalfe

Part I

Katie's Story

January 2001 was the time I decided I wanted to be more fit, healthier and slimmer. Just a stupid New Year's resolution made at the naïve age of fourteen – a time when I should have been rebelling against my parents, the school system and the law, not against my own body, mind and soul. I had no idea that a good intention, listed alongside 'do more to help the environment' and 'snog someone I fancy', would end with me in hospital and that it would change the lives of my family and myself.

Forever.

Chapter I

Young, Yearning For Perfection

My appearance and weight had never really been a big issue or concern to me before I turned fourteen. Of course, I did notice that I was bigger in the thigh and stomach region than most of my friends at school (or so I thought). I also acknowledged that I couldn't run as fast as my friends or be as good as them at sport. I didn't feel as attractive to the boys in the class as they were, not to mention the male species out of school. I felt like the 'tag on', the girl who 'wasn't quite right'. I wasn't pretty enough and didn't have quite the right figure. I tried hard not to let it get to me, but sometimes it was difficult, especially as I got older and the pressures to not only look good, but look amazing and to be popular too, increased immeasurably.

I couldn't jump the high hurdles in gym class without almost breaking a bone, or perform the perfect handstand without flashing my underwear. I was unable to shoot a pot shot in basketball without it being a fluke, or run for a mile without needing to stop and regain my breath. I would get sniggered at because everybody else could do everything so easily. My girlfriends would talk and brag about how little they weighed and what size trousers and tops they wore, patting their tummies and saying, "Look at this fat, isn't it horrible? No wonder I weigh so much." I wouldn't dare say how heavy I was; I wanted to avoid being humiliated. Little did I know that I was actually in the acceptable weight range for my age and height, and my friends were underdeveloped for their age.

The time I decided to do something about my weight, appearance and popularity was just after I turned fourteen, and was at a difficult period in my life anyway. The teacher I had had from the age of seven was leaving the school to go and live and teach in Germany, and all my school friends were leaving to go to other schools, a lot of them at boarding schools all over the country. I wouldn't be able to see them often. There was still another year left at school, and I was determined to see it through. I didn't want to change schools although I knew it wouldn't be easy. Unfortunately for me, I didn't get on with the three boys that I would spend the year with. I decided there was nothing I could do, other than to make the best of a bad situation. At least I'd got what I wanted, to finish my education at Botton Steiner School, even if it meant being the only girl in a class of four.

Throughout our year, for one reason or another, we had five different teachers, which didn't help the situation or our education. My classmates thought that it was their duty and God-given right to annoy and upset me. They constantly gave me a hard, often unbearable, time. They would ransack and tip over my desk, hit me for no reason, and call me obscene names such as 'whore', 'slag', 'fat cow' and others that I won't repeat as I cringe to think of them. They tried to make my life at school a living hell every single day and I used to wake up in the morning and dread getting up to face another day with them. My parents said I should leave school and take up my education elsewhere, but I didn't want to and felt that if I did the boys would have won. I also believe the thought of starting at another school scared me more than being with the boys. I figured that if there were three boys who could make me feel terrible inside as a person, how many would there be at a school of hundreds, possibly even thousands, who would be the same and possibly worse?

Over time, I became increasingly paranoid, and I always tried to make everything I did in life perfect. I thought that if I lost a bit of weight, got fitter and slimmer, then maybe the boys would be more pleasant to me, and not so horrible. But that didn't happen. The situation got no better. To tell the truth, changing my appearance made it much worse.

On the 1st January I weighed myself, I weighed eight and a half stone, and my height was 1.65m (5ft 5in). To me, that was far too heavy for my height and age. I made the decision that it would be wise to start cutting certain things out of my diet. I decided to construct some sort of a meal plan, which dictated the things I could and could not have. This would help me to lose the weight, which I figured was making my life a misery.

The first food I cut out was bread. I'd watched lots of brainwashing television programmes and read many magazine articles about how cutting carbohydrates out of your diet can help you to lose weight. I also had it in my head that bread contained masses of calories and fats and was an ultimate no-no if I wanted to diet. Cutting out bread was quite a hard thing to do, as it meant no toast, sandwiches or pizza: three things that I loved and enjoyed to eat. I replaced the bread with low fat, low calorie crackers, such as Ryvita and rice cakes.

After a short time, my family noticed that I was refusing to eat cheese on toast, fried egg sandwiches, and my favourite food of all – pizza, as well as various other things that I enjoyed. They started to question me. I would answer by saying that it was a New Year's resolution, and I wanted to see how long I could last (which was sort of true, in a way). They decided to leave it at that. I guess that my parents didn't think I would last very long and that I'd be eating normally within days.

Soon after I cut bread out of my diet, I also cut out sweets, all fried foods, chocolate, crisps and, gradually over time, simple things like butter, sugar, whole milk and normal cheeses. I refused to have a pudding after a meal and snacks after school became a thing of the past. It was hard at first not to eat these things, but it did make it easier when, each time I weighed myself, I found I was losing weight. I started adding more exercise to my daily plan and, in January, began going for long walks, from three to sometimes six miles, two or three times a week, and playing basketball in break-time at school. I ignored the sarcastic comments from the boys and other students. I was determined to stay focused and lose the weight and horrible appearance that was keeping me from being accepted and liked.

After a few weeks, I made progress with my exercise, going jogging with my mum regularly, playing football after school for a few hours, as well as basketball. I admit that I became totally obsessed with exercise and burning calories; a sensible one or two days a week of physical activity ended as being an obsessive seven. After a while of jogging with my mum, I decided to stop, because I got terrible stinging pains in my knees, as though pins were being jammed into the bone. I also thought people passing by in cars might laugh at my flabby bum, wobbling thighs, sweaty face and my feeble attempts to do justice to the word 'jog'. So I took up going on bike rides instead, by myself.

It became a regime that I couldn't break. If I missed out a day of my routine, I'd add it to my next day's exercise, doubling the amount. I would exercise in any weather too. Sometimes it would be raining so hard I'd be soaked to the skin within minutes of stepping out of the house, but I didn't care, as long as my exercise was done, that was all that mattered. I even rode my bike when there was six inches of snow on the pathway, and my hands were so cold, beneath two pairs of gloves, that I struggled to grip the handlebars. My body would regularly scream at me to stop, my legs aching in protest and my eyes streaming from the pain that jolted through my chest as I pushed myself further and further along unknown pathways and deserted roads, bumpy forest tracks and grassy slopes.

As time went by, I used knowledge acquired from science lessons at school to my advantage in losing weight. I would wear thin clothing, aware that the less clothing you wore when out in the cold, the more calories you burned. Naturally, this act of stupidity took a toll on my health and I started to suffer from terrible coughs and colds, which of course would be ignored. I had more important things to be thinking about than a dripping nose and throbbing head.

Life at school was no better, and to make things worse our house in Margrove Park was up for sale. I didn't want to move from the beautiful, peaceful countryside, which I loved, to the town. Although I had no friends where we lived, I loved the place, I loved the quiet, I loved our house, and I really didn't want to leave.

A few months had passed since I had started my new 'routine' and 'meal plan', and my dad was starting to get more and more suspicious of me because I was refusing to eat things like curry, chips, pasta and rice or anything I thought had butter on it, or had been fried in oil. He began asking question about why I'd stopped eating the things that I'd been happily eating a few months before. I just told him to forget it and to leave me alone. I knew what I was doing, and I didn't want him to interfere with my new daily life plan.

Chapter 2

The Friend Inside My Head

By March, I had become totally obsessed with food. Food, exercise and my weight were my life and all that I could think about. At meal times, I would eat really slowly, savouring each mouthful, often taking minutes to consume something that should take mere seconds. It was March when I was adopted by my new best friend: a trusted voice in my head, which told me what I could and couldn't eat and what to do. It was impossible to distinguish if the voice was male or female, but it had its various tones: soft and reassuring if I listened to it, firm when I was struggling, and vicious if I stepped over the line of its authority. It would tell me to eat my food slowly, as it would be a long time until I could have any more. I listened religiously, confident that it was my guide to achieving everything that I desired. Moreover, if I listened to it, then its tone would remain caring and soft, just as the voice of a best friend should.

I've always loved cooking, ever since I was a little girl, but now I was trying to do it at every opportunity, but rarely eating anything I prepared. I would get cookery books from the library and look at them for hours at a time, often writing out the recipes, and trying to think of ways I could make them low-fat.

I was totally obsessed with calories and fat in both food and drink. Whenever I picked up a packet of biscuits or a bottle of juice, I had to turn it over and look at the calorie and fat content and that would determine whether I was allowed to have it. The voice told me to look at the content and study it, and if it was too high in 'the bad stuff' then I wasn't allowed to have it, and I had to put it back without question. If I was ever queried by anyone about my 'packet scanning' I would casually claim that I was simply searching out the additives and E numbers, which seemed more of a natural thing for a vegetarian girl of my age to be doing.

As I ate less, exercised more and continued to lose weight, the voice grew stronger. Eventually, it took over my mind. For example, if I thought I'd eaten too much at lunchtime, and afterwards I went on a bike ride, after my usual six miles the voice would scream at me to do another mile because I'd eaten more than I should have. It told me that if I didn't do that extra mile, I would get even fatter than I already was, and my life would become all the more terrible. I believed this and obeyed it. No matter how tired I felt, or how bad the weather was, or how much my joints ached or how intense the pain in my head was, I did that extra mile to ensure I didn't get fat.

The more weight I lost, the more commanding and controlling the voice sounded in my mind. But I felt that I was in control and that the voice was just a firm, strict friend who was helping me to lose more weight and to achieve everything I wanted. I felt that at last I had control of one thing in my life.

In April, I hit an all-time low. I became incredibly miserable and depressed, and started bursting into tears for no apparent reason. Big arguments with my parents started, and would occur almost every day. We would argue about food, school and moving house among other family issues. Mum and I both noticed I hadn't had a period since January. Mum said it was because I was losing weight, and that I might now be underweight. She made me an appointment to go and see my GP, Dr Wilson. Naturally I disagreed and claimed it was simply my teenage hormones going slightly haywire.

When I went for my first appointment, I was weighed, but I was not underweight according to the medical scales. Dr Wilson thought my periods were just adjusting to the monthly cycle, even though I had been having regular monthly periods for two years! Dr Wilson said that I wasn't overweight, but was OK for my age and height, and that I shouldn't want to lose weight (I thought the complete opposite), but it was clear that I had some problems in my life.

As the weeks went on, my depression worsened and visits to Dr Wilson became more frequent. At my appointments she weighed me, and then we would talk about how things were going. We'd talk about most things, school, life at home, and my relationship with food and exercise. I'd tell her how I wanted to go back to being a small child, when life was simple and every day was happy and a new adventure. She replied bluntly that of course that wasn't possible, and I had to face up to reality and grow up. Often, I'd just sit there, not say a word and just cry for the hour. I'd let her do all the talking, but not take in anything that she said.

After the first visit, I found each time that I'd lost more weight; but I was still convinced that I didn't have a problem. The only thing I thought was wrong with me was that I was having a hard time at school with the boys, and that I was weak and pathetic for not being able to cope with it. And, of course, that I was far too fat.

When Dr Wilson told Mum I had lost weight, Mum tried her hardest to get me to eat more. But I refused. I became very secretive and sneaky, in the hope that I would be able to deceive Dr Wilson and my parents. I started to wear heavier clothes to my appointments and all my jewellery, even bracelets around my ankles. Then when I stepped on the scales, it would appear as though I hadn't lost weight. It worked for a while, but I was eventually found out and asked to take off my clothes and jewellery before I stepped on the scales. (I think it was my gaunt face and blue-tinged hands and nails which gave the game away.)

Seeing Dr Wilson helped get some things that were bothering me off my chest, but it didn't solve my problems. It made the situation at school even worse because the boys would question me about having to go home early, or missing lessons. When I told them why I had to go early, they would laugh and tease me. The teachers at school appeared to do nothing about the bullying. I think that some of the teachers thought that I exaggerated how bad it actually was. Even when the boys were told off, they didn't care and the teachers would be told to "fuck off" or "get lost".

I presume some of the teachers were afraid of my classmates because the boys could do nothing wrong, although the teachers suffered from constant verbal abuse. A blind eye was turned to the effects that the nastiness was having on me, as it was too complicated an issue. As the year progressed, so did the bullying and the teachers' denial of it. And so, anorexia's grip tightened around my life.

Chapter 3

A Lesson In Obsession

Every day, my diet was becoming all the more restricted. Instead of having six rice cakes at tea, I went down to four, and the spreads I put on them were also being reduced. I started to eat cereal at breakfast with the fewest calories I could find – the types dieters were recommended to have by doctors. Normally, I'd have the cereal drenched in milk, but the milk also became less, until I wasn't using any at all, and would eat my cereal dry. Doing this hurt my mouth, and soon my gums became sore and bled. I'd wet my bowl with water so that it looked as though I'd had milk with it. I hid my food too. I'd hide it in my room, wrapped in tissue paper and plastic bags, until the coast was clear to dispose of it. I wouldn't do it always, just when I felt I had to. I was caught a few times by my mum trying to throw away food, but I always talked my way out of it by saying something like I'd dropped it on the floor, or I didn't like it. I hated hiding my food and lying to my parents, and I guess I was lying to myself too. But, I'd be convinced by the voice, when I got away with hiding food, that I had done a good job. It was the anorexia that was in control. Not me.

My exercising became scarily obsessive, and I was doing more than ever before. Cold weather no longer affected me in the slight way it used to, it now bit hard into my bones, but I didn't believe that my weight loss was the cause. I was adamant, as was the voice, that I was still fat. Whenever I looked in a mirror, I saw two black dots driven into a mound of quivering blubber staring back at me. Before long my hair began to come out in clumps when it was brushed. In the morning, my pillow would be covered in hair. The long, thick, beautiful hair that had always been one of my best features was rapidly thinning. My nails and lips were blue when I went outside, although it was May, and my nails were becoming brittle and flaky and snapped at the slightest touch. I found all this devastating, but refused to believe it was a result of my dieting. My mum noticed that a downy blonde hair had appeared on my arms and back (lanugo, one of the common signs of anorexia). I was

11

showing classic symptoms of anorexia, but still refused to believe that I had it. So, I stuck to my crazy diet and exercise routine. I kept my appointments with Dr Wilson, but nothing she said convinced me that I was suffering with an eating disorder and becoming dangerously thin. Already my mind was warped by anorexia's main wicked way: denial.

In July, I came to the end of my year eight, and the end of my time at Botton School. On the last day, I remember walking into the classroom and going to my desk. All three boys' eyes were on me as I walked across the room, but I couldn't see what they were looking at, so thought they were being their usual pig-ignorant selves. When I sat down and tried to open the lid of my desk I found that it had been glued shut and I couldn't open it. The boys were in hysterics as they watched me struggle to get it open. When I finally succeeded, I found all the pictures I'd had stuck on the inside of Marilyn Manson, Metallica, Nirvana and vampires had been ripped out. All I could do was ask myself, why? What had I done to deserve this treatment? Why had they ruined the pictures of the bands I doted on and the culture I was part of? I felt the tears sting my eyes as I got up and went to tell the teacher what they had done. But she actually found it amusing, and didn't think it was such a big deal. And she LAUGHED along with the boys, and told me not to make such a fuss. It was meant to be a joke, and pictures could easily be replaced. This was the same teacher who, when told that I had an eating disorder, told me that it was better to be slightly underweight than slightly overweight. And I believed her. This was also the same teacher that I'd felt incredibly close to only a year before. She was someone I could open my heart to and tell everything to. She'd changed and now, to me, was a stranger. Slowly, all the people around me were changing into strangers.

I was glad to leave that class, but I was still very fond of Botton School, and didn't want to go because it really was a lovely area, and I think I was blessed to have had the opportunity to go to a school in such an idyllic place for so many years, even if the last year there had been a living hell.

The long summer holidays now stretched before me, which meant I could focus all my attention on losing weight, as I didn't have any schoolwork to worry about. So nearly every waking minute of my day was spent exercising, and I was eating less with each day that passed.

In August, we went on a family holiday to Tenerife for two weeks. This was the first holiday we'd had in five years and the first time we had ever travelled abroad together. We went all inclusive, which meant that all our meals and drinks were included in the holiday package. I was nervous about how well I would manage to stick to my strict eating plan and exercise routine, as I couldn't bring my rice cakes and bike along with me to Tenerife. I was also very excited about going abroad with my family for the first time, and determined to have a good time, as well as sticking to my routines.

Before we went on holiday, Mum and I went shopping for clothes to take with us. I was ecstatic that I had to buy clothes in sizes ten, eight and even smaller, and the fact that I had to use safety pins to hold up my new trousers and tops thrilled me all the more and made me feel as though I had achieved something fantastic. It was a wonderful feeling at the time, knowing that half a year ago, there was no way that I would have fitted into those size clothes. And so, with my new clothes, we set off to Tenerife.

But, our holiday didn't get off to a very good start. I was in the washroom at the airport when we had to hurry because our plane was due to depart in five minutes. All the passengers were ready (except me). So I hurried, and quickly dried my hands. It was only when we were running to board the plane that I realised that my thumb ring was missing. I stopped short and flipped. I begged Mum to take me back to the toilets to go and find it, but we had no time, as Mum and I were the only passengers not on the plane. I was in tears as the plane took off, as the ring had belonged to my Nanna, and it was very old and incredibly valuable to me. I never took it off. I couldn't work out how it had come off, as my fingers weren't *that* thin for it to *slip* off. So I decided that it must have come off when I was hurriedly drying my hands. My mum tried to persuade me that it was because my fingers *were* too thin, but I refused to believe her. My thumbs were the size of pork sausages; it simply wasn't possible for the ring to come off without being pulled by force. The voice naturally reassured me that Mum was wrong and that my perception of why it had come off was accurate.

The loss of my most loved piece of jewellery and the confirmation of my still 'pork fat' fingers, meant that I was miserable, irritable and horrible to be around for the entire flight there, and for days after we had arrived.

On the first morning in Tenerife, when we went downstairs to get our breakfast, I was amazed at the wide range of foods there was to choose from. I wandered around the serving area with my plate, past all the fried foods and the array of continental breads and cakes, trying to decide what to have, but knowing that I wouldn't have any of the things that I really wanted. I knew the voice simply wouldn't let me. In the end, I settled for muesli. It wasn't very nice, consisting of raw oats and hardly any fruit, but I knew it was the food with the least calories in, I didn't fill my small bowl up though, just in case people thought that I was a greedy pig. I did get a few strange looks from other guests as I walked back to our table with my little bowl and glass of orange juice; it didn't occur to me that it was because of the tiny amount I had and how thin I looked. I automatically assumed they were looking because I had far too much food on my plate.

After breakfast, we went swimming, to my relief, as I could burn off the calories that I'd eaten at breakfast. I was very, very paranoid about people seeing me in my swimming costume, because of my thunder thighs and elephant bum, so I wore a towel around my waist until I had to take it off to get in the pool. (If I could have, I would have gone in with it still around my waist.) Once in the pool, I swam for ages, up and down and up and down, until my legs and arms ached so badly that I had to stop and get out. I'd wait in the pool, until I was sure that no one was watching, leap out, and quickly wrap my towel around my bum and legs before anyone had the chance to see the disgustingly foul sight that was my body. It was like that every day of the holiday and my attitude towards my body in a swimsuit didn't improve in the slightest; it became far worse.

14

My mum noticed that my lips and nails turned blue when I got out of the water. So she ordered me not to swim for so long. But did I listen? Did I hell! The exercise was burning off calories and unwanted fat. Of course, I wouldn't do less! I felt, and the voice assured me, that I was putting far too many calories into my body anyway.

Another way I burned off fat was by *always* using the stairs, taking them two at a time, even if my body protested, and never taking the lift to our rooms on the sixth floor. My legs soon felt the pressure I was putting them under, and I would often fall asleep crying into my pillow because of the constant pain. Little did I know that by now the muscles in my legs were starting to digest themselvesThe voice reassured me that the pains were a sign of strength. Signs that I was progressing with my weight loss. The pains were something that all people who aimed to lose weight felt. Of course, I really believed this, and my legs continued to suffer the abuse I forced upon them.

Every meal time, Mum, Dad and I would argue over portion sizes, and they'd moan at me that I wasn't eating a variety of foods. I do remember, on the first night we were there, I'd done masses of swimming during the day, and I had satisfied the voice's 'appetite for exercise', so I decided, what the hell! I'll treat myself! So at dinner, after a small meal of salad and pasta, I went to get some pudding with my sister, Penny. I said I would, if she would. There were all the things that I adore, so Penny and I decided that we would each get a few different samples and share them. There was rice pudding, custard, chocolate tart and apple cake. So we both took a little of what we fancied, and went back to our table to share our puddings. I remember Mum and Dad's faces when they saw what we were doing. They were beaming with pride, relief and sheer joy. I automatically thought they were thinking I was a fat pig and laughing at me for being so greedy. I'd already eaten pasta, and salad, what right did I have to get anything else? What right did I have to stuff my face with treats? So, with these thoughts fixed in my mind, I stopped eating, left what remained of my pudding, which was almost everything I'd taken to begin with, and excused myself. I sprinted up the six flights of stairs to make myself sick. Kneeling before the toilet bowl, my hair messily tied back, I pushed two fingers down my throat, so forcefully that I scraped the skin. With the faint smell of urine and bleach it wasn't hard to vomit up the small amount I'd eaten. Yet I heaved again and again, until I could see small specks of blood among the regurgitated food and my stomach felt sore and empty of the foulness of food.

I shakily made it to my feet and splashed my face over and over with freezing water until it was numb with cold. Feeling less faint, I inspected the damage. I stared down into the toilet bowl, disgusted yet thrilled at the same time. I flushed the badness away, and smiled as it swirled down the drain. Swirling away with it was my interior pain. I observed the floor, and was impressed to find that not a trace of vomit had found its way there. I was an expert already on only my first attempt. The smell was vile, but was soon replaced by cheap perfume. Knowing now how easy it was to rid myself of the impurities of food, I was determined, as was the voice, to continue to use the skill whenever I needed to. No one would ever find out about it, and how could they? It wasn't as if Mum, Dad or my doctor could inspect my stomach regularly. How would they know if it contained food or not? Again, the voice in my head had ordered me to do something, and again I had obeyed.

It was nearly always my dad who started the arguments at meal times, saying that my portion "wouldn't feed a sparrow", and he would march me over to get more food. (But I know now that it was only concern for me that made him do it, and the fact we had paid over three thousand pounds for our holiday and he didn't want to sit back and watch me eat minuscule amounts of food.) But when he'd comment on my portion sizes and attempt to make me eat more, I assumed he was trying to make me fat, and there was no way I would let that happen after the hard work that I had put into losing weight.

All in all, it was an enjoyable holiday, minus the lost ring, and the arguments about food. I had successfully managed to stick to my routine and exercise every day, and keep to my meal plan, even eating less some days, which I thought was an enormous achievement. As did the voice. It kept reminding me, to ensure that I wouldn't lose track, to ensure that I would continue to abide by its rules to reach the state of perfection it had promised.

Chapter 4

Horrendous Heartache And Hospital Hell

We were home from Tenerife for one day before I started at my new school, Billingham Campus. (The school term had already begun while we were away.) I was quite excited about starting at a new school, but also was like a small child on its very first day at school. I didn't have a clue what the people there would think of me. I thought they might all think I was fat and stupid. But when I arrived, none of the boys called me fat or overweight, as I thought they would, and neither did the girls. People did notice my alternative appearance, a Nirvana hooded top, black nail varnish, black hair and silver jewellery, which did make me stand out. People who noticed shouted, to my dismay, 'mosher' and despite being the new girl, known for being quiet, I immediately corrected them, stating that I was a 'Goth' and not a 'mosher'. So I was called 'Goth girl' instead, which I didn't mind, because at least that was correct. I didn't take the 'mosher' comment as a form of bullying. It was nothing at all compared to what I had to endure a few months previously. I just felt it was important to be addressed as something that I actually am.

I managed to make quite a few friends in the first days that I was there, both boys and girls, alternative and not. It did seem to me, though, that being alternative was the 'in thing' to be at school which helped me and made me seem likeable to most of the students. A lot of the girls in my year asked me how I stayed so thin. I laughed and said 'I'm not thin!' Then just shrugged and said that I tried to eat healthily and exercise often. To me, I wasn't thin by any stretch of the imagination. I was still a blubbering blob. But I was thrilled that some people had noticed the effort I was putting into losing weight.

When lunchtime came around, I'd sit by myself with a packed lunch. All my new friends went home for their lunch, but that wasn't possible for me, as I still lived twenty miles away in Margrove Park. I'd pack my lunch at home in the morning myself. At first, it consisted of two thick rice cakes with peanut butter, two Ryvitas with Philadelphia Light cheese, and two Ryvitas with jam, and one or two pieces of fruit. Soon, it only consisted of two Ryvitas with a scraping of cottage cheese and a piece of fruit. (I stopped using peanut butter and jam, as the fat and calorie content was far too high.) Most of it would end up in the bin. I'd often get strange looks from other students as I sat there with my crackers and fruit; they had their ham sandwiches, crisps and chocolate. I remember the dinner hall was really cold because the doors were constantly left open, and it wasn't heated. You would have to take off your coat, even if you didn't have a jumper, and my teeth would physically chatter, because I'd only be wearing a school shirt. I requested a number of times to be allowed to put on my coat (despite the voice's demands not to – one of the rare times I ignored it) but my request was denied. I was told that it couldn't be one rule for one, and another for everyone else. I accepted this, and punished myself for being so selfish by taking another item out of my diet, and riding for an extra mile.

My concentration was getting worse by the day. I couldn't focus on my schoolwork because food dominated my thoughts all the time. I'd always be the last one to leave the classroom because I'd have to make my work perfect, and I wouldn't leave until it was.

To my absolute amazement I was put in the top set for every subject, including maths, which I hated the most. Maths was also the subject I found the hardest to concentrate on, and often I couldn't understand anything the teacher was explaining or telling us to do because the voice would be constantly nagging in my ear, telling me to swing my legs that little bit faster, and twiddle my fingers until they turned numb.

I'd often end up in tears, sobbing into my desk. I felt such a failure at not being able to understand. I wouldn't believe it was because my body and brain were starving and begging to be nourished. I didn't believe that being underweight affected the brain's ability to function. Well, I didn't believe that it affected *my* brain because I was certain I wasn't underweight anyway. Of course, it would have an effect on the starving children in Africa and girls with *real* eating problems and *real* mental illnesses. But me, I was having problems because I was thick, pathetic and useless and would continue to be so until I was as light as air.

After school, I had the same routine, day after day after day. I would get home after a silent hour and a half car drive with my parents. During the trip they'd ask me about school and how I was feeling, in a desperate attempt to get me to talk. But I would only murmur in response, too wrapped up in my own world, too preoccupied with arranging my routine in my mind. I knew that nothing would change unless the voice demanded that I altered it in some way. I would do at least two hours of homework, and then go for a six-mile bike ride (maybe more if I thought I had over-eaten that day), then I would have a tiny, healthy dinner (usually pasta and salad). This was a tiny portion by Mum's standards but huge to me. Dinner was followed by yet more homework, often till as late as eleven-thirty. All my homework had to be perfect; no letter wrongly shaped, no paragraph the wrong length, no number in a maths equation wrongly formed, before I'd finally allow myself to fall exhausted, into bed.

My concentration deteriorated as I continued to eat less and exercise more. A few weeks after starting at Billingham Campus, I began getting sharp, stinging pains in my heart and chest area during the day, which worsened when I exercised. I ignored them, and never mentioned them to anyone, for fear of being an inconvenience. (What a big mistake that was.) Generally they would fade away, but one evening, after coming back from an eight-mile bike ride in the pouring rain, the chest pains were far worse than before. I was doubled over in agony and could barely breathe. When I finally made my way through the garden in the pitch darkness I stumbled into the house, my hands clutching my chest. Mum had prepared my tea: a mushroom burger, peas, and boiled potatoes. I told her immediately, through sobs, about the pains in my chest but she thought that I was faking so that I wouldn't have to eat. I was made to sit at the table, and make at least an attempt to eat some of the meal.

"Eat it," my sister snapped. "Mum made it for you. Eat it."

"Yeah," my brothers cried in unison while smothering their own food in tomato ketchup and banging their tiny fists on the table in protest at my not eating. "You have to!"

I felt trapped and cornered with nowhere to run to or hide. With Mum hovering over the table, and my siblings glaring at me with their wide eyes over their forks full of food, I took one bite of the burger. One hand still clutching my chest, in some hope that the harder I clutched and wished, the more likely the pain would fade. I nearly choked on that first mouthful and spat it back out again. I refused to take another bite. Tears were streaming down my face as I tried to convince Mum that I was not faking the pain. It was then that she realised something really was wrong. She told my siblings to shut up with their comments and made me go straight to bed. She made me an appointment to go and see Dr Wilson first thing in the morning and prepared a hot water bottle and a mug of hot chocolate in the hope that I'd drink it. She spent hours stroking my hair and telling me that everything would be just fine while I continued to plead silently with the voice to make the pain stop. I felt as if I was five years old again, when, at times when I was feeling ill, my mum's attention, a hot water bottle and a drink would make things much better.

That was not the reality now. The illness would take a lot more than a mother's attention to beat it. The discomfort remained throughout the night, and at some points became so painful that I longed for my life to be cut short just so that I no longer had to endure it. I watched my mum's face contort with distress. Sleep never came that night, and, as my tired eyes saw the sun rise into the sky, I felt a sinking feeling in my empty, groaning stomach that the discomfort in my chest would be something more than just temporary pain.

After a failed breakfast, I went for my appointment and Mum and I explained about the pain, which had calmed down slightly. The doctor took my pulse and blood pressure, and found they were both dangerously low. My heart was under enormous stress. She explained that if I had not told Mum, and had just ignored the pains, it was likely that I would have had a heart attack and quite possibly died! That really shocked and scared me. I thought that it was only old people who had heart attacks, not girls my age. She told me that it wasn't safe to be walking around as I was, as I was vulnerable to having further serious chest pains and heart failure. She phoned South Cleveland Hospital there and then and told them that I needed a bed immediately. I was very anxious about going into hospital, as it would mean missing my exercise routine and being where everything was different again.

Mum and I went home to collect some overnight clothes and toiletries, and we didn't speak a word to each other in the car. Only cried silent tears. Mum would reach for my hand but I'd purposefully put mine out of reach. For some reason, I didn't want her touching me at that point. I didn't want her anywhere near me. I didn't want anyone at all, other than the voice. I wanted the voice to reassure me again and again that everything would be OK, that I would be able to exercise in the hospital, that I wouldn't be force-fed and that I wouldn't grow into an obese whale. It had already told me that the pains in my chest were normal, nothing to worry about. It told me that I should be happy that I was feeling them, as they were a sign of strength.

Mum and I drove to the hospital; I couldn't believe what was happening to me. I was confused and angry with myself for making such a big fuss. Of course, I wouldn't have had a heart attack. There was no reason for it to happen to me.

When we arrived, I had lots of tests for all kinds of things, most I didn't know the reason for, and eventually I was put into a bed and had heart monitors attached. They bleeped very loudly whenever I moved a muscle. It pronounced me dead about five times during the first few hours of my stay!

The first night was terrifying. I was petrified about what would happen to me, how long I would have to stay there and not be able to do my exercise routine. Worst of all, what if they forced food down my throat and made me fat again? Mum stayed with me in the hospital and Dad stayed at home with my brothers and sister. I didn't know at the time, but my siblings were convinced that I was dying and that they would never see me again. Hearing this confession from them, years later, proved their true feelings for me. Their true feelings of love and concern: two things, which I was sure had long since died.

I was in hospital under observation for two nights and three days. In that time, no one forced any food down me, but I was encouraged to eat. I tried my hardest to ignore the voice and to eat something as I wanted to go home. The voice snapped at me whenever I went against its wishes, claiming I no longer cared about my weight and image. Claiming that I would abandon its friendship soon, and become the overweight, hideous creature that I had been before it had come into my life. I did eat a little, but only because I made a promise to the voice that I would exercise the calories and fat off as soon as I got home. I didn't want food inside my body any more than it did.

I was allowed to go home when the pains in my chest had fully subsided, and the doctors treating me said there was nothing else they could do to help. They couldn't persuade me to eat more than half an apple. They couldn't stop my exercise attempts or climb inside my mind and pluck out my new 'best friend'. They couldn't approach anorexia and rip it from me. At this time in my life nobody could help. I was firmly trapped in anorexia's web. While lying in hospital, in a state half in, half out of sleep, I heard the nurse say to my mum, "Look at her – so peaceful. She looks just like an angel." I gave no indication that I had heard and kept my eyes closed. One thought flashed in my mind as I lay there. How could I be an angel? I was still a fat freak, gaining weight every second. I was an ugly nobody. I was nowhere near being as light as air, as that's what angels needed to be – light as air to fly.

The morning after I was discharged, I waited until the house was empty, siblings at school and Mum and Dad at work. No one could stop me from doing my exercise. I walked about three miles (walked because Dad had taken the shed key to stop me getting to my bike) although my legs ached with each step. I carried on, determined to burn off the fat and calories that I had consumed during my stay in hospital. The voice constantly congratulated me on my firm-mindedness and kept up my will to continue. I didn't notice the beauty of the countryside that before had left me awestruck. I didn't notice the graceful swans that glided on the smooth lake that I passed, making tiny ripples every now and then. I ignored the wild flowers swaying in the scented, light, cool breeze and the placid cows swishing their tails, chewing the cud and watching the world pass them by without a care in the world. None of that mattered to me any more. Satisfying the voice's demands was the *only* thing that mattered. Nature had always been my world, my escape from my family and the trials and tribulations of life. But to me now, it was nothing.

I returned home, moments before my mum arrived to check on me. I'd forgotten all about her returning, as exercise had been my focus from the moment my eyes opened. Mum never questioned my outside clothing, the gloves, hat and scarf. She had come to accept it as 'the norm'. She failed to question my sallow cheeks and purple lips too. But those were also aspects of me that she had come to accept.

I went to stay with my grandparents, for a few days' break. (I wasn't allowed to go back to school, as my heart was still very weak.) I promised my parents that I would try really hard to eat, and ignore the voice in my head. Lies, of course. I managed well for a few days, part of the reason being I didn't want to be a burden on my grandparents by being fussy and awkward, and a disappointment to them. My grandparents gave me a lot of encouragement, which while I was there I embraced. When I got back home, things soon returned to normal, with me eating as little as before, and often less. Along with eating less every day and drastically over-exercising, my depression sank to a totally new level. I became very anxious that I was getting behind with my schoolwork, so I made my mum go to Billingham Campus and pick up work for me to do, so I could try to keep up.

Arguments increased with my parents, and before long we were having rows more than five times a day. Most of the arguments were based around us moving house. Every time someone came to view it, I wished that they wouldn't buy it. I didn't bother praying. God, in my mind, no longer existed. The voice made it clear that if there was a God, then I would already be as perfect as I should be. I would be as light as air, beautiful and popular without a care in the world. If there was a God, I wouldn't have to eat, drink or sleep and I would still survive and be everything that I wanted to be.

I think my wishing helped, for a while anyway, as we had many people who came close to buying it, but then backed out for reasons unknown, which kept me happy for a short time. To put off potential buyers, I would wait until my parents were handing out coffee and offering them homemade flapjack, before slinking into the room to work my evil magic. I'd mention that the previous owner had hung himself in one of the sheds in the back garden, and that he had a passion for skinning mice and nailing their tiny mutilated bodies to the shed walls. Of course, I'd mention the fact that I had seen his ghost on numerous occasions too. Those comments almost always ensured that the flapjack was forgotten, and the coffee declined.

I confined myself to my room for most of the day, every day. I would work for hours on end on my schoolwork, and worried continually that it wasn't good enough. Mum had to work in the mornings, so when I wasn't doing schoolwork, I would be secretly exercising. When Mum came home from work in the afternoon, she would try to get me out of the house for a while, thinking that it wasn't good for me being alone in my room all day. I wasn't allowed back to school, as I was in such a state, emotionally, physically and mentally. I knew that something was wrong, but continually refused to accept that it had anything to do with my eating. As far as I was concerned, it was because I had a slightly 'dodgy' heart that would sort itself out sooner or later.

I was feeling the cold more than ever before, and so I'd do my schoolwork sitting against my radiator. I'd get scorching red marks on my back from the ridges that would last for days and sting terribly, but it was the only way I could keep warm. My mum noticed, after a couple of weeks of me being at home, that I was putting almost all my energy and concentration into my schoolwork. She encouraged me not to do so much, as I was wearing myself out and overdoing it. I disagreed with her at first, and we ended up having many full-blown fights over it. After a while, I realised that the time not spent on homework could be time better spent exercising.

"You don't burn many calories doing homework," the voice would inform me. "Take advantage of the situation. Rid your body of those nasty, horrible calories. Lose the fat that's keeping you from having a good life."

My eating was getting worse, and I took the opportunity of being at home by myself to eat nothing at all. But I was getting more depressed, and the less I ate; the more convinced I became that I was getting fatter and eating too much. My image in the mirror was becoming all the more distorted. A new chin would develop daily. Another layer of flab would flop over the waistband of my belted trousers. My eyes were gradually becoming pinpricks in a mass of pink putty. I was panicking that, soon, I would be unable to see anything at all; the mirror would simply reflect a mass of flesh with no identity.

In reality, my cheeks had sunken so far it looked as if I was permanently sucking on a lemon. The lanugo was growing and my complexion beneath the blonde down was deathly pale. My eyes were wide and haunted, set deep into my skull, and my hair – my long, lustrous hair – hung thin and lank over my visible scalp.

I hardly ever talked any more to members of my family, and I'd keep all my thoughts and emotions locked inside. Except when I went for my appointments with Dr Wilson. But even at my appointments what I told her, more often than not, was lie after lie.

As my health deteriorated, the arguments increased with my mum. Now, the only time I would really talk (or shout) was when I was arguing, and the only focus would be on what I hadn't eaten, my exercise and my exclusion of the rest of my family from my life. It often got so bad, I would go and stay with my grandparents in Ripon, so that my family could have some time away from me, and I could have time away from them. In all truthfulness, if we hadn't escaped one another someone would have ended up being seriously injured.

When I went to stay with my grandparents, they'd try to cheer me up, and make my stay happy, and so they would buy me the foods they knew I loved. I would exercise while staying with them, going out for runs in the nearby woods, claiming I was 'popping to the shop'. I didn't want them to worry about me getting lost or being abducted by some stranger. I also exercised late into the night in my room, when they were asleep and unaware. Whenever I couldn't dispose of the food that greeted me at mealtimes, I ate a small amount, excused myself, and visited my other familiar friend, the toilet. I had mastered the art of the anorexic, 'being sick silently', so they remained ignorant of what I'd been doing when I slipped back into the room. Neither of my grandparents had any idea what I was suffering, and supposed that I was simply going through a 'stressful time'. When they offered me a piece of flapjack for a snack, or a bowl of ice cream for dessert, I'd politely refuse. I hated seeing the look of disappointment and surprise on their faces, and I'd feel guilty, but there was no way I could have allowed myself those treats. Times were different when I stayed with them as a child. Back then, when I was showered with treats, I accepted them with shining eyes and a smile. Now, my sunken eyes stared down and my smile was a forgotten memory. The voice had coached me well in saying no and coping with the guilty feelings that came along with saying it. It assured me that my grandparents would understand my reasons for declining their offers once I was the perfect person.

I was becoming more and more obsessed with my main enemy: calories, and had mad theories about how they would enter my body, other than in food. I thought moisturising creams and toothpaste contained them, and they would get absorbed through my skin or down my throat. So, I'd only use moisturiser when it was absolutely necessary, and when brushing my teeth, I'd make sure I didn't swallow even the tiniest bit of toothpaste. I decided that moisturisers that contained things like avocado oil or cocoa butter would have more calories than plain moisturisers, so I only ever used the plain ones with no added nutrients or vitamins just in case. I also thought that salt and pepper contained calories, so I stopped using them altogether too. But when I found out that they have a fat and calorie content of nil I'd use them to the extreme to flavour the bland food that existed in my diet.

I also became obsessed with washing my hands after I had touched any food, even lettuce, as I'd worry that if I touched my lips with the hand that had touched the food, then I would have taken in unnecessary calories and fat. My hands soon showed the results of my new obsession. As my skin was paper thin and sensitive, tiny cracks appeared all over my hands, which oozed blood continuously. This was the beginning of my obsessive-compulsive disorder, which has taken me years to admit to. But, all the evidence is there; therefore, it is a fact of life I can't deny. Anorexia was ripping my body apart piece by piece, and my mind was wasting no time in following. Still I continued to play its game, adamant that my life was more normal than it had ever been before, because I felt that I was in control and had the best guide a girl could have to help me find my way in life. Never had I been more wrong.

Chapter 5

Screaming Silently Into The Snowy Season

As my depression reached darker depths, I talked even less and cried more than ever before. More than half of my day consisted of me sitting hunched up, sobbing to myself for reasons I couldn't understand. My mind was muddled on some occasions, clear as crystal on others. Dr Wilson decided I should be talking to a psychologist instead of her, someone who could understand the complexities of my 'illness' and what I was going through.

The appointment with a psychologist should really have been made much earlier. Talking to a GP about my illness had been useless. They're not trained to understand mental illnesses, so, in theory, the hours spent in her office had been hours wasted. Dr Wilson made arrangements for me to have appointments at the Rosewood Centre for children's mental health in Middlesbrough. My first thoughts when I heard that were, 'Am I cracking up? Have I really lost it? Am I a certified lunatic? Are they going to put me in a straight-jacket and lock me in a cell until I foam at the mouth and I have to be drugged into silence?'

Dr Wilson laughed when I relayed my thoughts to her. I, on the other hand, didn't. It wasn't funny to me. At my age, 'mental health' was straight-jackets and padded cells. She reassured me that it wasn't, but I didn't believe her. Only when the voice said that I might as well go and get it over with, so they could see there was nothing wrong with me, did I agree to go.

I started to have appointments with a young trainee psychologist called Beverly. She was friendly, and listened to me carefully when I finally got around to talking after a few weeks. I also started seeing a dietician, called Lia, who had a friendly air and took in what I told her. She said she'd had many girls with the same problem, and that it might take a while, but I could get myself back on the right track. I shook my head, again claiming I didn't have an eating problem. I was dieting, because I needed to. That was all. And everyone dieted at some time, so it wasn't unusual. Lia plainly told me that I was very underweight, and I had to try to gain some, otherwise I would become very ill. I weighed

39 kg at this time, just under six stone. We talked about my eating habits, and together we formed a meal plan, which I promised to stick to. I promised with my fingers crossed under my legs, as I knew immediately that I wouldn't be able to stick to it for long. I pretended to promise because I wanted Mum and Dad to believe I was making an effort. I was convinced that there was nothing wrong, but I thought if I played the game for a while, or at least pretended to, then I would be left alone to get on with my life, continuing with my diet, progress with my exercise routine, lose weight and become perfect.

In November 2001, to my dismay, we found a buyer for our house, and we moved to the town of Billingham. The only good point about moving for me was that I could have my own room with a lock on it, so I could exercise in there for hours on end without being disturbed. I was quite looking forward to moving to Billingham when I was at Billingham Campus, but now that I wasn't allowed back to school, I thought it was pointless being happy about it when I would have no friends there. Staying thin, and getting thinner, was my only concern.

Moving to Billingham meant that I had to change doctors, I didn't know the new doctor so I felt I couldn't trust her. It had taken a while to build up even the smallest of relationships with Dr Wilson, and now I had to start the entire process again, which added to my feelings of stress.

For the first few weeks in our new house, the arguments stopped. I suppose it was because we were all so preoccupied with unpacking and settling in, we didn't really have time to argue. But all too soon, they started again. The fights would often get so bad it would result with Mum and I not talking for days. Those were the times when my eating would go rapidly downhill, because I blamed myself for all the arguments. My mind was scattered. I couldn't decide if I wanted the voice or not. I started to try to hurt myself as a way of punishment, but it was never really drastic wounding, compared to true self-harmers. I would pull my hair out, punch myself in the stomach, scratch my legs, arms and belly with my nails, and sometimes, when I was really stressed and upset, I would bang my head against the wall, to make the pain I felt inside stop. I tried to make the voice go away as well, but it didn't. Nothing would make it disappear.

I was getting weighed regularly at the Rosewood Centre, and I was continually, unsurprisingly, losing weight.

As we were nearly into winter, the weather was getting colder. Whenever I went out (which was hardly ever) I'd wear thick tights underneath my trousers and socks, at least two jumpers over a T-shirt, a coat, hat, scarf and gloves. I would also wear them inside when I was really cold, which was quite often. In the house, I'd have to stand next to the fire to keep warm, and sometimes, when I went out in the car with the whole family, I would take a hot water bottle with me because the rest of the family couldn't stand the car heater as it made them all feel nauseous.

Christmas was getting closer by the day, so there was a good excuse to do lots of baking. I baked trays of mince pies and biscuits, loaves of Stollen bread, etc. I tried to be excited about Christmas, and get into the spirit, although I was still very depressed. I felt that I had to make an effort for my family. Plus Christmas had always been my favourite time of the year. When Mum was not at work, I would beg her to take me Christmas shopping so that I could look at all the gorgeous food and urge Mum to buy it, and promise her that I would eat what she bought, knowing full well myself that I wouldn't. Part of me felt good that I could control myself around all this lovely food, and not be tempted enough to have some, but another part of me wished that I could allow myself something, and wished that I could be how I had been two years ago, eating what I wanted and enjoying it, and not caring about it.

As well as looking forward to Christmas, a part of me dreaded it, as I knew I would be surrounded by all my favourite foods, and everyone else would be eating and enjoying themselves. I might get tempted, over-eat and get fat. I tried to ignore those thoughts, and be positive about the festive season while it lasted.

A few days before Christmas Day, I had my last appointment with Lia and it wasn't a good one. I had not been sticking to my meal plan, and my weight had dropped since I'd last seen her. I was now dangerously underweight, weighing just 38 kg and Lia, along with the Eating Disorders Team, decided that I should be admitted to hospital (The Newberry Centre). I would be admitted after Christmas.

At first, I wouldn't believe it. I thought that I was just being threatened with hospital, but I soon realised that it was true, and I knew that I must have a serious problem. I was absolutely devastated. I couldn't believe that this was really happening to ME. Two years previously I'd been reading a book about an anorexic while I was eating a bowl of ice cream, thinking, 'The girl in this book is so stupid. That's NEVER going to happen to me. I'm never going to deprive myself of things that I enjoy. I am NEVER going to prevent myself from having a happy life.' How wrong was I? I couldn't believe that I had let a New Year's resolution get so out of hand. I felt so stupid.

I really didn't want to be admitted, but I realised that it was for the best. I was making my entire family's life a living hell, as well as my own, and my family could no longer cope. Neither could I.

Christmas Day went relatively well. I tried my hardest not to start or get into any arguments with my family. I helped Mum and Dad to prepare Christmas lunch, and I tried to eat some of each of the vegetables that were put on to my plate. Although I felt like a greedy, fat cow, I wanted to please Mum and Dad, and avoid any arguments about food. I had the smallest portion; I still finished last, eating one pea at a time, and savouring every morsel, as I was starving. But I didn't want to look like a pig at a trough by finishing first. I couldn't believe at the end of Christmas Day that I had managed to resist all the temptations and carry out my exercise routine. I felt really proud of myself, but I could tell my parents were upset.

The day after Boxing Day, I was back at the doctor's for blood tests. They had never hurt as much as they did on that day. Because I was so cold, it was very hard to find a vein to draw the blood. I had to bite my tongue to stop myself from screaming. The pain was horrendous as the needle was stuck into my vein and the blood was slowly drawn out. I knew it had to be done but my bad eating habits, obsessive exercise, routine crying and the arguments continued until I was admitted into hospital.

Chapter 6

Admitted, Defeated And Bed Rest

On 4th January 2002, I was admitted into The Newberry Centre. I couldn't believe it had come to this. So much for New Year, new start! Mum, Dad and I had an appointment with the Eating Disorders Team in the morning, and it was decided that that afternoon would be the best time for admission.

I was shown around the ward where I'd be staying, and I met some of the patients and staff, who all seemed friendly. But something I noticed was that the doors were kept locked at all times, and the windows could only be opened to a certain width. (I soon found out that it was done to prevent people climbing out and running away.) It made me feel like a prisoner even before I had moved in. Every bedroom was decorated identically, except for people's personal belongings, and the boys and girls were separated – girls down one long corridor, boys down another. There was a kitchen, which you were allowed to enter and use under supervision; a small gym which, to my dismay, I was not allowed to use; a lounge with a TV where people could sit to relax or have debates and arguments (there were often arguments to be had), it was also where the Community Meetings were held; a pool room; and a dining room, which I never ate in once.

There was also a large garden, surrounded by a high wooden fence, which reminded me of a prison yard, as there was nothing there except grass and an old, miserable-looking tree standing in the centre. Beyond the hospital was an enormous cemetery, which made the place seem all the more depressing and morbid. It was also a dark reminder of where, if I continued to lose weight, I would end up.

Connected to the unit, situated near to the psychologists' and doctors' offices, was the 'School', where I would spend many an 'inventive' half an hour as I got stronger, creating cross-stitch and writing poetry. It consisted of about four rooms, and one lovely, friendly 'teacher' called Catherine, with whom I made firm friends.

I quietly sobbed as Mum and I packed a suitcase and drove there that afternoon. I apologised over and over again to her for what I had done. I felt so bad for putting her and Dad through such hell, despite not knowing exactly what I'd done wrong (the voice insisted everything I was doing to lose weight was OK). My brothers and sister didn't think much about me going into hospital. They imagined I was only going to be there for a few days, and that I would be home again soon. So they never really said anything when Mum told them. I have since found out that they were very scared for me, and were certain I would die.

I was weighed when we arrived, and because I was at such a low weight (I weighed 37.1kg) I was immediately put on to bed rest. At first, I couldn't understand why. An hour earlier, I had been walking around, doing my own thing, and now I wasn't allowed off my bed. I even had to keep my feet up, and wasn't allowed to dangle them over the side, as I would apparently burn essential calories. I was told if I needed to go to the toilet I had to ask, and a nurse would take me there in a wheelchair. I found that humiliating, as I could walk and I didn't need to be wheeled anywhere.

I cried for all of the first day. I couldn't believe that it really was happening. I didn't want my mum to leave, and I held on to her hand tightly, squeezing her firm, strong fingers with my frail, weak ones, begging her not to leave me. But, when I saw the tears in her eyes, I let go of her hand and allowed her to go without further argument. I saw that she was tired, upset and needed her rest and it was not possible for her to stay. It was a hospital rule. I would have to face up to my fear of this strange new place, alone.

If any of the nurses came into my room, I didn't talk to them. I just mumbled replies to their questions, and shrugged. I was also terrified that because I wasn't allowed off my bed, I would instantly get fat. My plan to exercise while I was in the shower room was foiled on my first night as I wasn't allowed one because of my unstable condition. I was fuming that I was being told what I could and could not do by people I didn't even know.

I was also put on five-minute observations so I couldn't exercise in my room, which angered me even more. My life had changed in a matter of hours. From doing what I liked, when I liked, where I liked, I was now being treated like a baby who couldn't look after itself.

The first night in hospital was the worst night of my life. I had to have my door open so that I could be checked all through the night. It made it impossible to get a good night's sleep, as there was someone coming in every half an hour to make sure that I wasn't exercising. I kept waking up from my interrupted sleep, and thinking I was having a bad dream, and that my mum would come in and hold me, stroke my hair and tell me that everything would be all right. That never happened. It wasn't a bad dream. It was a living nightmare.

On my first morning, the curtains were ripped back and I was exposed to the bright, early morning sun. I opened my eyes to see a woman I had never laid eyes on before in my life. She introduced herself as Alicia. I was taken to the toilet in the wheelchair, where I managed five minutes of vigorous exercise, stopping only when Alicia starting banging on the door with her fists and telling me to hurry up. I guess she had suspicions as to what I was actually doing.

When I returned to my room, I was made to sit on my bed again, and was given my breakfast on a bed rest table. I couldn't believe what I was seeing. There was thirty grams of bran flakes, drenched in semi-skimmed milk, and a huge apple. And I was expected to eat it all. This was what was on the meal plan that Lia had given me but as I'd never followed it, I had no idea what the amount of food looked like. I nearly burst into tears. There was so *much* food. There was no way I could eat all of it. The last time I'd eaten breakfast, it had been fifteen grams of dry bran flakes, and a glass of ice-cold water.

Alicia sat down in the armchair next to my bed and attempted to make conversation with me. But I wouldn't talk. I felt her eyes on me as I pressed each individual bran flake against the side of the bowl, attempting to drain off the milk, and then slowly, put it to my mouth. I felt tears sting my eyes. I hadn't taken a full mouthful yet, and I already felt like a greedy pig for even contemplating doing so. I was also sure that Alicia was thinking the same thing – that I was a fat and greedy pig.

As I was on bed rest, unlike the other patients who had to make do with the television in the lounge, I was allowed a television in my room, and I tried to focus my attention on GMTV as I ate flake after flake.

I had eaten about five soggy flakes when Alicia said to me, "Katie, you have GOT to put more on your spoon."

I lost it and shouted at her, "At least I'm bloody trying to eat them, aren't I?"

I don't think I'd managed a quarter of my cereal before I put my spoon down and refused to eat any more. I was sure that I had put on at least a stone by eating that much. I managed to scrape the skin off about a quarter of my apple before I put it down, and it was all taken away. Alicia never said anything to me about not finishing my breakfast, she just gave it to the cleaner to dispose of and sat down to supervise me.

I then had to have a rest for half an hour, which meant lying on my bed and not moving at all. I was supervised for the whole half an hour, so that I had no chance or opportunity to exercise or make myself sick. I wasn't allowed to go to the toilet until my rest was over. I attempted to move my legs and feet constantly, in a desperate attempt to burn off the calories I had just consumed, a habit I still have now when I sit for any length of time, but Alicia kept giving me disapproving looks while she focused all her attention on me, which made it impossible to continue. Much to the voice's and my complete and utter dismay.

After my rest, I was allowed fifteen minutes on my own to have a wash and get dressed. I used that time to exercise and move around as much as possible. After fifteen minutes, it was straight back on my bed with my feet up. But, I didn't keep my feet up. Whenever possible, I would dangle them over the side of my bed and swing them back and forth in a desperate attempt to burn off calories. The voice in my head was screaming at me to move all the time and not stay still because I would get fat. And, of course, I listened and believed what it was saying.

That day, I remember two girls coming to my door, and introducing themselves as Phoebe and Louise. I noticed that Phoebe had bandages all the way up both arms, so I guessed that she was in hospital for depression and for harming herself. But I couldn't see anything *physically* wrong with Louise. She was incredibly pretty, with shiny golden curls and rosebud lips, a slim figure and looked perfectly happy with herself and life. But I did think that she was too young to be in a hospital like this, as she only looked about eleven or twelve. (I later found out that she was seventeen.) They both seemed like really nice people, and I muttered hello to them, and that was about it. I think they got the idea that I wouldn't be very talkative at the time, so they both said goodbye and went. (I found out that Louise was in hospital because she had been depressed and suicidal. I then realised that you can never judge people's emotions and feelings just by looking at them.)

At every given opportunity, I would get off my bed and stride up and down my small room. But, I was nearly always caught, as people were often walking past because my room was close to the main office, where all the staff would congregate. I was caught so often I was told that if I didn't cooperate, I would be put on constant observations. It felt as if I was already.

At my second meal, lunch, I was equally shocked as at breakfast. The portion size was a hundred times bigger than I would have at home and the actual food items were things that I would never have dreamt of touching. There was a large piece of cheese quiche, a scoop of mashed potato, and a huge helping of carrots, as well as a pot of low fat Muller Rice. Again, I nearly burst into tears. How was I even supposed to attempt to eat it? In the end, I picked at the cheese on the quiche, not even touching the pastry, poked at the carrots, and didn't even bother with the mashed potato. I was so scared that it had all been smothered in butter. Although I couldn't see any I was positive that it had been added secretly. They were on a mission to make me fat anyway, so, of course, they were going to try sneaky tactics like that. It was the same routine as breakfast with a nurse sitting with me while I ate, which made me feel even worse because thoughts would go through my head such as, 'Does she think I am being greedy? Does she think I am being a pig?' So eating was even more difficult. I managed to eat a quarter of my Muller Rice, after which I felt greedy and fat, and as if I had put on two stone.

I had half an hour to complete my meals, and I had barely touched mine when thirty minutes had ticked by. The nurse took it away. Nothing was said, only disapproving looks at the plate and me. The food in the hospital was actually delicious, but I was so scared of over-eating, and of not knowing every calorific and fat detail. I then had to have another rest, but this rest period was an hour. To me, these rest periods were like being punished for doing nothing wrong.

Sunday came – visiting day. I was secretly hoping I'd be taken home. My grandparents came to see me, which cheered me up a little. But I wasn't even allowed to get off my bed to give them a hug. During visiting, a nurse came in every five minutes to check on me, and to see whether I was still on my bed. I wasn't even allowed a few hours' personal time alone with the ones dearest to me. I mean, what did the nurses think I would do? Climb into my Nanna's handbag and try to escape! Well, actually, if it had been big enough, that's one thing I would have attempted. It made me very angry and upset that I couldn't have any private time alone with my family, but what could I do? I was powerless in every sense of the word.

My grandparents' visit passed incredibly quickly, and before I knew it, they were ushered out and gone. And as my grandparents went out of my door, to my utter dismay, my next meal came in through it.

Chapter 7

Routines, Rules, Regulations And Deception

I was given a care plan on my first day on the ward, which I had to follow until my situation improved, and it was changed to suit my needs. On it was a seemingly endless list of what I was or wasn't allowed to do; how long I had to eat my meals; how long I was allowed in the shower, etc. When it was presented to me (I had to sign it to say that I agreed, even though I didn't), I couldn't believe that some random person had written rules for me to follow every day. I also had the meal plan which I was given by Lia, the dietician, before I had been admitted, which now included two Ensure Plus drinks (Ensure Plus is a high calorie, high fat concentrated milkshake drink to assist weight gain) a day on top of everything else that I was supposed to eat. I was certain that there was absolutely no way that I would even manage to finish half of one, let alone two. No hope in hell.

I was weighed twice a week: Monday and Thursday first thing in the morning, while I was still in my pyjamas so I couldn't hide anything. I started to deceive the nurses before long, by slipping my bracelets around my ankles, making it seem as though I had gained weight. I had to go to the toilet before I was weighed, in case I tried to drink vast amounts of water, because that too would make it appear as though I had put on weight. The first few weeks I was weighed, I didn't look at the scales, I was too petrified, but after a while I started to make a record of whether my weight was increasing or decreasing. If I had put on weight (even with the addition of my bracelets), I would try my hardest to lose for the next time that I was weighed. If I had lost, I would try hard for a few days to gain it again, but then I would get back into the routine of losing it.

The weight I needed to be was 38.5 kg, but I was terrified of coming even close to that weight. Though I knew I HAD to put on weight to get off bed rest, the voice in my head would tell me to keep on losing, and if I put on weight, I would be losing my battle to stay thin. And for five months, five long months, I listened to it and remained on my bed. I would phone my family immediately after I had been weighed, to tell them the news. When I told them that I had gained weight, they would be thrilled, even if it was only a tiny amount, 100 grams for example, which gave me a rush, but only for a very short time. And when I told them that I had lost, they'd be incredibly disappointed and upset, but always tried to give me all the encouragement they could. It didn't help that my mind was focused on pleasing the voice and satisfying its needs rather than listening to my family and their words of love and advice.

Visiting in the hospital was on a Tuesday and a Thursday, 6pm to 8pm; and Saturday and Sunday, 2 pm till 4 pm, and 6 pm till 8 pm on the dot. Normally, my whole family would come and see me, and we would sit and watch TV and chat.

Mum recently has told me that I would often sit and rock backwards and forwards for the entire visiting time, ignoring everything that was happening around me, and, when I looked up, my eyes would be wide and wild and my lips moving silently. I was talking to the voice, telling it that I would continue with my weight loss. This would apparently scare my siblings and make my parents cry. Often, visiting times would get very emotional, especially if I'd had a bad day, and I would beg Mum to let me come back home, but in my heart I knew there was no way that could happen.

I asked my mum to bring in my posters and pictures off my wall at home, and stuck them up all over my new room, covering every inch of the drab, pale brown and yellow walls. Having my pictures of Kurt Cobain, Marilyn Manson, Seth Green, Orlando Bloom, vampires, American Indians, bats and wolves made my room feel a little bit more like home, a little bit more like my own space, and not like the bare prison cell it did when I was first admitted. Even having familiar things around me didn't make up for the loneliness I am sure any prisoner feels when in the same room, day in, day out. I had people in my room ninety-nine per cent of the time during the day, had my pens and paper, my books, a TV and CD player with my music, but I still felt afraid and lonely with only the voice for company.

The first few weeks were definitely the worst, and I would wait in anticipation for the post to come, to see if any of my friends from my old school had written to me. I received a few cards from relatives (mostly from my nanna who would make me a card and send me it every week along with a little present) and one of my friends wrote to me. One friend, in all the time I was there. Thea was the only friend who wrote and came to visit me, along with her Mum, Monica. (My pen pal Seveana who lives in Martinique also wrote to me, but she didn't know that I was anorexic, let alone in hospital. I only told her when I had been discharged.)

I would listen out when the phone in the nurses' office rang, to see if the call was for me. But the only people who would ring me were my friends Thea and Matt (an old friend I'd met in Margrove Park and who had introduced me to the delights of Death, Thrash and Heavy Metal), my parents and my grandparents. None of the friends with whom I had spent years of my life before the terrible trauma of class eight even bothered. And it broke my heart. I'd always relied on these people and they on me, to get through the tough times in school when we were young. I stopped hoping after about a month, the tears for them dried, and I relied on my 'true' friends and family to stay in touch with me. My Nanna's daily phone calls and weekly cards and my family's and Thea's visits would be the sunshine in my darkness.

I had the same routine, day in, day out, for five months: get up at 8 am, have my breakfast (well, what I could manage of it), supervised, of course, then half an hour rest, also supervised. Fifteen minutes to change and have a wash, then back on my bed. I spent my time writing in my diary and writing stories, reading, watching TV and listening to the loudest, darkest and most miserable music I have, until 10.30 am, when a nurse would come into my room with my morning break. (Often, my morning break was forgotten but I would never remind anyone. The voice in my head would scream at me not to. I was escaping unnecessary calories, so why say anything?) When my break was remembered, I was given an Ensure Plus drink to try to finish. Normally, I would manage about a quarter of the carton. A supervised rest would follow my break for half an hour, and then I would continue with writing in my diary, or stories, until midday, when someone would come in with my lunch. I would usually manage a quarter to a half of it.

Most of the nurses who sat with me while I tried to eat wouldn't constantly stare at me (I think they knew how uncomfortable it made me feel) but there were a certain few who would lean over my bed as I ate, just in case I tried to hide food in my lap. Another hour's rest followed, and then I did the same as before, writing, etc. until 2.30 pm, when a nurse brought in my afternoon break – another carton of Ensure Plus, and a Nutri-Grain Bar. Again, I could only manage about a quarter of the Ensure Plus, and only a nibble of my Nutri-Grain Bar. That was followed by yet ANOTHER supervised half an hour's rest, and then the same as in the morning until 5 pm, when my tea would be brought in: three thin rice cakes, with peanut butter or cottage cheese, and a bowl of bran flakes with semi-skimmed milk. I tried to scrape as much spread as possible off my rice cakes, and hide it in a napkin when the nurse wasn't watching. If the opportunity arose I would scrunch up the entire rice cake, put it all in the napkin and then hide it under my pillow.

I wasn't aware of it at the time, but this must have been noticed by the nurses, as they would have known that I couldn't possibly have managed to eat a full rice cake in that short period of time. Yet nothing was said at the time. It was, however, brought up by Alicia after a number of weeks – the nurses had apparently relayed everything to her.

I would also drain off as much milk as possible before eating. Nurses noticed this, and certain ones would leave the milk to soak into the bran flakes before giving them to me as soggy mush which made it made it even more difficult to eat. Tea was followed by yet another supervised hour's rest (this is getting boring now!) then writing, reading, etc. until I was allowed twenty minutes for my shower. Half of that time would be taken up by exercise: sit-ups, squats, press-ups, running on the spot, etc. I followed the routine I had done at home. After my shower, I would have my supper, if it was remembered, which was a cup of Cadbury's Highlights, followed by yet another supervised half an hour's rest. Then at 11 pm it was lights out.

So that was my life for five months. Boring, wasn't it? I did not leave the hospital building in all those five months. The only times I went out of my room were to go to the toilet, for my shower, to the once a week Community Meeting in the Lounge, which all the patients and nurses attended. Here, we discussed if there were any problems with the building or our rooms. Also, if there were any problems with patients, for example, if we felt that someone was bullying or simply being irritating.

My parents and I did request to have complementary therapies in the privacy of my own room, which we would most certainly have paid for. However, The Eating Disorders Team answered with a strict no, not under any circumstances. They stated clearly that the reason was because the therapists were not part of the Eating Disorders Team. At the time, both my parents and I were furious, as we knew for a fact that complementary therapies treated the person they were being performed on, at their emotional, physical and mental level. However, the rules were set and there was no way we were able to make changes to them. I was baffled as to how people who claimed to want to help me in my recovery were able to refuse me therapies, which were certain to help.

There were many days in those five months when I would just break down and cry for almost the whole day, asking myself 'Why the hell is this happening to me? It's not fair. I want to be normal again. I want to be at school, with friends, leading the happy life I should be.'

The voice would take on a soothing tone at times like this, insisting that I was normal and the people around me weren't.

As I gained a little weight – one hundred to two hundred grams (which was inevitable because I couldn't make myself sick) I was allowed to attend the hospital's 'school' in the wheelchair, once a week for half an hour. There, I would do simple handicraft things, supposed to help take my mind off my weight and food. They never did though, and the temptation to prick my fingers with the needles or press a pair of scissors across my wrists was overwhelming. I needed to punish myself for not being sick and disposing from my body the foul food that was invading it. The only thing that stopped me was Catherine hovering over and watching my every move, ready to pluck the scissors or needle from my twitching fingers.

Once a week, I had an individual session with my Key Nurse, Alicia, who had coincidentally been the first human I encountered on my first morning in hospital. A Key Nurse is someone who constantly reviews your care plan and is a person to talk to when the need arises. You keep a diary for them to read, in which you're supposed to talk about any problems you're having. I wrote in a diary that I would show her every session, but I would never write the whole truth about things. I would never tell her about hiding my food, or how I exercised in the bathroom. I wouldn't ever mention my obsession with having all my books exactly lined up or my obsessive touching of my bed when I made it in the morning, or having to have my toiletries positioned in a certain way. That would have been stupid. Sometimes I developed an urge to tell her about hiding food, my obsessive behaviour and exercising, but the voice would scream, "Are you mad? Do you want to give your secrets away?" I wanted the secrets and lies out of me, because I am not the kind of person who likes to lie and have never done it naturally. I hate lying to anyone; I feel terrible about doing it. But at the time, the voice still had control over my thoughts, feelings and everything I did. Therefore lying was part of the deal, and more often than not, every second word I spoke was a lie.

The sessions were often useful, but they were also sometimes a frustrating waste of time. I had so many days when I was feeling really low, and Alicia would come in for my session and give me a lecture about how I should try harder and make an effort with 'battling against the voice' and 'eating more'. I'd switch off during her lectures, and stare into space. Her voice became a stream of nonsense to my ears, yet the voice in my mind rang clear.

It was a month after I was admitted that I began to drink different drinks instead of just water. I'd have a cup of tea in the morning with my breakfast. I had deprived myself of it for such a long time, that it was absolute bliss when I drank it!

After about two months, I started opening up to people, and had full conversations that consisted of more than just a mumbled hello, with the nurses who supervised me for my meals. I'd brought in my *Lord of the Rings* book collection when I was first admitted, along with an enormous box of other books that I was determined to plough through during my stay. I was halfway through *The Two Towers*, the second book in the trilogy, when

Jackson, a nurse I found incredibly irritating, came into my room and made an announcement.

It was his passion to watch horse racing and football when supervising me, or read the *Daily Star*. Despite mimicking my so-called 'posh accent' – especially the word 'wanker' which I used on various occasions when I wanted to walk to the toilet or I was in a genuinely bad mood, Jackson was interesting and very friendly. The announcement he came to make was to admit, to my complete and utter delight, his own obsession with JRR Tolkien's work. I was ecstatic about finding a 'book mate' as no one else, or so I had thought, adored *Lord of the Rings* as much as me.

We discussed the books for hours at a time, bickering over who we believed to be the best characters. He brought in his sacred collection of cassette tapes containing twenty-six half hour stereo instalments of *Lord of the Rings*, broadcast by Radio 4 in 1981. He agreed to bring them in on the promise that I worked hard at eating more. I agreed to his blackmail on a handshake, although naturally most of the extra food I promised to eat was hidden away on the voice's strict instructions. I'd escape into my own world when listening to Ian Holm portraying Bilbo Baggins and Michael Hordern speaking as Gandalf, or reading my books. I'd escape from anorexia, my illness, the hospital, the people there and all the other problems in my life and the world besides. For a few hours I'd have no worries, cares or concerns other than what was happening in the stories. Climbing mountains with Frodo and battling against armies of Orcs was far preferable to facing my own difficulties.

Phoebe made visits to my room almost every day. We would chat about a range of things from music to movies, our illnesses and what we felt were the causes of them. She'd constantly encourage me to try to get off bed rest, reminding me of the many things that I was allowed to do once I was off. I would nod my head and agree with her, promising to work at my weight. I knew secretly that the promises I made would come to nothing. No matter how hard I tried to ignore the voice in my head, and eat just a little bit more, it always won in the end. And I have to admit that I felt safe and secure allowing that to happen. It was my routine, and I didn't want to see that being disrupted. I didn't know what lay ahead, in a world without the voice, and I wasn't in a position to find out.

Chapter 8

A Friend In Need Is A Friend Indeed

A few weeks after coming into hospital, Dawn, another anorexic patient, came to my room in her wheelchair (she was also on bed rest) on the way to the toilet. I instantly thought she was far, far thinner than I was, and couldn't possibly imagine myself weighing less than she did. When she smiled, all her amazingly white teeth shone back at me, and her skin was taut but flawless over sleek cheekbones. To me, she was a beauty, and I felt like hiding in shame at my 'fatness'. Now I realise, when I browse through old photographs, that actually she looked just like a clothed skeleton, and so did I.

Dawn started writing letters to me shortly after we met, encouraging me to ignore the voice. She wrote that she knew exactly what I was going through, and she knew just how difficult it was to keep on fighting and ignoring the voice when you feel confused whether you actually want it in your life of not. I'd write back, sending my love, support, and encouragement. Often, we'd write as many as ten letters in one day, particularly if we were both having a terrible day when nothing seemed to be going right. Days when we felt like bloated pigs after having something more to eat than usual. The letters could be, and often were, pages upon pages long, displaying our fears about what we were going through, and how no one understood what we were trying to achieve. I'd sometimes spend up to two hours composing a single letter.

My obsessive-compulsive disorder not only interfered with my everyday activities, such as making my bed, but it interfered with my writing too. Every letter had to be written in black and shaped perfectly to suit my formal Gothic style. Every word had to be spelt correctly; there could be no errors although it was simply a letter going to a friend down the corridor. When I folded it in half, the line needed to be exact. There were times when the line was fractionally out, and I ripped up a letter that had taken me an entire afternoon. When it was placed in the envelope, I licked my finger and wiped my saliva over the seal. Stamps contained five calories. There was no way that I would risk taking in the calories from the enormous seal on an envelope. There was a chance it contained well over twenty calories.

In our letters, we'd tell each other how well we had done at hiding food, and about accidentally-on-purpose spilt drinks, compare our weights and give each other tips on how to dodge and burn calories.

All this time, we were still giving each other encouragement to gain weight, which, looking back at it now, is most peculiar. I suppose that just indicates how very disillusioned we were. We would get other patients to transport the letters to and from our rooms, or nurses whom we knew we could trust not to look at them. As we were both on bed rest, the only times we'd see each other were when we'd pass each other's rooms in the wheelchair on the way to the toilet or shower, or at the Community Meeting where we'd both sit shaking our legs and fiddling with our fingers trying to burn calories. We became firm friends, even though we hadn't spent more than an hour in the same room together!

As my time in hospital went by, I developed good relationships with most of the staff on the ward. After Jackson had brought in his tapes, a young nurse, only a few years older than myself, called Lisa brought in old tapes and CDs of Goth bands from the 1980s. She introduced me to many bands that I had never heard of before, taking my mind off weight loss for a short time. I was re-introduced to aspects of my life that had been ignored because of my dedication to losing weight. Lisa was a friend of Nina, another young nurse who supervised me but hardly looked old enough to be out of college. She was caring and considerate, and constantly had my needs and interests in mind. She delivered cards from herself and little gifts in an attempt to help keep my motivation high. They would both arrange activities that revolved around things I found enjoyable such as cooking (how ironic!), for example. I'd be wheeled down to the kitchen and allowed to grate cheese for a pizza or break a few eggs for a sponge cake mix. Nothing too strenuous, of course! Strictly no whisking or beating allowed. I developed a relationship with both Lisa and Nina, which I never imagined possible with anyone other than people I'd known for years. I'd proved myself wrong, in a good way.

My long period of almost complete silence was more or less over; there were some nurses I still struggled to exchange a sentence with. I preferred the nurses I got on better with, including Lia, Nina and Jackson (when the horse racing or snooker wasn't on) to sit with me when I had to be supervised, as they wouldn't constantly stare at me and make me feel paranoid. They understood how I felt about being watched, almost as if they had been through something similar themselves.

We'd watch the TV and act normally, sometimes having conversations about things that we shared in common such as *Lord of the Rings*, and heated debates about things that I didn't care much about, such as *The Daily Star*, meat eaters and *Star Wars*.

I had many arguments with certain nurses, as they'd accuse me of hiding food when I hadn't, and would give me lectures about how I had to try to make an effort. I would get so angry with them. They had absolutely no idea what it was like to suffer with anorexia. (Or did they?) They had no clue what it was like to constantly deprive yourself. They had no inkling of the pain of splitting skin; the numbness of freezing fingers and toes, or radiator and hot water bottle burns on thighs and arms.

I would only hide food when I was having a really bad day and felt as though I had eaten far too much already. I didn't like doing it at first, as I was nervous and convinced that I would get caught. But the more I did it the easier it became to just slip the food into a napkin and hide it in my lap, under my leg, or behind my pillow, until I could dispose of it. It became a sort of skill. It was obviously easier to hide food from certain nurses than from others. We would have training nurses come on to the ward, for example, and they would be left to sit with me. I'd start up a conversation that would involve laughing on both sides, when heads went back, and eyes closed during the fit of laughter, away the food went. Or I would ask for the television to be turned over so it would give me a few seconds to close my fists around the food, scrunch it up and slip it inside some tissue. They were oblivious to my sneaky tactics, making hiding food as simple as blinking. When I hid food from Lisa and Nina, I felt guilty about it, genuinely bad. But those feelings lasted only for a few hours at the very most. The voice would remind me that it didn't matter who I was hiding food from, as long as I did it without being caught.

It was a lot easier to dispose of food at home, mainly because I had freedom of movement, but also because my parents never suspected that I would do such a thing. I was their daughter. I wouldn't lie to them. I never did in the past, why would I now? Of course, they never realised quite how much power the voice had over my mind and actions. My parents were simply people to the voice. They were not anyone special. That was how I needed to see them: as people I needed to deceive to achieve my goals – anorexia's goals.

During the first few weeks in hospital, the nurses didn't say anything to me about finishing my meals, but now that I had been on bed rest for a lengthy period, and my weight wasn't improving, I was being encouraged to finish my meal or at least try to eat a bit more than before. Some nurses would be pushy and more forceful than others, which I hated and it really pissed me off. Of course, at that time I didn't even consider that they were simply trying their best to help me get well. All I knew was they wanted me fat so they could laugh and joke and make a mockery of me, and there was no way that I would allow that to happen.

I was eating just slightly more than when I first came into hospital, but that was because I was threatened with being tube fed; but I still wasn't eating enough. I would now eat the same amount at every meal and break: half of my cereal and apple at breakfast; half an Ensure Plus drink at my morning break; half of my lunch, depending on what it was (if it was quiche or something else with quite a high fat content, I would eat less, or hide it); half of my afternoon break, etc.

I didn't dare take one more mouthful than usual. I thought (and the voice told me) that if I did take just one more mouthful, I would instantly put on loads of weight. It was the same with drinks. At first, I drank only water, and thought that if I drank too much of it, it would start to contain calories and help to fatten me up. So I would only allow (well, the voice would only allow) myself to have a certain amount each day.

When I had bad days I'd look in the mirror and see a fat moon face staring back at me, with rolls of fatty blubber instead of a slim, graceful neck, and thighs that looked like tree trunks. But other days, I could look and see what was really there: a gaunt, pale face with almost transparent skin, and a bony bird neck, and thighs which looked as if they were going to cave in as they had no support. I would see the ghostly image that I was, but my visions of myself changed from day to day. One day I could be a quivering mound of flabby flesh, and the next, a skeleton just risen from the grave.

Because I wasn't gaining weight and had been on bed rest for a considerable time, the nurses and my parents began to get extremely suspicious. There were quite a few occasions when my mum would lose her patience and demand to know why I hadn't moved forward with my recovery. I simply sat there, smiling at the wall. I was in my safe zone. I hadn't gained weight. The voice was still patting my bony back and congratulating me on my success. But sometimes the emotion would hit me, and I would collapse in sobs, screaming that I didn't know why I wasn't gaining weight. It was rightly assumed that part of the reason was that I was secretly exercising in the shower room. It was discussed in a Ward Meeting with the nurses and doctors that I should have my showers supervised by a female nurse, so that it would be impossible for me to exercise.

I couldn't believe it when they told me. It also didn't help that the nurse who came to tell me basked in my misery. She was one of the few for whom my hatred ran deep. My shower was the only privacy that I'd get all day and they wanted to invade that and take it away from me as well as everything else. I was so upset and angry about it, that I remember bursting into tears, and shouting abuse at everyone that tried to come near. My life wasn't getting any better at all. It seemed to be getting progressively worse. I had always been very, very paranoid about people seeing my body, any part of it, since I had become anorexic. I didn't even let my mum see me in my bra and knickers, as I was so scared that she would laugh at my fat legs, flabby bum, and saggy stomach. I was petrified that the rumours would spread around the ward like wildfire that I was a grotesque sight to behold, and that all the food should be kept under lock and key.

The first supervised shower I had, I was a nervous wreck. I very nearly didn't have it. (I considered refusing to have a shower until they let me have them unsupervised, but then I reconsidered, as I don't think I could have endured not having a proper wash.)

To my amazement, having the supervised shower wasn't as bad as I thought it would be. Sabina, one of the nurses I got on really well with, supervised me the first time. She was very understanding about me feeling paranoid, and sat in the wheelchair and faced the wall, so I wouldn't feel that she was watching me. I stripped off as fast as I could, and jumped into the shower, quickly pulling the shower curtain across. I managed to do some squats and lunges while I lathered and washed my body, not even stopping when I slipped and almost cracked my head on the showerhead. When I finished, I got out and dressed as quickly as possible. Sabina had no idea about my exercise in the shower, as the water had successfully muted the thudding I created on the shower tiles. I was glad the first ordeal was over, but I was positive that she'd seen some of my body and so I couldn't look her in the eye. But she reassured me over and over again that she had seen absolutely nothing.

Over time, having to be supervised in the shower became less of an issue (even though I still hated it) and I became skilled at undressing quickly and showering in under five minutes. I continued with my exercise while in the shower though.

When my mum came to visit, she would take me for my shower, but I made her face the wall, as I was still paranoid about what she would think if she saw my fat body. Even though she was my mother. I assumed EVERYBODY had the same image of me in their minds: an image of a fat, lazy, greedy, ugly, selfish slob.

After two months in hospital, I was allowed to join in the group activities held in the lounge or the kitchen, but not in any that involved going outside or walking or exercise, and I had to remain seated at all times – which was unbelievably frustrating. It was fantastic joining in the activities though. It meant that I could see and talk to the other patients and get out of my 'cell' for an hour or so.

We would do a variety of self-esteem and positive thinking exercises; many were not as constructive or successful as the nurses imagined they would be. For example, once we were all told to create collages of things we admired in life and which we aspired to be. A mountain of magazines was set before us and, naturally, the thin models were plastered over my cardboard.

Seeing their waif-like bodies decorating the pages of these glossy death wish lists only encouraged me to strive to weigh nothing at all. Maybe if that happened, I would be the ethereal beauty that famous designers decorated. The models were plastered over my work. Layer upon layer of bones and haunting eyes, astronomically expensive garments hanging off slight shoulders and impossibly high heels clutching tiny ankles.

My finished work was placed underneath my bed for easy access. I'd remove it every day, and study the pictures. Sometimes, reality would coat my eyes and for a matter of moments I would see just what was there: ill girls sacrificing their health and often their lives for fashion and fame. The rest of the time, I looked through a green tint, and simply longed to be one of the paper-posed images of perfection.

Chapter 9

Making The Choice To Change

Time went by, and something suddenly clicked in my mind. I consciously realised that things weren't changing. I wasn't putting on a sufficient amount of weight; I wasn't off bed rest; I wasn't allowed to go out of the hospital; and I was still having supervised showers. What I naively thought would be only a few weeks in hospital had turned into months. My mind had shifted to another level, and I was beginning to see the reality of my actions.

I believe that the fact that I'd started opening up to people and sharing with them my emotions and feelings had helped this mind shift. A number of the other patients gave me their trust and would upload their worries and concerns, in the hope that I could help. I didn't mind this in the slightest, and would offer them my views on what I felt would be best for them. My advice ranged from advising them to increase their calorie intake (something I now knew a heck of a lot about) to what to do when gagging for a cigarette. I never smoked, members of my family do and I had spent hours in the past researching into ways they could quit with the assistance of friends, family and their own willing minds. Phoebe constantly offered me support in all forms. She would hold me when I cried, restrain me when I would scream and want to hurt myself, and take away calorie counter books and glossy magazines when she knew that I needed to gain weight, and that looking at the content of food and the shapes of supermodels would do me no favours. It wasn't often that I would see her break down and struggle to manage her own difficult situation. She always had the persona of someone who cared and coped. The seeping bandages on her arms revealed the fact that she was 'coping' secretly, and not wishing for involvement from others.

Another friend I made through the Community Meetings was seventeen-year-old Lauren. She'd been in hospital since she was thirteen, and her health problems stemmed from before then. Abuse from her family had created demons in her mind that I suspect will never fully fade, no matter how long she is connected with psychiatrists, care and love. There was one occasion during my afternoon break when a number of nurses on the ward were ill and there was also an important meeting scheduled to take place. Therefore, there were fewer staff to take care of patients. I was dividing my cereal bar into numerous pieces when I noticed the flash of a smiling face pass by my window. I dropped the piece of cereal bar and peered out to see Lauren hurtling across the car park, her long brown hair flying out behind her.

"What's wrong?" Jackson asked, looking up from his newspaper. I opened my mouth to tell him what I'd seen. But then closed it again. What would Lauren say if I told on her? Would she ever be able to trust me as a friend? Would she hate me forever? On the other hand, what if she was going to do something beyond stupid? What if she was planning on hurting herself, or even taking her own life? How would I be able to cope knowing that I might have saved her by simply telling someone where she had gone? The guilt would remain with me for ever. I would never be able to forgive myself for my act of stupidity. I would have to tell Jackson. There were no two ways about it.

"What's wrong, Katie?" Jackson repeated, his eyes still trained on my face. "Something is wrong, I can tell. You look petrified."

"Lauren just… " I began.

As if on cue, Norman, a training nurse, appeared at my door.

"We need some help," he said breathlessly. "Like now."

Jackson looked at him and then at me. I nodded in indication that I could be trusted with my food. So he dropped the paper and ran.

I later found out that Lauren had run for three miles to Newport Bridge, one of the largest bridges in Middlesbrough, that spans the River Tees, and had tried to throw herself from it. Miles, a schizophrenic patient and another friend of mine (except every now and then when his illness sparked up and he hated everything that existed) had followed her out of the hospital to the bridge and managed to keep hold of her arms until the police and ambulance service arrived. Hearing Lauren being carried back inside the unit, watching through the gap in my open door as she struggled to get free, listening, as she demanded to know why they'd stopped her jumping, I realised that I was one of the lucky ones. I still wanted to live. I had the enthusiasm to continue with life.

The following day, Lauren was back to normal, apart from looking slightly more drawn than usual. She was at the Community Meeting and when I sent a smile her way, she sent one back. Although I knew it was only a mask. Inside, she was still screaming.

Meanwhile, Dawn had managed to gain enough weight and get off bed rest, which encouraged me enormously to battle with the voice that was still controlling me.

Seeing her having a brilliant time simply doing normal things, such as taking a walk to the shop, inspired me and I thought, 'If she can do it, then so can I!' I was getting sick and tired of my life on bed rest and the same routine day after day after day was taking its toll on what remained of my sanity. I began to listen more to what the doctors, nurses and my family had to say, not that I agreed with all of it. I was told, and I now knew, that it was me, and only me who could change things. I was the one who had to do the eating and ignore the voice in my head. Nobody else could do that for me. Nobody could reach inside my mind and pull anorexia out by its thin tail. No one else could wave a magic wand and make the voice vanish. I knew then that if I didn't start eating more and put on weight, I'd be in hospital for a very, very long time. I was absolutely petrified of change and knew for a certainty that I would keep delaying my decision.

Nanna phoned me every day, to see how I was and encourage me. She'd also regularly sent letters and hand-made cards begging me to try harder and telling me how important I was in her life, and sent little presents through the post. She played a big part in helping me to battle harder and keep on fighting.

I was constantly encouraged to change my meal plan. I had previously refused to change anything at all. But now I was having second thoughts. I pulled myself together and after a few days of agonising 'Should I? Shouldn't I?' I decided to go for it, although I knew I would feel shit about it, and the voice would give me hell beyond belief.

An appointment was made for Lia to see me in my room. We decided that it was a good idea to start small and make changes to my morning break. I normally had an Ensure Plus drink, which contained 330 calories and 10 grams of fat (I had memorised the content!). So I decided to try to have chocolate instead, as the

Ensure Plus had the same calorie and fat content as an average chocolate bar. I hadn't eaten chocolate in well over a year, and it was a tremendous step for me to take. Everybody, including Dawn, encouraged me, saying that it would be fantastic if I could, and it would mean one step forward to beating the voice. The voice, naturally, screamed at me not to, to ignore other people's advice and only listen to what it had to say. Of course, it used the old tactic too, saying that I'd gain masses of weight within moments. I attempted to block my ears, but still its scream rang shrill and unstoppable.

For three days I agonised over which chocolate bar to choose. I saw an advert for Cadbury's Dream Bars, and I thought they looked absolutely delicious. So on 22nd February 2002, I gave Lisa some money, and she went to the shop and bought me a Dream Bar. When it was placed in front of me in all its glory, I stared at it for about ten minutes and panicked and nearly backed out of even opening it. It looked less frightening tucked away in its wrapper. Although it had the same amount of calories in it as an Ensure Plus I was petrified of trying something new. The voice was screaming at me "One bite of that chocolate and the bed will break under the weight of your lard! Don't you dare eat it! DON'T YOU DARE!" But I did my best to ignore it. I even talked aloud to myself with Lisa sitting by me (speaking aloud to myself with someone in the room was something I'd never done before, but I knew it was necessary), telling it to sod off and leave me alone to get on with what I needed to do.

Eventually, I picked up the bar with trembling fingers. I felt tears prick my eyes as I slowly opened the wrapper and broke off one of the white chunks. I stared at it for a moment, taking in its simple beauty – a perfect piece of pure, white chocolate. I couldn't believe what I was doing as I closed my eyes and bit into half of the piece in my hand. I let it slowly melt in my mouth, and I was in heaven, the chocolate lived up to its name, I felt as though I was floating in a dream of happiness.

I'd never tasted anything as good as that half a piece of chocolate. I rang my mum and nanna as soon as I had finished the piece to tell them the great news, and they were both ecstatic. I managed to eat four of the six pieces (the equivalent of about half an Ensure in calories and fat), and I was really proud of myself.

But I also felt a tremendous amount of guilt, and my stomach felt bloated and sore. The temptation to throw up in my sink was enormous, but I was denied time alone, and despite claiming to need the toilet desperately, Lisa said I wasn't allowed to go until an hour had passed and the chance of throwing up the chocolate was slim as it would be digested. As for the remainder of the day, the voice screamed at me, calling me a fat, greedy fool, who was losing control and who didn't care about gaining masses of weight; a fool who'd given in to temptation for the forbidden food. The food, the voice told me, 'of the fatties'.

But a little part of me knew that I had stood up for myself. I had done what I wanted to, what I needed to. I did find it difficult to stick to my meal plan for the rest of the day, as the guilt hung over me like a black cloud, and every glimpse of myself in a mirror would fill me with sickening horror, as I would observe a pulsing mound of flesh and not a young girl.

The following week, Lia came back to see me and was all smiles and hugs when she heard that I had managed the chocolate. I made another change to my meal plan and altered it so that in the evening I could have soup, a slice of bread and a piece of fruit instead of my usual rice cakes and cereal. That was another huge step to take; I hadn't eaten bread in well over a year either, but Lia, through sheer determination and skill, persuaded me to give it a go. Although it would contain the same amount of calories as my rice cakes and cereal, I was still scared of changing my routine and of eating bread.

A few days after making the changes, I went for the soup and bread for my tea. It was put in front of me, but I had waited too long after making the decision, and the voice was overpowering, reminding me of the complex carbohydrates and calories, so I couldn't manage even a bite of the bread. I did eat some of the soup though, which I thoroughly enjoyed. The bread didn't find sanctuary in my stomach; it ended up with the other rotting food in my bin.

Chapter 10

Fighting But Still Failing

As days went by after my two big changes, my determination to get off bed rest grew all the more powerful, and I pushed myself harder to eat more and to battle with the voice. My determination showed and I now managed to eat an entire low fat Müller Rice, instead of half. Occasionally I still hid food though, especially when I'd had a bad day, and was tired of battling with the voice, thinking 'enough is enough, you can't win this fight today.' But I still felt as though I'd achieved something when I successfully hid food.

I thought that because I was now eating more than when I was first admitted, and I was eating chocolate, I would have put on a sufficient amount of weight. But I hadn't. I couldn't understand it. I couldn't do my full exercise routine in the shower because I was supervised, and I was still on observations, so exercising in my room was out of the question. I couldn't make myself sick because my door was constantly open. How was I losing weight still? Then I remembered all the little bits of food I'd hide. They all added up, each individual calorie and gram of fat. My little bits of exercise also added up, and as I was still at a very low weight, small things made a difference. Although I was eating, the calories I was taking in weren't enough. The doctors told me if I didn't start putting on weight, I would have to be tube fed, and I would have absolutely no say in the matter as I was under eighteen and was putting my life at risk.

I couldn't believe it when I was told this. I *was* eating, and trying my best to eat new foods despite all the horror that I went through in my mind and the sickness and disgust I felt when I looked at myself in the mirror. Not to mention the physical pain I put myself through because my stomach felt bloated and my limbs heavy and sore after I thought I'd eaten too much. After all this, they wanted to punish me. I felt as though I was fighting a losing battle, and seriously considered giving up altogether and allowing the voice to take complete control. I had always said that I would NEVER get so ill that I would have to be tube fed. The thought of it sickened me to the bone. Dawn had told me that she had had it done when she was first admitted, and said that it was hell.

"It is much better to eat by yourself," she told me.

I decided there was NO WAY that I would have a tube stuffed up my nose, pumping me full of calories when I could eat by myself. I used to hear Dawn screaming and crying, smashing her fists against her bedroom walls and threatening nurses when she was held down and the tube inserted up her nose. My blood would run cold. I didn't want to be in that position, ever. Having someone sit by my side for hours at a time, watching me, waiting for me to do the smallest, most insignificant thing wrong was bad enough. To have four people hold my body down so that I couldn't move and ram something up my nostril was something that was never going to happen. I was adamant about that.

So I cried, and shouted, and swore, and cried some more while I forced myself to eat more food. My stomach felt sore and swollen, but still I continued. I needed to. The pain was deceiving. It wasn't real, it was only in my mind because the voice wanted me to feel it. I'd eat an apple and feel as though I'd consumed a six-course meal. One day, I'd be full of determination, and the next, I would feel like, 'Why should I bother? What is the point of fighting this when all I really want is to be light as air and the voice's perfect child?'

But the tube threat really made me think: I've got a lot more to do with my life than sit on this damn bed day after day. I've got more to do than watch people watch me sitting, screaming and staring. It made me think of the hell I'd put my family through for years; the hell that I'd put myself through, and all my teenage life that I was wasting and would continue to waste if I didn't make an effort. I mean, I hadn't been out of the hospital in months. What kind of a life is that? A terrible and lonely one, I can tell you. I wasn't a teenager, I was simply being, existing, just in the clouded bubble of a possessed mind.

So I battled the voice a little more each day. And instead of feeling as if my world had ended when I gained a bit of weight, I made the effort to be thrilled and positive about it. I constantly wrote down the positives of getting well and wrote hateful letters to the voice, claiming I was managing fine without listening to its orders. Of course, that wasn't always the truth. Often, I'd long to allow it to take control again, and guide me to where I thought I wanted to be.

I thought of gaining weight as being a step closer to getting out of hospital and going home. It felt terrible when I had to ring up my family and tell them the news that I had lost weight. But it was fantastic when I'd ring them and tell them that I had gained. To hear them sounding so pleased would fill me with pride instead of fear as it had done before. That helped me to carry on with the battle, and get off bed rest. The added support from the hospital staff made my weight gain easier to deal with. I'd become very close to certain members of staff such as Lisa, Sabina and Jackson, and I looked upon them almost as family. I could speak to them about anything that concerned me, and they knew when I was in need of a hug or general attention. I would accept it with open arms, most of the time, unless the voice brainwashed me into believing that I didn't deserve any attention.

The first time I was allowed out of the hospital, was on 10th March, Mother's Day. (That's the reason *why* I was allowed to leave the hospital.) It was discussed with a number of doctors and nurses, and they decided that I was allowed two hours' leave (how kind is that! Not) on the agreement that I would promise not to walk around, as I was still on bed rest, and I had to sit in the wheelchair at all times.

I found it humiliating going out in the wheelchair. I saw people I knew, and who knew that I could walk perfectly well. I also felt guilty when I saw old people struggling to walk, and I was being pushed along. But going out in the wheelchair and putting up with embarrassment and guilt was much better than not going out at all. The excitement bubbled up inside of me for days before I went, and I was shaking with anticipation as my parents came to collect me. A burst of relief flooded through me as my dad pushed me out through the hospital's front doors and, as I breathed in the cool smell of fresh air, I couldn't help grinning from ear to ear.

We went to our local pub for a drink, and then home. It was very strange going home, because I hadn't been there for such a long time it didn't feel like *my* home. I felt slightly awkward and out of place. Like I didn't belong, and I shouldn't be there. It was weird seeing our cat, Del, because the last time I had seen him he was only a kitten and now I barely recognised him – he was a strapping young tom cat (with one hell of an attitude problem!). I don't think he recognised me either. He seemed to look at me as though he was thinking "Who the hell are you, stranger? What are you doing here?" But it was great to be with my family and outside my small, stuffy hospital cell.

I cried when Mum had to take me back. My two hours of leave had flown by, and I didn't want the time to end. I begged Mum not to take me, but when I saw her eyes fill with tears as she tried to explain that I had to go back to get better, I pulled myself together and I realised that I couldn't stay at home. I had to go back. It was how I would get better. Staying at home was not an option. It just wasn't possible, and if I did stay, well, I would have given up all the hard work I'd put into my recovery. I would have finished worse off than when I was first admitted. To put it bluntly, I would have ended up dead.

I arrived back at the hospital in time for my tea, and I was still crying as I ate my rice cakes and cereal. Although going home should have inspired me to finish my tea, it didn't. I really wanted to eat it all, but I just couldn't. The voice wouldn't allow me to, claiming I had indulged in too many treats already that day and needed to pay for my stupidity. In the voice's opinion, spending time outside the hospital, in the company of my family, smiling and laughing with them and drinking a can of Diet Coke at an unregulated time in a 'strange place' were all classed as treats, that I hadn't earned.

I cried myself to sleep that night, wishing that I had been strong enough to eat all my tea. Wishing that I could be at home. Wishing I could make the voice in my head go away forever and leave me to be Katie; free. Wishing that hospital and my illness was all just a bad dream, and that I'd wake up and I would be a normal girl, living a normal live, with a normal soul, body and mind.

On 28th March 2002, I had some fantastic news. I weighed 38 kg, only half a kilogram away from my target to get off bed rest, and I was allowed to be off five-minute observations! I was over the moon as I now only had to be looked in on every half an hour or so. This was evidence that the hospital staff were starting to regain their trust in me. I guess that it was because it had been a while since I had been caught hiding food or exercising. Plus, I was managing to gain weight, even if it was a stupidly tiny amount, instead of constantly losing it. After my visit home, I gradually started to put on weight, but I would get scared at my own determination to get well and I would lose what I had gained again. Half of me would be pleased, while the other half would be devastated. In a way, I was terrified about coming off bed rest. Part of me had this mad theory that I would be sent straight back to Billingham Campus (although I had been reassured that I wouldn't be) and that because I was off bed rest people would think I was well again. They'd think I could cope with anything that was hurled at me. I can see now that those were the anorexic thoughts. My thoughts would tell me all the positive things about coming off bed rest, such as not having to use the wheelchair, having showers alone again and going out of the hospital on visits. I could join in with the activities on the Unit and be able to prepare my own meals instead of eating what the hospital provided. But the voice would tell me that these positive things weren't as good as staying thin, so it was a better idea to stay on bed rest. It was far easier to stay in the voice's routine and only change when it commanded me to.

But on 26th April 2002, I was having my afternoon break with Alicia supervising me and I had drunk half my Ensure when I put it down. Alicia turned to me and asked, "Have you finished it?"

"No," I replied simply, as I swung my legs back on to my bed, reached for my book and leaned back for my rest. She shouldn't have even asked such a stupid question, I thought. I would have made far more fuss if I'd even considered finishing it.

She went on to tell me all the good things that would happen if I came off bed rest. So I told her all the things I had listed in my mind and diary, and she said, "Well, how do you expect to get to those positive things if you keep listening to the voice and not finishing your Ensures?"

"I will get there," I replied confidently; flicking open my book and focusing on the chapter I was reading.

"You'll not get anything if you don't finish your Ensures. Now try!" and she went on and on until I shouted, "OK! I'll bloody try!" With tears running down my face I slammed down my book, picked my drink up and sipped through the straw until the carton was empty. I then threw it on my table and shouted, "Look, it's finished! Are you happy now? Are you happy that I feel like fat, lazy shit? Are you happy that the voice will give me grief until I want to slit my wrists?"

She just smiled and said, "It will help you to get off bed rest."

I flung myself down on my bed with a sob and faced the wall. But inside, a tiny bit of pride was growing.

The following day I asked, well pleaded, again for a few hours' leave, as it was the Goth Festival in Whitby at the weekend which my sister and I go to every year. And I wasn't prepared to miss it, even if I did have to go to it in a sodding wheelchair.

I very nearly didn't make it, but after a couple of nurses (you know who you are! And thank you!) put in a good word for me, and my mum said that she would take me out whether the doctors liked it or not – I was allowed to go.

I spent hours putting on my make-up, velvet, lace and silver and allowing the butterflies to flutter inside, but it was all over in what felt like a matter of minutes. My parents pulled out the wheelchair when we arrived, and I sat in it for a maximum of five minutes, before I was up and away with my sister amid the sea of black clothing, fangs and silver piercings. Although it felt like such a short time, it was fantastic being out again in the real world, the Goth world. This was my world – where I rightly belonged, and I wanted more.

Soon after my visit to Whitby, after an emotional phone conversation with my nanna which ended with us both crying, I decided that I would talk to Alicia in my Individual Session about how much I wanted to get off bed rest, but I really needed more focused help to get the voice out of my head. We discussed, in depth, how I felt and what we could do about it. Alicia saw how determined I was, but she also understood how hard it was for me. We agreed that I would try to finish one meal a day. That would help me get off bed rest and make the voice weaker, she assured me. I decided I would try to finish my tea, as that seemed the easiest at the time. I was very nervous about finishing a meal, and it took me a few days after our talk to actually do it.

It took me almost an hour to eat my three rice cakes and my bowl of bran flakes and afterwards I felt really fat, greedy and worse than shit. But a little part of me was pleased and proud that I had managed to beat the voice. My family was over the moon when I told them and that made coping with the guilty feelings slightly easier. The voice was still strong in my head, and the day after I had finished my tea, I felt a sudden need to lose weight and cut back on what I was eating again. My weight went down, down, down, up, down, etc. I was determined in my mind, but I was finding it really hard to put my positive determination into positive action.

My parents couldn't understand why I was still on bed rest after such a long time. They would get upset and angry when they visited and ask why I wasn't getting my life back on track. Their often harsh words upset me and I would try extra hard to please them, but I always ended up back at the same point. I didn't want to be back there; it was a battle I was continually losing.

Many visits from my parents ended with them storming out in a flurry of tears and torrents of abuse from everyone. My siblings came less frequently now because my mood was constantly up and down. I would smile and laugh one moment, engaging in conversations and jokes with them, but the next, I would be screaming and shouting, claiming nobody understood me and everyone wanted to see me fat. Another reason my brothers and sister found it difficult to visit was the other patients and their behaviour. It wasn't a rare occurrence for them to be confronted by a suicidal schizophrenic being restrained by at least four members of staff in the corridor. Or be deafened by the screams of an anorexic fighting against the tube.

I was again threatened with tube feeding, but this time I took it even more seriously. I decided that no matter how shit, guilty, confused or fat I felt, I would eat more and gain weight. Only I could do the eating, and only I could ignore the voice. It was me who could gain enough weight to put two feet on the floor and have the right to walk. It was my battle and only I could fight it and win. And I was determined that I would.

Chapter 11

Rising Out Of The Shadows

After five months of being on bed rest, having supervised meals and showers, restricted outings, using the wheelchair, and relying on others to help me get through my daily routine, I fought. I fought the hardest battle I have ever had to fight in my life. I challenged the voice every single day. I decided to change more things on my meal plan although it terrified me. I fought against the voice's wishes and did it. The sense of power and pride was huge when I managed to ignore the voice and do what I knew in my heart was right. This gave me a massive confidence boost (most of the time). I was now finishing my Ensure Plus drinks and all my meals regularly. The amount of praise I got from the nurses and my family when I ate everything on my meal plan was enormous. It really helped me to continue. I discovered though that if I made the tiniest slip, the voice would try to worm its way back into my mind and take over again. The battle was ongoing and constant.

The date I came off bed rest (a date I will never forget!) was Thursday, 2nd May 2002. That day was the happiest day in months but terrifying too. I was confronted with many aspects of life that had become alien to me. Here is the page from my diary on that day:

OH MY GOD! I AM OFF BED REST! I weigh exactly 38.5kg! I am over the moon! All my hard work has paid off. I was allowed to prepare my own breakfast for the first time in over five months, and I managed to eat it all! I spent all my morning readjusting my room exactly how I wanted it (I wasn't allowed to when I was first admitted), and WALKING, yes WALKING to the toilet without having to ask.

I was asked if I wanted to eat my meals in the Dining Room, but I said I still want to eat all my meals in my room, as I am still really paranoid about eating in front of a lot of people. I now have so many things to be happy about. I can now have unsupervised showers and much longer leave at the weekend!

I did really well with my eating today, which included finishing an Ensure Plus again! There's NO WAY I am going to go back on bed rest, so I am keeping up the hard work. Even if I feel crap about finishing my meals, life is too good off bed rest to go back on it.

This evening I had my first unsupervised bath in months; actually, it was the first bath I had since coming into hospital. And I can tell you I didn't want to get out, it was heaven! I feel different, alive. I have never experienced these feelings of complete and utter joy before. It is scary too, all these new things at once – Very scary.

The next few days I was on a constant high. I kept thinking that I was in a dream, and that I would wake up any minute and be back on my bed. It was so fantastic not having to ask whether I could go to the toilet or have a shower, and it was brilliant being allowed to prepare my own meals. (No more soggy bran flakes for me!) It also made it much easier for me to eat and cope with the guilty thoughts and feelings now that I could walk and move around freely.

The nurses did advise me not to walk around too much though, as I was still at a low weight, and I could lose what I'd gained very quickly if I did too much activity. I tried to follow their advice, but it was hard, as I been stuck on my bed for five months. All I wanted to do was move around. I was free, and I wanted to move and let my legs 'breathe'.

My entire family was overjoyed that I was finally off bed rest after such a long time. It felt like an amazing achievement being able to greet them at the front door of the hospital instead of them coming to my bedside.

At the weekend, I went out with my family for the first time without the wheelchair. We went into Middlesbrough, shopping, and despite the fact it was such a mundane event, to me it was beyond exciting. It felt as though I had never done such a thing before, and I was discovering shopping for the very first time. I drank a full Ensure Plus in front of my dad, and seeing the smile appear on his face when I finished it, feeling the gentle squeeze of his hand in mine and the shine in his eyes gave me such an amazing feeling of happiness and pride that the voice's words were reduced to incoherent babble. The feeling in my stomach is best described as a Catherine Wheel whizzing round and round. It felt so wonderful to see my family truly happy with something I'd done after such a long time of disappointing them and letting their hopes crash and die.

Before I knew it, weigh day was upon me again like a black storm cloud. I had tried to convince myself that I wouldn't be back on bed rest, but I knew, deep, deep down that I would be. Although I'd been trying really hard to stick to my meal plan, I knew that I hadn't done as well as I could have done. I woke up on Monday weigh day with a feeling of dread in the pit of my stomach. I had tried to be as inactive as I possibly could be the day before, and I hoped and prayed that it had helped. I considered putting my bracelets around my ankles again but resisted temptation. I knew I would be lying to myself, and so remained strong against the voice.

I stood on the scales and looked down at the digital numbers, and the disappointment hit me like a smack in the face. I had lost 300 grams, and my weight had dropped to 38.2 kg. It wasn't an enormous weight loss, but it was enough to put me back on bed rest until the next weigh day. I was so angry, upset and disappointed with myself that I sprinted back down the corridor, not giving the nurses the chance to get the wheelchair to bring me back in. I rushed into my room and slammed the door. Tears were streaming down my face like Niagara Falls. I didn't want to ring my family because I'd promised them and myself that I wouldn't go back on bed rest, and I knew how devastated they would be. I'd already ruined my day, and there was no way that I wanted their day to be a miserable one too because of my stupidity.

I made an effort to gain the weight by finishing all my breakfast. It was humiliating and degrading to have to ask to go to the toilet again, and to use the wheelchair to get there. I was fidgety and restless, sitting on my bed once more. I wanted to be up and moving as I had been a few hours previously, and I was determined to be back off bed rest by Thursday weigh day.

All my focus went into finishing my meals and coping with the guilty feelings and thoughts, and the voice, of course. And I did it! By Thursday, I'd gained 500 grams, and I was back on my feet! I had the same great feeling, and I felt proud that I'd coped with the guilty feelings, ignored the voice and taken one step away from anorexia and closer to home.

Chapter 12

Feeding My Fear And Feeling It Fade

That weekend, it was my dad's birthday, so I went home for a special birthday meal. It was the first time that I had eaten a meal in front of my family for months. It went better than I expected, although I still felt unbelievably paranoid. It was hard to imagine ever having sat down and eaten normally with them. We had spaghetti, Quorn Bolognaise and salad. I didn't eat a lot, but it was better than nothing. None of my family said anything when I pushed my almost full plate away, as we all wanted to keep a good and happy atmosphere. I felt quite proud of myself when the meal was over. I had just taken another positive step and done something I hadn't done in a very long time. I had faced another one of my big fears and conquered it.

Despite trying my best, I ended up back on bed rest again the following Monday after losing 300 grams. This time I felt like giving up, and not bothering any more. I was trying so very hard, but it seemed as though I was going round in one continuous circle. It wasn't right or fair. But I had a sudden change of heart and mind and I didn't give up and managed, with a struggle, to fight on. I owe so much to Dawn and Phoebe, Lisa, Sabina and

Jackson who reminded me hourly why I needed to fight, why I needed to get out of hospital and why I needed to take my life back from anorexia. They continually praised my writing, emphasising that I couldn't be a successful writer while stuck in a room in an adolescent mental health unit. I needed to snatch my health back and make myself known to the world.

I made a really determined effort to gain the weight I had lost. By this time, I was completing all my meals, except for my lunch, and on occasions I'd finish my morning break too. I still needed to make a huge effort to ignore the voice, which was continually going on at me, saying things like, "If you finish that Ensure Plus, you'll get fatter than an elephant and they weigh tons! You'll break the bed! You'll fall through the floor! You'll be the fattest thing on earth!" and I had to keep on repeating to myself over and over again, "You are eating and drinking to get off bed rest. You are not a pig! You are eating and drinking to get better. You are not an elephant! You are eating and drinking to survive. You will not get fat."

I was incredibly nervous when the time came to be weighed again. I was physically shaking and had to have assistance to stand straight on the scales. I wanted so badly to have put on weight. I just wanted to have gained enough to get back off bed rest.

I'd gained 500 grams, and my weight was 38.9 kg. I was thrilled, but I was also very concerned about my new weight. I felt fatter than an elephant. A beached whale fitted my perception of my body. I was very uncomfortable at this new weight, and I was convinced that people would look at me and think 'Bloody hell, look at Katie! Isn't she getting fat! What is she doing in hospital? What is she doing taking up precious space?'

I tried to ignore these negative anorexic thoughts and feelings, and thought of all the positives of being this weight. Things such as overnight leave off the ward, more freedom to do what I wanted, and another step to going home for good and of course regaining my periods. I found when I calculated that there were far more positives than negatives for gaining weight.

On the same day as coming back off bed rest, I asked whether I could have my evening drink unsupervised. I wanted to see for myself how well I'd cope without being watched. I wanted to battle the voice alone. The reply from the doctors was "Yes!" and I was overjoyed! At last, people had trust in me again. My request for longer leave at the weekend was also a positive "Yes". It was a fact that my life was now really starting to look up!

That evening, when I'd prepared my mug of Highlights, and brought it to my room, the voice in my head said to me, "Go on, pour it down the sink. No one will find out. Go on! You're unsupervised – you can't be caught. Go on!" At first, the temptation was enormous. The voice was right. How would anybody find out? But I ignored it and said aloud to myself, "No! I will NOT pour it away. I will drink all of it!" And I sat down, with the voice still nagging at me in my mind, and I started to drink.

When I swallowed the last mouthful of 'chocolaty goodness', I felt an enormous amount of pride well up inside me. I had beaten it! I had beaten the voice! And there was nothing to stop me doing it again. I can do it! I can beat it! The feeling of the drink warmed me like a hug from inside. I felt nourished and unusually content, feelings that I had been alienated from for a very, very long time – feelings unfamiliar but wonderful. Oh so wonderful.

At the weekend, I went home again for another meal. I found it much easier this time than previously, and I had a number of mouthfuls more than before, too. I challenged myself again that day, by eating my tea at home as well as my lunch! I felt really proud that I'd achieved such a lot in (what I considered to be) a very short time. My family was also ecstatic that I had made these changes. Knowing they were pleased made me feel even better and made the feelings of fatness and failure fade slightly.

The day after my second meal at home I became ill with sickness and diarrhoea. (I am not blaming your cooking, Mum!) I couldn't believe it. I was trying my very best and doing so well, and this was my reward? Grossness coming out of both ends! Everything I ate went straight back up (or down) again. A few months ago I would have given anything to be in this situation – but not now! Not now when all I wanted was to fight *against* anorexia. I tried my hardest to keep everything I consumed inside. But it had a will of its own, and wouldn't co-operate. Anorexia had taken the ball in its court again, and I was unwillingly tagging along.

The following day, which was weigh Monday, I had lost 1.2 kg and my weight had dropped to 37.8 kg all because of a bug. Had I been well, at a normal weight living an everyday life, the bug would probably have given me a slight stomach ache at the most, but because of my unnaturally low weight, my immune system couldn't fight back. I was back on bed rest, and was well and truly devastated. All my hard work and energy for nothing; all the tears and tantrums, trauma and terror of confronting my worst fears – all of it totally wasted. Again, I felt like giving up and quitting my battle. I was filled with the desire to lie back and let anorexia take its hold again and let it keep hold until I was limp and lifeless.

It took me a long time to come to my senses and realise just how stupid I would be if I went ahead and did that. I realised that if I quit fighting my battle, if I were to lie back and die then my time on earth would have been a complete waste of time, space and energy. I had the world to live for. There was so much I needed to do, so much I wanted to achieve. A bug, I decided, would not be the death of me.

So I made a huge effort to eat, but continued to throw it back up again. I was told I would have to wait for the sickness and diarrhoea to pass, and then put all my energy back into eating and putting the weight back on that I had lost. I begged and pleaded with the doctors to allow me to go home until it had passed, but was told that, for my own safety, I had to stay in hospital. I was in such a fragile state that if I collapsed a doctor needed to be immediately at hand. And to be honest, I felt as though I were at death's door, preparing for the end.

Luckily, the sickness and diarrhoea lasted only for three days. But in that short time, the weight dropped off me, so I knew I obviously wouldn't be off bed rest for Thursday. When I was weighed, I had maintained at 37.8 kg. I was disappointed, but the nurses, my family and I knew that it wasn't my fault this time. Now I could eat again without throwing it back up, I concentrated on completing my meal plan. After months of drinking Ensure Plus, I was getting sick, literally sick, of them. I found that now they tasted vile, really sickly and sweet. I don't know why I began to hate them all of a sudden, but I think it might have something to do with having too much of one thing. I asked if I could change my meal plan around so that I didn't have to have them any more. The problem was that to consume the same number of calories the amount of food would be phenomenal. So I put up with them for a few days. But the last straw came when I nearly threw up after two sips. The nurses didn't believe me at first, but when I went a sickly shade of green and heaved, they hurried to find a doctor who could prescribe an alternative.

The doctor came, and with him he brought a prescription for a meal replacement drink called 'Build Up', which is a milkshake drink and comes in loads of different flavours. They were 100 calories less than the Ensures (also contained less fat, not that I mentioned that to them!) so I was told that if I had them instead, I would have to add another 100 calories to my meal plan.

Lia was called, and we talked about what would be the easiest food for me to eat which had 100 calories in. We decided that biscuits would be the easiest. I could have them with my evening drink. So we put our heads together and decided on Fig Rolls, as they are my favourite biscuits. We worked out that I would have to eat one Fig Roll and three quarters of a half to make 100 calories. (Petty, wasn't I!) Lia attempted to persuade me to venture past my safeguard of 100 calories, but her efforts were fruitless as I refused point blank.

I started with the Build Ups that day, and to be honest, they were gorgeous. Much, much nicer than the Ensures, and they remain one of my favourite drinks to this day. I thought that adding one and three eighths of a Fig Roll would be quite easy, but boy, was I wrong. I was so scared of eating more, that it took me over a week to eat the full 100 calories. It was only when I plucked up the courage to eat it that the voice, giving me hell, quietened down a bit.

Although I'd lost weight and remained on bed rest, I was allowed the same leave as the previous weekend, and I was told I could eat a meal unsupervised if I wanted to! I realised that people's trust in me was increasing with every day that I did well. The first unsupervised meal was my breakfast, and initially, I was tempted, as I had been with my drink, to dispose of it. But I banished those thoughts and ignored the voice. Dawn had recently blocked her sink with various foods including rice pudding and bread, and had to have plumbers in her room to unblock the mess. The smell of rotting food that wafted down the corridors and lingered on the ward for days was atrocious. Through sheer determination and will power, I'd earned the trust of the staff on the ward as well as my family, and I had a strong desire to keep it. There was no way I wanted to face the humiliation of watching as my sink was unblocked. I didn't want to lie to anyone any more. And so I ate all the breakfast, and it was a hell of a lot easier to eat it without being watched over, I can tell you.

Putting back on the weight I'd lost was really, really difficult but I forced myself to ignore the feelings, and to keep fighting on. I would constantly try to think of all the positive rewards that I would get at the end.

At the weekend when I went home, I ate all my lunch for the first time in months! I felt incredibly guilty, but seeing the proud look on my parents' faces made the guilt easier to cope with. It also made me feel proud of myself.

I forced myself to eat everything on my meal plan the few days before I was weighed again. Although the guilty feelings were almost unbearable to the point that I wanted to let the voice take over again, I kept on pushing myself harder. I wanted to be sure. By completing my meal plan, I gained 900 grams and my weight was 38.7 kg. This was enough to be off bed rest again! It was really hard at first to eat *properly* after gaining that weight, but I was so determined and focused on not going back on bed rest ever again, that I completed my meal plan every day. Once my weight gain had sunk in, I had my goal set and I wouldn't give it up for some voice in my head, even if it had controlled me for well over a year.

My determination, will and focus paid off. I stayed off bed rest the second successive weigh day for the first time EVER! I had even managed to gain 200 grams. I knew my gain was another step in the right direction towards giving myself a better life and banishing the voice from my brain forever. Now my Care Plan was changing almost weekly, allowing me to do more things, and granting me more freedom than I'd had since my admission.

At home that weekend, I decided I was ready to take another step forward in my recovery. The step this time was to eat a meal out in public. It was nobody else's decision but my own. I had been encouraged to attempt something as extravagant as this by nurses, friends and my family but had paid no attention. I shrugged it off and muttered "Sometime, maybe," of course not meaning a word. It was only now that I was actually listening and taking action.

My parents and I went to a restaurant, and I studied the menu for over ten minutes, calculating the calorie and fat content of everything I could. Eventually, I ordered a jacket potato, no butter, with baked beans and salad. It appeared to be the healthiest and lowest fat meal on the menu. I remember feeling waves of paranoia sweep over me while I was eating. I was sure that every single person in the restaurant had his or her eyes on me and was sickened by what I was doing. Watching me, and thinking, 'Bloody hell! Look at the amount of food SHE'S got on her plate! What does that fatty think she is doing eating all that food?'

But of course they weren't staring at me and thinking those things. It was the voice, whispering and taunting. My paranoia faded a little during our meal, as Mum kept on reassuring and pointing out to me that, clearly, no one was taking any notice of what I was eating (which was a first in a very long time!). I didn't finish my meal, but I still felt proud of myself for taking another huge step forward. My parents were supportive as I had done something else I hadn't done in a long time. I did leave the restaurant feeling bloated and sick, yet it was anorexia's frail fingers prodding my sanity and convincing me that everyone saw me as an obese whale. I wrote page after page about how I was feeling and the inner pain that I was going through. Although I also observed the positives, writing them down too. Those included the happiness I'd felt in my heart when my parents smiled at me taking my first bite of potato and the delicious taste of achievement.

The next day, I ate my lunch and my tea at home again. Eating at home and in front of my family was becoming gradually easier the more I practised. I was slowly beginning to realise that they weren't interested in watching me. All they wanted was to see me eat again, to see me smile and laugh, be normal and happy around food and, of course, around them and our home.

They wanted to see Katie, how I had been before anorexia had taken and twisted me into something nightmarish and unforgiving. It was too late for the 'old Katie' to come back and make an appearance. That time had passed and was never returning; a new Katie was slowly emerging. Slowly, slowly as though rising from an early morning grey mist to evolve from a shimmering shadow into a shining sunbeam.

By the next weigh day, I had gained 800 grams. I felt unbelievably terrible and enormously fat. I tried to continue completing my meal plan, although often I found myself not taking my breaks if I wasn't reminded. A part of me wanted very much to take them to prove that I could be trusted and ultimately to prove my strength to the anorexia. Yet, another part of me wasn't sure, and the voice said a definite "NO!"

When I'd gained weight, I found it difficult not to listen and obey what the voice said to me. So calories continued to find their homes in the milkshake mix packets instead of in my body where they needed to be.

Chapter 13

Sleeping At Home

I had lost 200 grams but remained off bed rest (much to my delight and relief!). It was the fourth time I'd kept off. Although I'd lost a bit of weight, the doctors decided that, all in all, I was keeping focused and determined. I was granted another two of my requests: to have another meal unsupervised, and an overnight stay at home at the weekend!

Though I still had the voice plaguing my mind at most mealtimes, I was genuinely stronger-willed at the meals I ate alone. I was determined to maintain the trust that people were giving me.

As the day for my home overnight stay crept closer, my nerves rapidly increased. I am not sure why I felt apprehensive and on edge about staying in my own house. It was probably because it had been such a long time since I had spent a whole night with my family, and away from the safe and secure Unit.

I was positively excited and equally nervous on the day, but my parents and I went out for another meal, and the feelings of paranoia were not as bad as before. I also ate slightly more than before, which eased some of my anxieties about this enormous step.

The night at home went amazingly well. It was wonderful to sleep in my own bed again. It was a lot more comfortable than sleeping on the air-filled, rock hard mattress (which I had to have on my bed during my time on bed rest, to prevent me from getting bedsores). Mum came in throughout the night to check that I was all right, and to see her face smiling down at me, well, it was as though an angel was watching me. Her smile, of course, disguised the fear she felt about my health and her concerns over whether it had really been a good idea for me to come home for the night.

When Monday weigh day came around, I had lost 400 grams. I was frustrated, as I'd been trying phenomenally hard. Although I have to admit that a tiny part of me was glad, as I had been feeling really fat and the weight loss helped to get rid of some of those 'fat feelings'. Obviously, I shouldn't have been thinking like this. I should have gained weight and lived with the 'fat feelings'.

Over the next few weeks, my weight went up and down in small amounts, but I was still keeping off bed rest, and showing no signs of going back on. I was now trusted to eat all my meals unsupervised, and to have overnight leave at home every weekend and all weekend. It is hard to imagine now the incredible feelings I experienced back then about being able to do such simple things. It just goes to show that life really can get put on hold.

A few weeks later, it was announced that the TV in my room would be removed permanently. I freaked out and instantly started to panic. I had it on at every mealtime, as it helped to distract me while I was eating. (The only times I hadn't watched a TV while I was eating was when I went out with my parents.) They couldn't take it away! How would I manage to eat? How could I accomplish anything else without my trusted supporter? It was as though they wanted to make my life even more difficult than it already was. I was told that now I was off bed rest, some other patients were complaining that I had a TV in my room. I couldn't imagine which of my friends on the unit would have done such a thing. I assumed that it had been made up so that I would co-operate. Also, the doctors and nurses wanted me to eat without having to watch the TV. I was told that if I still wanted to be distracted while I ate, I could use my radio. I decided to try, but knew that it would be nowhere near as effective as the television.

The first meal without the TV in my room was nerve-racking. But when I'd finished, I'd done quite well. Not as well as I would have done with the TV, but OK none the less. It wasn't as bad as I thought it would be, and with each meal it became a little easier.

One day, Dawn came to my room looking overjoyed. Her eyes were shining, her smile wide and she gave off an all-round feeling of happiness, joy and success. I guessed it had something to do with her being discharged, and it was! (She'd recently had her eighteenth birthday, so she would have had to leave anyway to go on to another hospital specifically for adults.) I was overjoyed for her. She had worked incredibly hard at battling her demons and winning the war with food. I was also heavy-hearted that she was leaving as we had become so close, almost 'sister close', and I didn't know what I would do without having her to talk to and to have my daily moans and groans with. It may sound despicable, but in many ways I felt closer to Dawn than I did to my own sister. The relationship between Penny and me hardly existed any more, to my utmost dismay, of course. The previous closeness that had existed between us seemed only a happy memory.

Despite being upset about Dawn leaving, I was positive and happy for her. It also provided an incentive to continue with my own fight against the voice. I did have my own personal doubts about her discharge at the time, though. I was still ill at the time, and my mind was not my own. I had niggling thoughts that she was still too thin to go home. There was something about the way she continued to swing her narrow legs backwards and forwards when she sat down at the end of my bed, and something about the way she fidgeted with her frail fingers non-stop. She would also constantly twist towards my door to see whether anyone was there, as though she was petrified of being caught doing something wrong. I know these facts today, the fact that she was fidgeting and twisting because anorexia still demanded that she did so. The fact that she had hidden jewellery on her body because the voice claimed it would ensure a fast discharge. If I had been more aware at the time, I may possibly have prevented her from being discharged too early.

Now that I'd been off bed rest for a considerable amount of time, I was granted permission to make visits to the 'school' section of the hospital, for a few half hours a week. To begin with, I was petrified, as I believed I would be treated as though I was back at 'normal school' and the thought of 'normal school' terrified me to the point of tears. I discovered it was actually easy, gentle work (the same as I'd been given to do on bed rest). Catherine continued being kind, friendly, and caring. She didn't transform into the bad-tempered, fire-breathing dragon that most teenagers associate their teachers with. I found that spending a short time at 'school' helped take my mind off food and other things that were happening to and around me. It also helped me block out the nagging voice most of the time because my thoughts were concentrating on something completely unrelated to anorexia.

I was also allowed to take part in the more so-called 'active' activities, which involved going for short walks, trips to local parks and the shops in town. Despite the fact it was only once a week, the more weight I gained, and the stronger I became, the more frequently I was allowed to go. It was wonderful to get away from the unit for a few hours. At first, the time was very restricted, sometimes only ten minutes, and I would always beg for more. When I went out with other patients, we'd be stared at and often people would point and laugh at the jumbled, dysfunctional group of teenagers. Some members were far too thin, others obese, or covered with bandages hiding their self-inflicted wounds. We were certainly seen as 'the odd crowd'.

On one occasion, in Middlesbrough town centre, a woman approached Phoebe, asking if she had considered getting compensation for her accident. She had assumed that the bandages on Phoebe's arms were the result of a car accident and had pounced on her like a cat on a bird. She had no idea that they were actually the consequences of an engagement with Phoebe's trusted friend, the penknife. After Phoebe had calmly explained her situation, the woman hurriedly apologised, but stared after us while we walked away as though we were from another universe. It was at times like this that I felt most alienated from the world. As if I truly was a creature from another planet and that feeling made me feel sick to the bone.

Inside the unit, the sense of depression is suffocating, as though a plastic bag has been placed over your head and you are only supplied with a limited amount of air throughout the day. All you think about is your difficult situation, and other people's sadness and complications. No matter how colourfully the unit was decorated; no matter how many beautiful pictures they placed on the walls, nothing could take away that sense of doom and destruction, death and devastation. To me, the colours and the pictures on the walls, the smiling nurses with their chirpy conversations, the wide-screen TV, pool table and video games masked a blackness that could only be seen by those suffering. It was a blackness that filled every patient's soul. I would *always* dread going back after a weekend at home. I dreaded going back to the sadness and depression, the blackness that would instantly swallow me on entry, and back to where strangers had the power to tell me what I could and couldn't do with my life.

Chapter 14

My Revealing Review And Possible New School

On Wednesday, 10th July 2002, I had my first Case Review since being admitted. It was suggested that if my situation continued to improve at the same rate as it was currently, I would probably be discharged at the end of August, early September! I was delirious with happiness, but also slightly frustrated, as it seemed such a long time away and I wanted to go NOW! I wanted to get away from the bleak bedlam where I had been imprisoned for such a long time. Yet I knew in my heart that it was necessary that I remained there until anorexia had been abolished from my head and body, and I was prepared to face the 'big, wide world' again.

They also discussed me starting school again in September, at Abbey Hill College for anxious pupils. My parents were satisfied about how my review went and told me that both they and my brothers and sister couldn't wait for me to come home permanently. They made it clear that they didn't want me home until they knew it was Katie who they were accepting back into the house; their daughter, who had no intention of inviting an old 'friend' to stay again.

After my review, I went to visit Abbey Hill. I was hesitant yet curious, as I had major doubts, although I'd been reassured by Catherine that it was a wonderful place, and all the teachers were caring and friendly.

When I arrived with my parents and Catherine, a lovely lady called Fay showed us around. (She was eventually to be my Class Tutor.) The site wasn't what I'd expected. It was significantly smaller than I anticipated and very run down. The people, nonetheless, welcomed me with open arms, pupils as well as teachers. The warmth I encountered from the people and, to my surprise, the 'shack-like' buildings, encouraged me to look past my initial impression of the place and reconsider my first thoughts and emotions about it. I developed a strong gut feeling that Abbey Hill was where I would like to go when I was eventually discharged and well enough to focus on school subjects again. I believe that the size of the site and the student body were two of the things that most appealed to me. I was also given a guarantee that I would be allowed to work at my own pace. Of course, the fact that there would be people there who had been in the same situation as me assisted in my decision, as I knew that I most certainly would not be viewed as a detached weirdo. Many students there, I'd say about eighty-five. had severe learning difficulties, affecting their speech, learning capabilities and general everyday living. All the more capable students were polite and understanding towards them, accepting their differences with open minds – all the students were treated as equals by both fellow students and teachers.

During the summer holidays, my parents planned to go and stay at Primrose Valley Caravan and Holiday Park in Scarborough. We used to take short breaks there when my siblings and I were younger. I think my parents wanted to try to recreate some of the happy times that we had as children because they were now few and far between. I was eager to go, as I would then be able to spend some quality time with my family, away from everyday life at the unit. It would also be a superb opportunity for me to prove that I could succeed with my coping strategies in the outside world. Therefore, the possibility of a holiday for me created another topic of discussion in my review.

It was decided, after much debate, especially from Alicia who was adamant that I wasn't quite ready yet, that I could go, on the strict condition that I stuck to my meal plan and did not go to extremes with my exercise. I promised the doctors, Alicia, and my parents that I would exercise my utmost determination to stay focused. I'd prove to everybody that I could cope being away from the unit and from the watchful eye of its staff. I was anxious beyond belief about staying with my family for an entire week, but I was also enthusiastic and resolute that everything would go according to plan.

On the first day of our holiday, I ate my first ice cream in over a year! It was a Magnum Classic (my favourite) and it took me over an hour to decide whether to have it or not. The first bite was indescribable bliss. I had well and truly forgotten how good they tasted. My whole family cheered as I took my first bite, and Mum held on to my hand. They were all over the moon that I had finally managed to overcome another one of my long-time fears. When I had finally finished, my feelings were a mixture of extreme guilt and immense achievement. My mum told me that words could not describe exactly how proud and happy she was, and both of my parents' enormous grins, cheeks and eyes shiny with tears, ensured that the guilt that raged through me was softened. It was difficult to comprehend the fact I had actually eaten a full Magnum ice cream, so I made Mum take a photograph of me holding the wooden ice cream stick, I could now keep the memory of my achievement for ever. The voice made me suffer for my 'dreadful deed' by manipulating my thoughts so that I believed, again, that I would transform into a mass of quivering blubber and then, whenever I saw my reflection, that is what would stare back at me.

The caravan we stayed in was the largest type available on the site, but where our family are concerned it was minute. It was bizarre having to share a room with my sister again after being apart from one another for such a long time. It was almost as though two strangers had been thrown into a room together and were ordered to get along. Well, you can't really call what we stayed in a room, more like a cupboard! Our beds touched, and only one of us could stand at any one time. After reintroducing ourselves, so to speak, Penny and I got along better than I'd expected. It was wonderful to talk again of an evening, like we used to when we shared a room when I was well. That was something I had missed immeasurably: our hours of discussion about all manner of things, from boyfriends to spots, periods to kissing. Our conversations had, of course, changed drastically, and now focused on music and clothes; my Goth culture and Penny's Punk one. Of course, sometimes my illness was dredged up and those discussions inevitably ended with arguments, tears and tantrums or, on many occasions, a melancholic silence.

Throughout the holiday, I bent over backwards to be as perfect as I possibly could be, so that I hoped every moment we spent together would go superbly and there wouldn't be a chance for any major disputes or quarrels.

I managed my meal plan as I was determined to prove that I could do it and make it my own responsibility. I remembered to take my 'breaks' out with me whenever we left the caravan site, and ensured that I always had enough stock of the food I needed. The time of 'being at one' with my family was over all too soon and, before I could blink, we were on our way home. It felt as though time purposely had speeded up to annoy me. Who knows what might have happened if we'd stayed a second week? The relationship between by sister and I might have moved that notch higher on the ladder we were climbing to renew sisterly love.

During our holiday I had my first swim in I can't remember how long. I didn't stay very long in the pool as I soon discovered that my arms and legs refused to follow instructions from my brain, creating great difficulties. Also, I was utterly convinced that every single person in the pool had their eyes trained on me and was thinking, 'Look at that fat girl trying to swim! She won't get anywhere with those thunder thighs! Look at her flapping and flobbing. She's a pathetic excuse for a human being! Her head should be bobbing under the water, not on top of it. And that's where it ought to stay.'

After I climbed out of the pool (my head was whirling and my body tottering and trembling although I'd been in the pool for less than twenty minutes), I had to keep on reminding myself that my body was not a blubber beast and that I was not a pathetic excuse for a human being and I did have the right to breathe. Why would I have been put in hospital otherwise? If no one believed I deserved to live, I wouldn't have been granted a bed and care for the many months I had.

I was dreading going back to the unit, but I knew that I had no choice in the matter. A few days after we returned from Primrose Valley, I went back, and was weighed. I discovered, to my delight, that I had gained 400 grams during our holiday, and my weight was now 40.4 kg! I had proved myself! I COULD manage out of the unit for a long time. I did feel regretful for gaining weight, but relief and achievement rose above that. The voice in my head (which was getting gradually fainter the more weight I put on) nagged at me to erase food from my meal plan, and concentrate on doing more exercise. "LOSE THE WEIGHT!" It would scream at me. "You're getting FAT again." But I would answer it back aloud to myself. "NO! I WILL NOT LOSE WEIGHT! I am not getting fat; I am getting better!" And onward went the battle.

Chapter 15

Extended Leave

I maintained my weight at 40.4 kg for an entire week. The doctors, the nurses, my parents and I agreed that I was coping extraordinarily well, and that remaining at the unit with the heavy, suffocating misery, pain and despair was doing my body and spirit no good whatsoever. So I was allowed home on extended leave and only needed to return to the unit to be weighed or for appointments! I hadn't been discharged yet. I still had my room at the unit in case anything went wrong, or if I felt that I couldn't cope and wanted to go back.

I was thrilled and enthusiastic about going home, but also slightly apprehensive. I wasn't sure how I would adapt to life outside with all the new routines that I would have to learn. But I was delighted to be getting out and leaving all the depression, sadness, rules and regulations behind.

Being at home exceeded my expectations. It was amazing seeing my family every day instead of only at designated times on set days. It seemed unnatural sleeping and waking up in my own bed again and, sometimes, I would wake and think that I was dreaming. Cooking and preparing my own meals again was superb, as I didn't have a nurse hovering around me as I did it. (Just my mum sometimes! But, naturally, I preferred that.) I started to explore the delights of shopping with my sister, not realising, until I was doing it, just how big an effect little things had on me. Even simple things like going food shopping or for a walk excited me, and it felt as though I was going out on an adventure whenever I stepped outside the door! I was anxious at first about going out of the house, but once I'd done some normal things again, such as shopping, I always wanted to be doing more to make up for all the time I'd lost. I wanted to cram as much as I possibly could into every minute of every day. About a week after coming home, I had an appointment with the dietician about increasing my meal plan so I could do more energetic activities, such as going on short bike rides, or using my rollerblades for brief periods of time. I was scared about adding more food, so we came to an agreement – I

Chapter 16

Seeing School In A New Light ____

On 5th September, I had my first morning at Abbey Hill. I started going for half days, and then, over a period of weeks when I'd built up my courage, I would go in for the full five days a week.

Catherine came to pick me up from home and took me in her car. I was really nervous but also giggly with excitement. I imagined that this would be a brilliant opportunity for me to make new friends. Being back at school and learning again would help me ignore the voice as my mind would have different things to focus on. Catherine noticed my nerves as soon as I got into her car and reassured me that everything would be fine. She said that if I wanted to come home early, I could just call her and she would come and pick me up.

Catherine was right, as my first morning at Abbey Hill went better than I had expected. Fortunately, I already knew a girl there called Amanda, who had been in hospital with me suffering with depression. She'd recently been discharged, and had started at Abbey Hill a few days before I did. It eased my nerves enormously to have someone there I already knew and helped break the ice with both teachers and other students. Amanda was quite a talker and was liked by everyone, so she was the perfect person to have by my side. I made a number of friends on my first morning, with the assistance of Amanda, but I was shy and so didn't talk much, allowing Amanda to take the lead role.

As I was at school for the entire morning, it meant that I had to eat my morning break there, which I found difficult. I tried to stand with Amanda and the other kids, to act normal and just talk, but I found it way too hard because the voice was screaming to me, "They're all staring at you, Katie! They're all thinking what a fat, ugly, greedy pig you are! They all think you're eating *way* too much." (I was actually only eating two plain oatcakes and a Strawberry Build Up out of a water bottle.) "Go and put your break in the bin. Go on! Go on! GO ON!" It continued to scream at me, but I refused to listen and wandered away from the 'Smokers' Area' and finished my break where no one could see me. I tried to reassure myself at the same time that I wasn't a greedy, fat pig. It was just a persistent voice in my imagination that was telling me so.

My review was set for the afternoon after my morning at Abbey Hill. I was a bag of nerves, but tried to be positive about what the outcome would be. I was weighed because my newest weight would have an effect on the decisions made. I'd gained 100 grams since my last weigh day, and I was now 41.3 kg. I was thrilled and breathed a huge sigh of relief (completely the opposite of the voice which was fuming with me) as I stepped off the scales. Something good was bound to happen now!

There were many people present to discuss my future: my parents, Catherine, Fay, and Alicia, two doctors, myself and a nurse called Laurence whose job it was to write up the notes. My time in hospital and the amount of progress that I had made since going on extended leave was discussed as well as when I would be starting full-time at Abbey Hill. Dr Edwards, who was the main doctor in my case, asked me when I would ideally like to be discharged. It was two days before my sixteenth birthday so I jokingly said, "Tomorrow. I would love to be discharged tomorrow before my birthday."

"All right, then," Dr Edwards replied. I couldn't believe what I was hearing! "Actually," he said, "Let's make it one better than that, shall we? Let's discharge you today!" I couldn't speak. I opened my mouth but couldn't form any words, and I sat there looking like a goldfish. I really couldn't believe it – it took ages to sink in. I wanted to hug every person in the room, but instead I just sat there mute, with my mouth now closed, but grinning. I was transformed from a goldfish to a grinning Cheshire cat. I finally had what I wanted more than anything in the world. I was discharged. I was free from the 'hole' of despair, depression and sadness, rules and regulations where I'd wasted nearly nine months of my life. It wasn't all wasted, of course. I'd made some new friends and they'd helped me to fight the battle with the voice, and to not give up. I thanked every member of staff who'd helped me and wished the other patients all the luck in the world with their own recoveries.

It was odd but amazing at the same time, sitting at my own leaving party. For months it had been other people receiving presents and cards and walking through the double doors for (hopefully) the last time in their lives. Now it was my life that stretched out before me. I was the person stepping through the doors and into the sunlight that held so much promise. It was now the beginning of *my* new life experience.

It felt unreal, packing my things into boxes to take home. The last time I'd packed it was to move from one room to another – it wasn't even me doing the packing that time, it was the nurses; I'd simply sat and stared. This time it was a real move. Not a move down the corridor, it was a move back to the home I'd earned the right to return to. I'd earned the right to be with my family again.

The amount of random stuff I had to pack was unbelievable. I think I had accumulated there every single one of my belongings in the months that I was in hospital. When I'd finished packing, my room looked bleak and bare without the pictures, cards and posters that had adorned every square inch of wall. I felt as though much of my sorrow had seeped from my soul into the foundations of the building. The core of my illness would live there forever, alongside those of all the others before me.

Now that my things were packed, it was ready for the next unfortunate patient to fill and adorn the walls with their belongings and emotions. The walls were ready to accept new pains. A minute part of me knew that I would miss little things like having my own sink (it's much better having your own than having to share, I can tell you!) and being in possession of space where I knew that my brothers and sister couldn't annoy me. But at this point, I couldn't care less if my brothers and sister antagonised me or not. I couldn't care less if they invaded my space. They could annoy me all they wanted to, they could shatter my silence and corrupt my tidiness – because at last I was going home! We would be a family again. And families annoy each other and argue sometimes, don't they? We were never going to be the same as we had been. I'd never recover the role of 'big sister Katie'. It broke my heart that we'd become like strangers to one another, but I had to face the facts and piece not only my heart back together again but the pieces of our fragmented family.

It was as though I was living a dream, being at home for my birthday. My dad had promised me on the day that I went into hospital that, as soon as I was discharged, he would buy me an electric guitar, and, on my birthday, that promise was fulfilled. It made me realise just how much faith he and the rest of my family had in me, and to what extent they wanted me to recover. I made a promise to him that I would never again set foot over the threshold of a psychiatric hospital carrying a suitcase. He had bought me my guitar, and I would keep my part of the deal.

Two weeks after I was discharged, I began full days at Abbey Hill. I did better than I imagined I would, and I slowly made new friends. It got slightly easier to eat my break in front of other people, but now I also had the big challenge of lunch. I tried going into the dining hall and eating my packed lunch, but the sight of so many people made me turn around and walk straight back out again. So for the first few weeks I'd stand outside next to a bench and eat my lunch there. I'd wish that I was invisible, as I thought that everyone walking past was staring in disgust at what I was eating. I know now that it was just my imagination, and the voice telling me, in the hope that I would throw it into the bin. A few people did ask, out of general interest, why I ate outside, and I told them the truth, that I didn't like eating in front of people, but I would come into the dining hall when I was ready to. They got the picture and left me to it. Of course, when the rain started and still I insisted on standing outside with my food, people grew more curious and my unusual behaviour appeared to be even more abnormal.

Chapter 17

The Boyfriend

Shortly after leaving hospital I met Louis, a friend of my sister's who I knew from Billingham; I fell for him instantly.

What made the combination of Louis and me so appealing was that we were interested in the same things: the same music (Rock and Heavy Metal); the same films (Horror); the same idols (Kurt Cobain and Marilyn Manson). Louis even played the electric guitar, same as me! So we always had stuff to talk about. It really felt as though my life was piecing itself back together.

It took me about two days before I eventually plucked up the courage and asked him if he would like to be my boyfriend. All through those two days, the voice taunted me saying "Why would he want to go out with you? You're an ugly, disgusting freak! You're FAT FAT FAT! No one would ever want to go out with YOU! YOU'RE GOING TO BE SINGLE UNTIL YOU DIE!" I tried very hard to ignore its taunts, and anyway, it was wrong, because when I did ask Louis, he said "Yes!"

I was both over the moon and shocked. I had a million and one things going through my head at this point. I really couldn't understand why he wanted to go out with me. ME, of all people! At first, I thought it might be because he felt sorry for me, but I banished those thoughts from my mind, as he didn't seem that kind of guy.

Louis was the first proper boyfriend that I ever had, and, the first time we walked down the street holding hands, I felt contented and tingled with happiness and joy. I felt the most positive that I'd felt with myself in a very long time. The first time he kissed me was the most wonderful feeling and experience, and I was the happiest girl in the world. When he told me, after a few weeks of us going out, that he loved me and thought I was beautiful, well, the feeling was indescribable.

It gave me the incentive I needed to increase what I was eating, and gain more weight. (How weird does that sound!) What boyfriend wants to see his girlfriend's ribcage? Unless, of course, he is some sort of weird thinness fanatic who believes that girlfriends should be kept as trophies and are not real people with true feelings.

As the weeks went by, I did start to struggle, and feel that my diet was too loaded and that I was putting on weight too quickly. (My weight was actually yo-yo-ing, but I managed to gain more often than I lost and kept above 'bed rest weight'.) The voice told me every day I was getting fat – insisting I would be dumped soon if I didn't make the effort to cut out the calories and boost my exercise.

I had weekly sessions with my psychologist, Marie, and I told her about these fears. We discussed them, and she helped me to cope, giving me helpful advice on how I could ignore the voice by doing various writing exercises and mind games. We also discussed my fear of eating in front of Louis. I'd miss out on quite a few meals or breaks in a day, if Louis was at my house or if I was at his, and it was resulting in weight loss. Marie reiterated the importance of not missing any meals or breaks as it would lead to my ultimate downfall. We agreed that, when I was ready, I would try to eat in front of Louis. Otherwise, I would just have to see him before or after I had eaten. I couldn't risk the possibility of all my accomplishments slipping away.

It took me a number of weeks, but eventually I ate in front of Louis (I mean, he was my boyfriend, and I had to do it sometime!) and it wasn't as bad as I had imagined it would be. He didn't stare at me or make any sarcastic comments. It was just a normal thing to him. To begin with, the foods I ate around him were snack-type foods, but as it became easier, I ate meals with him around and sometimes he would eat with me. That made it even better, as then I didn't feel greedy.

I felt immensely proud, but he had no idea how much I had struggled, and just how big a step I'd taken. I guess it was a good thing in a way as it's a normal thing not to make a fuss about eating and that's what I wanted to be – normal again.

I talked to Louis about almost everything, including the time that I had spent in hospital. It didn't bother him at all and I don't think he saw that part of my life as a big deal, to be honest. If people don't make a big deal of someone being in hospital, then that is sometimes a good and positive thing. A sign that he was aware I simply wanted to move right away from that aspect of my life. It was wonderful and convenient being able to go around to his house whenever I needed to get away from my family for a while. He would never pressure me into doing anything that I didn't want to, which made me feel respect for him and love him all the more.

Louis was the first person in my life that made me feel truly special and worth something. Whenever we'd kiss or walk down the street holding hands, I'd love it when people took a second look. I knew it was because I'm a Goth, and he was a Skater, but I just loved getting noticed. I thought Louis fulfilled all the requirements of a loving, caring, supportive and understanding boyfriend.

After almost four months into our blissfully happy teen romance, Louis became cold and distant, and he didn't seem to want to be around me any more. It was clear, no matter how hard I tried to deny it, that our relationship wouldn't last much longer. I instantly assumed that it was because I was getting fat and he was repulsed by me. (It couldn't have been, as I had recently lost a little weight and my clothes were looking and feeling looser.) Then I realised that there was probably another girl involved. Louis spent a lot of time chatting to people on his computer via MSN Chat Room, and I was aware that he chatted to a girl in his class on a regular basis, but I never thought that there might be something going on between them.

For a while after, I was distraught, and couldn't understand why (I had the voice in my head saying, "It's because you're too fat! It's because you wouldn't have sex! He's got someone better and thinner than you! He's found a girl who'll do everything and anything for him!"). At first, I thought it was something I must have done, and I wondered if the things the voice was saying were true, but I forced myself to remember that the voice is only in my imagination. It's not a real thing.

By December 2002, I was managing to increase my weight. I would still have 'off weeks' where it would fluctuate. Sometimes my anger would flare up, my stress levels soar sky-high and my emotions would scatter like leaves in an autumn wind. So my family would need to deal with the devil. That's all part of the long and frustrating recovery process. Things aren't always comfortable and a simple walk in the park. There are many ups, just as many downs and hoards of bumps along the way. My diet consisted of all the nutritional elements that I needed, and it was still considered, by everyone other than myself, to be too little.

I had settled in at Abbey Hill well and I enjoyed going every day (I never thought I would say that about school!). By now, I was also eating both my morning break and my lunch in the dining hall with the other pupils. (The days were getting colder, so I didn't have much choice if I wanted to keep all my fingers.) When I first had thoughts about going inside the (now much fainter) voice went on at me, saying, "Everyone will look at you and think you are a pig! They will all want to know why you, fat pig, are not outside rolling in the filth where you rightly belong, eating everything and anything that you can get your disgusting trotters on!" I found some inner strength and pushed the voice to the back of my mind. I discovered that when I eventually did go inside, the voice didn't plague me with those taunts any more. It was quiet, for once. I had shown it who was boss! I didn't sit with the other pupils; I would just stand in the corner and try to look as if it was a normal thing to do. It was a big improvement from standing outside and, with time, I knew I'd sit with everybody else, share conversations and eat normally – but one small step at a time.

I was still seeing Marie every week. I'd get weighed, and we'd discuss life at home with my family. We'd also talk about any problems I was having and about how I was managing to ignore the voice and was continuing with my recovery. This was also when I allowed myself to eat more 'new' foods. I managed to eat my favourite sandwich, egg mayonnaise, and an egg toastie, which I hadn't had for two years. And, as I said before with the chocolate and the ice cream, the taste was indescribable, and once again brought tears to my eyes and a feeling of complete and utter confusion as to why I had deprived myself.

It was four months since I had been discharged, and family life was slowly returning to a sort of normality. I had got through the worst of my anorexia and was looking towards the future.

Chapter 18

A New Start?

It had started as a New Years resolution, but could it end as one?

I woke up on the 1st January 2003, with it in my mind that my life would have changed completely overnight. I thought that I was a whole new person! That I would be able to eat normally once again, without feeling fat, greedy and disgusted with myself and without having to experience terrible guilt trips that would last for hours, if not days. I thought that I would be able to do a simple thing such as sleep for a few extra hours on a weekend if I wanted to, and not care. I thought that I wouldn't be bothered about how long I would allow myself to sit down for. I thought that I would once again be attracted towards members of the opposite sex and they towards me. I thought that because of the progress and all of the things I had managed to achieve in my life during the year 2002, then life would be back to how it had been before I became anorexic, and this year would be a brand new start for both me and my family. I thought that the anorexic voice would have disappeared overnight. Dissolved into nothingness. Ceased to exist, leaving me to be Katie, inside and out once again. But I couldn't have been more wrong.

I woke up at exactly the same time as I would normally wake up, and I had to get up immediately. It was an automatic reaction; my feet swung over the side of my bed and were on the floor and walking before I could even open my eyes fully and think straight. There wasn't even a glimmer of a thought about a lie-in.

When I went downstairs for my breakfast, I found myself reaching for the box of branflakes, and not the cornflakes which I really wanted to have, and weighing them out to the exact gram and measuring out my milk to the exact millilitre, just as before. I realised that things were exactly the same as they had been. There had been no miracle transformation overnight. I wasn't cured; all better and well as I had imagined I would have been.

I looked down at my hands to see that they were still cracked, bleeding and sore, my nails still ripped. I touched my hair and it was still thin. The languno all over my body was still thick. My joints ached and the skin, which covered my protruding bones, was stretched and still parchment thin. The overwhelming urge to step on the scales again and again and again was still constant, as were the thoughts of food, calories, and exercise. Oh yes, anorexia was very much still with me. It was still a part of my being. The voice hadn't dissolved into nothingness. As much as I hated to admit it, it was still there, niggling in my mind. Keeping its control over my body. It still played the main role in the stageplay of my life. Katie was off stage, out of view, and out of mind.

I couldn't for the life of me understand it. Visions of my hair being full and glossy faded away, as did the hopes that my hands would no longer bleed and crack with the smallest movement. The hope that the languno would have vanished, leaving my skin silky smooth and hair-free died too.

By the end of the day, I felt as though nothing had changed in the slightest, and, to be honest, nothing had. I never had put my positive attitude into action and I was still giving into the anorexia's demands, listening to its loud and strong voice. I was still the same possessed Katie as I had been the day before, and the week before, and the many months before that. I was still the Katie who was sharing her mind, body, soul, life and family with the demon by the name of anorexia. I wasn't the Katie with her own voice, her own body and soul, life and family. That Katie was still lost, still wandering through limbo. Still wanting to come home but not knowing the way.

As I lay in bed that night, after my routine exercise schedule, on the first evening of the New Year 2003, looking back over my day, I felt as if I had really, well and truly, let myself down by not being able to start anew with my life, and not worry about what I was eating, or feel guilty about doing something that I enjoyed doing. I felt furious and hugely disappointed that the voice hadn't disappeared like I had planned it to, and it was, in fact, stronger than ever. It didn't take me long to crash back to the real world, where I realised that my recovery wasn't going to happen overnight, I couldn't just recover from an eating disorder and gain three stone simply because a New Year had started. And the voice definitely was not going to disappear of its own accord just because it was a new day. I felt stupid, as I had discussed so many times over a number of years, with various psychiatrists and psychologists, that my recovery wasn't going to happen in the space of a day. It was impossible. I came to terms with the fact that it was going to take time, a lot more time than I had originally anticipated.

I knew that to destroy the voice, and along with it my fear of becoming fat, and to make real my dream of being slim and healthy again, with the added bonus of having my periods back again, I was going to have to work the hardest I had ever worked in my entire life, with the exception of getting myself off bed rest and out of hospital. One of my main motivations to get well was the fact that I didn't want to mess up on my GCSE exams, which were due to take place at the end of the year. Getting good grades was incredibly important for me, as I was determined to go on to higher education. I knew that my concentration was going to have to be of the highest standard possible for me to manage my revision and pull through the final exams, which I had already heard were hell. I couldn't allow myself to be focusing on food, calories, fat and exercise when I was supposed to concentrate on Shakespeare, algebra, enzymes and how to create a pie chart using Microsoft Wizard. I was focused on having a career as a writer and there was no chance that I was going to have anorexia blocking the way to my dreams. Having missed a full year of school because of my illness meant that I would have to work twice as hard, if not more, as everyone else to catch up on work that I had missed and to make up for lost time.

It was going to take a lot of hard work and effort from my family, my doctors and myself to rid me of the anorexia demon once and for all. anorexia didn't want me to do my exams. It didn't want me to lead a happy, normal life. It didn't want to see me having a relationship with anything or anyone other than it; anorexia wanted me to focus on losing weight and hovering close to death where it was able to keep complete control over me. But I was more determined than ever to be Katie once again and live life by my rules.

Chapter 19

Back To School... For Some

I guess that I felt the same way every teenager does about going back to school after the Christmas holidays: miserable, unenthusiastic and exhausted after the celebrations. I didn't particularly want to go back, especially as we were heading closer towards our GCSEs and the work set for us was going to become much more intense and mind-numbing. And the anorexia definitely did not want me going back. It had enjoyed the days spent over-exercising and going to bed at ungodly times. Little did I know, even though I was going back to school, anorexia still planned to have me over-exercising every day, and not going to bed until the early hours of the morning. It was going to take more than a shift in routine to make the anorexia give in and let go.

Despite the fact that I was petrified about how on earth I was going to cope with my GCSEs and the mountain of revision that I was going to have to tackle, I was still determined to try my hardest and do the very, very best that I could do under the circumstances.

As I got back into the swing of school at Abbey Hill again, Penny, at fourteen, got into the swing of not making the daily journey to her school. She used every excuse known to mankind in order to avoid going. Eventually, her excuses stopped, and every morning she would simply say:

"I AM NOT GOING TO SCHOOL, FINAL, SO YOU CAN GET LOST!"

Cue slammed door and the sound of falling plaster.

I couldn't understand why Penny had all of a sudden decided that she was not going to make an effort to get out of bed in the morning. She had friends. People liked her. She was really smart and did very well in all of her subjects. And to top it all, she had the bonus of being extremely attractive. What was wrong with her? I, on the other hand, didn't have many friends left, wasn't particularly popular and wasn't physically attractive as my curves had long since been consumed by anorexia. My face was often stony and cold due to the ongoing battle inside my mind. I assumed the way she was acting was my fault, and that my illness had had some kind of mental effect on her that was kicking in now, after being hidden for such a long time.

Yet again, I was faced with the thought of 'what if?' What if I lost more weight and became thinner, would everything turn out perfect and great? Would life be good again? Would our family be happy? Most importantly, at this stage, would Penny change her ways if I changed too? And would she respect me again?

Instead of starting my Macbeth essay that evening, I calculated the calories I could easily cut out of my diet, without my parents noticing. Anorexia urged me on, speaking sweetly in my ear, telling me all would be OK, if only I lost more weight.

I shredded the paper into tiny pieces, watching as they fell to my bedroom carpet like scruffy confetti. Anorexia's sweet words turned to snide, hateful comments as I did this. As Mum hugged me, and told me that I had done the right thing by telling her about the voice's demands, I was torn in two, and unsure of what to do. Penny's problems were by no means solved, and by the look of things, mine were beginning all over again in the all too familiar daily cycle.

One weekend morning I woke up and, to my absolute horror, found that snow had fallen through the night, leaving a blanket of white so thick that the curb had merged with the road, making it impossible to determine where the path ended and the road began. A few years ago, when I had been well, I would have been thrilled to wake and find such a scene, but now, it was just an inconvenience. I knew my parents hated me cycling in the snow; however, I needed to go on a bike ride in order to be able to cope with eating for the day. And of course, the voice still nagged, nagged, nagged away. I attempted an inner argument, saying to the voice and myself that it was dangerous outside, and I could fall and injure myself. However, on the other hand, I was a careful rider. I'd be OK. The voice assured me that I was correct in that assumption.

I ended up falling off, whether it was because of a stupid manoeuvre or I because blacked out for a moment, I'll never know. I found myself underneath the bike on the side of the road, but fortunately I was close to home and the cuts and bruises to my arms and knees were easily hidden. Although the bruising around my eyes had to be explained. That, I told my parents, was the fault of some little brats throwing ice balls.

The same day as my fall, my mum went out with her friends to a party, and decided, that after five years of not drinking, that she wanted to break her abstinence. It was only when she returned home, laughing hysterically and stumbling around that I realised. I was furious and shouted at her, telling her exactly how I felt about it. She instantly bit back and stated that she wanted to kill me, that I was ruining everyone's lives and tearing the family apart. That I should never have been discharged from hospital.

I was hurt beyond belief, and despite the fact that she was drunk, I believed every single word she said. The voice told me she was speaking the truth. Everyone wanted me out of the family.

Fortunately, the day afterwards, we both admitted we had been wrong, apologised to each other, and things returned to normal. The voice, realising this, ceased its vicious backstabbing. However, there have been other occasions where Mum and I fought, and the silences would last for days on end. Those occasions would be truly awful, as Mum is the main person I turn to with my problems, and without her there to talk my worries over with, I would crumble and admit defeat to the voice.

After a few weeks of the 'not going to school' routine, I began to feel that it was my duty to try and make up for Penny's behaviour by doing everything that I could to please and help my parents. I started to try and be strong, well behaved and good for both Penny and me. Often, after a day at school, I would tell my parents that it had been a really great day, and nothing at all had gone wrong. However, a lot of the time I would have terrible days, and it felt like everything that could have gone wrong had done so. For example, I had thrown food away because I had done terribly in a maths test. But I wouldn't leak a word. Instead, I would act as though everything was fine. I didn't want them to have something else to worry about in their lives. Their hands were already far too full to be worrying about me again. Often, I decided that I would have to handle sticky situations on my own, without any help. Which now, after having done it, I would not advise anyone to do, under any circumstances, as it leads to far more harm than good, believe me.

It was around this time, early into the new year, that our family received heartbreaking news about a family friend in America, who was dying from cancer. He was undergoing every treatment that was available, but the disease was spreading all through his body, and his time left on earth was short. Hearing about how this man, who had been tall, strong, healthy and happy, was now being destroyed by a disease put my life into perspective. I made the decision that I really had to start living again, and enjoy and be forever grateful for every individual day given to me. Every single ray of sunshine, every free breath of air, every unique droplet of rain to fall on my skin was something to be thankful for. Life really is too short to waste, especially with an illness which I had the ability to overcome. I took advantage of this sudden bout of willingness to get well, and allowed myself to try new foods as well as increasing the calories in my diet. An egg toastie was my first achievement. It had been three years since I had allowed margarine and normal sliced white bread to pass my lips, and, when I did so, as had happened all of the other times in the past when I had allowed myself a 'new food' I cried with joy and delight. It was difficult to imagine that egg toasties had, once upon a time, been a staple part of my diet.

Chapter 20

Feeling Extinct

As well as working like a Trojan towards my GCSEs, I started hunting for a part-time job. I wanted to save towards my trip to America, which I was planning to take when I reached seven stone. I also felt a job was a necessity because life at home with my siblings would often be unbearable, especially at the weekends when everybody (except Dad) would be at home and under each other's feet. The arguments with my siblings seemed to have lessened before New Year. We had all been getting along with each other most of the time, and they had appeared to be showing me slightly more respect. But the wind had changed, and all of a sudden, for reasons unknown, we were fighting and arguing once again.

One major factor that I noticed which has changed in my relationship with my siblings is that, before I developed anorexia, the three of them looked up to me and respected me as 'our big sister Katie'. They would ask me for advice as individuals about every kind of topic imaginable: clothes, hairstyles, music, boyfriends, girlfriends, you name it, they asked me. To them I was the queen of knowledge!

I am able to recall a time when they would even tell bullies that if they were horrible, I would come after them! And back then, there were quite a few incidents when I actually did go and 'sort bullies out' for picking on them, by using physical strength and a whiplash tongue. Those incidents ceased when anorexia came into my life. I became small, feeble and weak, unable to defend myself, let alone my brothers or sister from bullies. Penny was now the sister Tony and Sam both looked up to, and she was the one they ran to asking for advice about what to wear, how to have their hair cut, what new CD to buy and who to go out with on a date. She was the new queen of knowledge and their new protector. Penny no longer consulted me about anything either; it was her new friends on the MSN chatroom who knew it all, who had all the advice and knowledge about every single tiny thing. I was totally out the picture.

I felt as though anorexia had robbed me not only of having a great life, full of fun and excitement, but it had also robbed me of respect from my brothers and sister as well as my official duties as a 'big sister.' I know my siblings thought that, because I was anorexic, it meant that I didn't deserve respect any more, as I couldn't even take proper control of my own life. And as for advice, well, I am sure that they thought, 'who takes any kind of advice from an anorexic anyway?'

At Abbey Hill, I began to discus with my teachers the prospect of leaving and going on to study at college after I had finished my GCSEs, instead of staying on at Abbey Hill for another year as originally planned. I felt as though I would really benefit from a complete change of scene, and was desperate to make more friends I could share interests with. The teachers all praised my determination and supported me in every way possible. They also made it clear that I still had a place reserved at Abbey Hill if I found college too stressful to cope with and felt the need to return. I was very grateful that they had given me that option, as I did want to move on with my life, but I still wanted to know that there was somewhere that I could go back to if it didn't all work out as planned. I am the kind of person who needs a plan Z, let alone a plan B!

A trip was arranged to go to an open day at Teesside Riverside College, where there would be a large collection of different colleges advertising their prospectuses and all they had to offer. The Riverside College was brand new at the time of our visit. It was enormous, and incredibly overwhelming after the tiny, run down Portakabins of Abbey Hill. However, it was the perfect setting for the event, filled with people wishing to make a new start in their lives.

By the end of the visit, after I had inspected each college's table, I was excited and thrilled about all the fantastic opportunities that lay before me, just waiting for me to grab them with both hands and haul myself aboard. That very same day, I sent three application forms off to different colleges, stating I wanted to study English at A level. All I had to do then was wait for invitations to interviews and try and do the best I possibly could in my exams.

I wanted to achieve the best GCSE grades I could possibly manage, partnered with doing my best with eating too. But saying you've got to do it is far, far easier than actually doing it and sticking to your plans. As I still wasn't eating enough food to make up the calories needed to gain weight, I was meant to drink three Build Up drinks a day. I forced myself to have these, and I would make them up feeling positive and determined. However, when the last mouthful had been swallowed, guilt would set in like a sickness.

The guilt was not as pressing as it had been the previous year, also I was slowly learning to cope better with it. I would sometimes cry myself to sleep at night after having all three drinks, despite the fact that I knew that having them had been the right thing to do. I would often go to Mum and collapse into her embrace, as I felt I could get strength from her. I knew that I was able to concentrate a lot better on my revision and everything else in general after having all three Build Ups, and the food I was supposed to have, but the thoughts of 'eating too much' nearly always managed to worm their way in. I would often feel that I was eating much more than a 'normal' person would. Of course this was the anorexia attempting to haul me back into its clutches.

Chapter 21

The Miracle Of Massage And Art

To try and ease the constant stress I was under, as well as to help me forget about my illness for at least a couple of hours, my parents offered me the opportunity to have complementary therapies, which would work alongside the therapy work that I did with Marie, my psychologist. I practically bit their hands off with my enthusiastic response.

As I had been in Steiner education, I had already experienced many of the benefits that complementary therapies had to offer.

So, for the months ahead, I had weekly art therapy sessions planned, as well as weekly massages. The therapies did not come cheap; however, my parents were more than willing to spend money on treatments which they were positive would help me on so many levels. And they did. The art therapy helped me to release trapped emotions on to the paper and helped me greatly to cope in stressful situations. Moreover, my therapist was an old teacher of mine, and a fantastic friend who would listen to my troubles and offer me her shoulder to cry on in support.

The first time I had a massage, by someone other than my mum, I felt paranoid and insecure about my body, convinced that it was too flabby and hairy. Therefore I insisted that my clothes were allowed to remain on. I removed my jacket and jumper, but refused to remove my T-shirt, vest and bra, for fear that the therapist would see my languno-covered back, and as the voice felt it needed to remind me, roll upon roll of flab.

Despite the fact that my clothes were still on, and the massage therefore wouldn't be as effective, the pressure applied over my body was pure bliss. The burning candles and calming music soothed me, and the smell of the oils in the room, and those that were used on my arms (which I had allowed to be uncovered) made me want to lie upon the massage couch for eternity.

The following visit, I was asked whether I would mind removing anything else, and to my own surprise, I agreed to removing more of my clothing. However my feet always needed to be covered, as to me they were the most horrific part of my body, and not allowed to be seen by anyone. When the hour was over, and my massage completed, I felt at ease with myself, and slightly less afraid of the changes to be made. For some amazing reason, having someone touch me in that way, with oils, and managing to relieve such an astronomical amount of aches and pain, both inside and out, made me realise that worrying about what other people thought about my body was pointless, as were all the things I allowed to make me stressed, angry and upset. It was as if they had been taken out of my body through someone else's fingers and palms. What a mistake the hospital had made by not allowing complementary therapists in their midst. If only they could know the wonderful positives that come out of something as simple as a massage or a session of art therapy. Such amazing qualities out of something so small and so readily available.

Of course the treatments did not solve all of my problems, far from it, and they needed to be done on a regular basis to have a long-term effect. But they helped me through many difficult situations and tough times, and they are treatments which I think everyone should have access to.

Chapter 22

The Man With The Blackened Heart

Soon after I had sent away my application to Riverside College, I received a reply inviting me to go for an interview. I was ecstatic, and determined to make a good impression when I went. I asked my teachers at Abbey Hill for my predicted grades, and practically wrote an essay and practiced over and over again just how I would explain to my interviewer about the situation concerning my illness, and my ambitious plans for the future.

I went for my first interview, imagining that the people I would be meeting would fully understand why my grades were not predicted to be of the best standard, and they would see my motivation and willingness to work hard to reach my goals in life. I thought that's what their job was all about: realising the potential in people, despite their backgrounds and pasts.

When Mum and I arrived, I instantly realised that the college was a LOT bigger than when I had first visited. I had forgotten that the previous time it had been an open day, and the place had been packed to its unbelievably high glass ceiling with students from all parts of the north-east of England. I started to feel the nerves wrapping around my intestines as we waited for my interviewer.

When he eventually arrived, I was ready, prepared, and determined to get myself a place, no matter what. When we sat down for the interview, he had a brief flick through my application forms while I sat there grinning, happy and immensely proud that I was beginning to make these huge changes in my life.

"You have lots of aspirations, don't you?" he said, with a slight snigger and one grey, pruned eyebrow raised.

"Yes," I replied seriously. "Yes, I do." Which was the truth. Why bother lie when I knew exactly what I wanted out of my life?

"Yes, but you don't know what you really want to do, do you? You're unsure about your future career. Aren't you?"

Puzzled, I replied, "Erm, well, no. I'm not unsure actually. I do know exactly what I want to do in my future career." I explained in detail what I had put on the form, and described my ambitions. My interviewer glanced at my predicted grades, and told me what Riverside College had to offer me.

"Basically," he said in a bored and unenthusiastic tone, "you can do re-sits here."

"E... e... excuse me?" I stammered. I thought I had misheard him. That couldn't be right. That couldn't be right at all.

"You are able to do re-sits here," he repeated slowly as if I was a small child unable to understand.

I felt my smile falter slightly and my stomach begin to tie into twisted knots yet again.

"Yes, but I want to do A Level English," I explained, equally as slowly. He glanced down at my application form again.

"Well, I'm sorry, but with your grades looking like they do, there is no way that you are going to be able to do so. Anyway, Miss Metcalfe, it's not a case of what you want to do, it's a simple case of what you can do."

I swallowed, hard, and felt the knots twist tighter, squeezing my insides into pulp.

"But I've explained to you about my past situation," I said desperately. "And I work really, really hard. I will be able to do English at A Level. I know I can manage it. I know. I'm positive."

"I'm sorry, but there is nothing that can be done. There is no way you would be able to cope with the amount of work set out for A Level English, and the college is not obliged to teach A level English to people with these kinds of grades." He tapped a pen loudly on the paper. "Bad past situations or no bad past situations."

How could he know what amount of work I could cope with? He didn't know me, therefore wouldn't have a clue. I persisted with my begging.

"Yes, but I'll work really, really hard, and I can cope with a lot of work. I'm a very hard worker. Please believe me." By now, he looked as though he was getting very irritable and wanting me to close my mouth.

"I am sorry, Miss Metcalfe, but it is just NOT possible," he said through gritted teeth. "Now, you have the option of doing re-sits, and then next year, if, that is, your grades have improved, you should be able to do English at A Level." I felt like bursting into tears, and I seriously struggled not to. "Now," he said, a small smile on his face, as he handed me back my forms, "you have plenty of time to decide if you would like to join us here at Riverside College, although it would be wise if you would let us know as soon as possible, as places are going fast, as you can imagine. May I remind you that we are one of the top colleges in the north-east of England."

I attempted to smile, but couldn't. My face felt as though it were cast in stone.

"Thank you," I said in a choked sob, not meaning a word, and knew when he shook my hand, said goodbye and strode away without a care in the world, that Riverside College was NOT the college that I wanted to be attending, especially with people like him teaching there. There was no way I was going to go through GCSEs again. EVER. I had had enough of them already, and my exams weren't even completed yet. I was determined to be able to do A Level English. I knew that I could cope with the work. And I wasn't going to let what anorexia had done for me in the past wreck everything all over again. As hard as it was, I was determined not to be downhearted, and get depressed like I normally would have done when a bad situation arose that was out of my hands. I still had my interview at Bede College, and surely they would understand about my grades and everything that had happened to me in the past, as their motto was 'We are here to care and listen'. Surely I would be able to convince them that I was a hard worker, and that I didn't need to do re-sits in my GCSEs? That I would be able to cope with the amount of work any student would have to cope with?

Chapter 23

New Hope

I went for my interview at Bede College the day after my disaster at Riverside, to find that it was pretty small in comparison. There were only about five hundred students compared to the one thousand or something that went to Riverside, and it was many years older, quite shabby and run down, too. But that didn't really matter to me, as it had a friendly, warm atmosphere to it, and you didn't feel tiny and insignificant when walking inside. However, this time, I asked Mum to come with me into the actual interview, to help explain about my past, the situation with my grades, and everything else about my complicated life. I felt that if I didn't have Mum there, then there would be a 99.9% chance of me breaking down.

The Principal of Bede, who happened to be my interviewer that day, understood everything that Mum carefully explained. She told us both that she could clearly see how motivated I was to get my life back on track, and do well in my exams. She told us that Bede would welcome me with open arms and gladly take me on to do my A Levels, no matter what my GCSE results turned out to be. I was ecstatic, and so was Mum. I was told to come along to the two preview days that were to be held in a few weeks' time, where I would try out the courses that I had chosen to participate in. It would also be a good opportunity to meet the new people with whom I would be starting college in September. I was wished the best of luck with the rest of my exams and my results, and I left Bede with a smile on my face, a spring in my step, and new hope in my heart.

Now that I knew for definite that I had a place at a college to do what I wanted to do more than anything else, I felt a lot calmer and less stressed about my exams, as I knew that even if my results weren't exactly what I wanted them to be, then I would still be given a chance to move forward with my education and my life. I was given a whole new belief and faith in the education system, not to mention in mankind's care and hospitality towards its fellow beings. However, before long, that belief was once again ripped savagely from me.

When I wasn't revising for my exams, I was working hard on my writing. I managed to complete a short teenage novel during my spare time, which I was overjoyed with and thought good enough to try and find a publisher for.

I bought a copy of the Writers' and Artists' Handbook, and went through it, scrupulously, page by page, searching for suitable publishers. I emailed more than I can remember and sent at least seven manuscripts by post to publishers, who emailed me back saying they were interested in having a look at my work, as well as to publishers who I was certain would find it appealing. I felt amazingly confident when I sent them off, positive that at least one of them would enjoy my work, and see that it had enough potential to publish. I waited with bated breath for replies, and was always the first one at the letterbox when the postman arrived in the morning, ripping into the pile of post like a demented dog.

The first rejection for my novel came within two weeks. I tried hard not to get disheartened, as I knew that I was still waiting for replies from others. However, as everybody knows, rejection from anything is tough to take, and I did have a cry and a major sulk about it. The second rejection came exactly a week after the first, and that hit me like a bullet in the heart. I was quite stressed out at the time with the maths exam I had just taken, as I knew I could have done better had I been at a higher weight, enabling me to concentrate and remember things better. I needed something to cheer myself up, boost my self-esteem and keep me trekking on through the rest of the exam papers. Looking forward to Bede was one of the main things that kept me from becoming depressed and crawling into my shell once again. I was also determined to keep on looking for the right publisher for my work. I told myself, 'Nothing in life comes easy. You need to work for your dreams.' And that was something I was prepared to do.

I applied for a job at a small, newly opened café in Billingham, and a few days after handing in my application form, was invited for an interview. I was determined to make a great first impression, as I wanted some positive feedback now, no more rejections. I had managed to complete my book about my experiences with anorexia; *Sticks And Stones (Will Break My Bones And Words Will Forever Hurt Me)*, which became the basis for this book, and along with my teenage novel manuscript, began to send that one out too.

I received the impression that the owner of the cafe was very impressed with my application and aspirations, and, on leaving, my interviewer said, "We'll call you soon," with a large smile on her face. I felt as though I had already got the job, and I practically skipped home.

A week later, the letter came. I opened it, expecting to read, 'We are pleased to inform you...' There was a first class stamp on the front of the decorated envelope, so I assumed the best. However, it was yet another rejection. My heart sank. I couldn't believe it. The interview had gone so well, and I had felt so sure and positive. Where had I gone wrong? Despite the fact that I was incredibly disappointed and upset, I kept on looking in all the newspapers, the Job Centre and shop windows, and continued to fill in application form after application form. I was determined not to give up on finding a job, just as I was filled with determination to find a publisher for my book.

Chapter 24

Leaving A Sense Of Security

I managed to struggle my way through the final exams, and, on completion of the last one, I felt as though a giant weight had been partially lifted from my shoulders. My teachers told me not to think about my exam results, and how I had done with them. They said it was just important to remember that I had tried my hardest, and that's the best anyone can do. I took their advice, however much I doubted its truth, and I reminded myself, whenever I started to worry, that I had tried my best, and that I did do the best I could at the time. However, it wasn't always a comfort, as I am a perfectionist and despised the fact that there were parts of my papers which weren't perfect, and there wasn't a hope in hell of being able to ever look upon them again and make them better.

I left school and Abbey Hill for ever on 10th June, 2003. It was peculiar going home for the last time in the taxi, knowing that I would never, ever have to go back to school. The thought actually made me quite giddy with happiness. It was a day which I had never imagined would come. When you're in school, you're constantly thinking that you're going to be there for ever and a day. You imagine you'll have to do algebra and Shakespeare every single day of your life and play by someone else's rules. You never imagine that one day it will actually all be over, and you will be responsible for your education, and what you do with your time, day in day out.

Even though I felt over the moon about having left school, I also felt insecure and awkward, as if I had grown up far too quickly, and my childhood had gone by in a lightning flash. But I suppose, in a way, my childhood had done just that, as I had missed almost all my teenage years due to the fact that anorexia wouldn't let me live my life. Now I felt as if it was my official duty to always act grown up and mature, like an adult. Although, inside, a minute part of me felt like a young, vulnerable child, not wanting to be let out into the big wide world to start a whole new chapter of the book of my life as an older person. A small part of me still wanted to be in school where I was safe and secure. A small part of me still wanted to be tiny enough for Dad to hitch me onto his shoulders and go walking. A fraction of me wanted to be the innocent, unaware and unconcerned child of my past.

The first few days after I had left school, I basked in the knowledge that I was free (from school at least). I was intent on having a good time, allowing myself to do things that I wanted to do for the fun of it. I knew that because I no longer had to be at school for a certain time, and that the days were free to do what I wanted, I was able to put much more effort into eating more and gaining weight. Times that were set for my breaks and for my meals no longer had to be interrupted by exams or schoolwork. However, changing my routines took longer than expected.

And I wasn't the brave, carefree girl I thought I could be.

Now that I had free time on my hands, and to help me from thinking about my results 24/7, I took up my writing full-time, continued to hunt for a job and focused steadily on beating the demon. On top of everything I was trying to regain and maintain good relationships with all of my family.

While the atmosphere at home was bearable, my parents decided that it would be a good idea for the family to take a holiday together abroad. So with fingers crossed that we would remain distracted from killing each other and threatening to run away, they booked a holiday to Kefalonia. I was thrilled, as I adore travelling, and seriously needed a break away after my GCSEs.

Mum and I went shopping for clothes, and I was hit with a variety of confusing thoughts and emotions about my body. As I picked swimming costumes and shorts, vests and T-shirts, thoughts raced through my mind, 'would these shorts look better if my legs actually filled them' or 'would this swimsuit look sexier if my chest was actually visible and not so flat?' Un-positive thoughts immediately followed 'I'm far too fat to fit into that T-shirt and there is no way my bum will squeeze into those shorts.' The voice, naturally wholeheartedly agreed with my negative outlook on my body, and joined in the chorus.

My attempts to ignore the un-positive thoughts and emotions about my body, and focus solely on the positive ones, failed miserably, and my weight dropped an entire kilo in less than a week. However, after speaking with my psychologist in an extended session and talking things over with my mum, as well as doing charts and diagrams about my feelings and current thoughts, I came to the conclusion that my clothes didn't and wouldn't look better with weight loss. As a matter of fact, they looked awful: my skirts held up with safety pins and my bra straps falling down my arms. My swimsuit sagged around my bum and my shorts slid down over my hips. Due to my recent loss of weight, I looked even more of a bedraggled mess. I knew it was important to ask the necessary people for help, and not to try and handle the situation completely by myself. So I asked for help, and received the encouragement and boosts I needed to pull myself together, gain the weight back and change the anorexic puppet I had become once again.

Chapter 25

Dreams Come True

Four days before the Preview was due to take place at Bede, I spent almost an entire day trying to decide what to wear. I was worried as some of my clothes still had to be pinned and looked terrible as they hung off me as though I was a rag doll. The voice tried to convince me that they didn't look awful at all. But they would look awful if I gained an ounce of weight, as the pins would pop, and my flab would flop out, displaying itself in all its monstrous glory. You may think I was pathetic, but I wanted to make a fantastic first impression with everyone I met, as well as a statement about who I am. I also wanted to be noticeable to other Goths, in the hope that they might come over and chat to me, as I was desperate for new friends.

As I made my way to Bede, I realised that I was physically shaking with nerves. Nevertheless, I was determined that I wasn't, under any circumstances, going to be shy. I would go up to people and make conversation. I would be sociable, friendly and chatty. However, once I was inside, my nerves worsened, as did my shakes, and my determination to try and be sociable vanished instantly. I became like a statue. My stomach was tied in knots, and a part of me felt like sobbing. I had made a promise to myself that I wouldn't be shy, but it was all so new, so different, and so strange; I felt so out of place, so odd, so not right. I felt nothing like I had done on my first visit. I didn't feel welcomed any more.

People surrounded me, many of them Goths, but they were all gathered in groups, chatting and laughing, hugging and messing about. They were all friends with each other already. As I stood there, statue still, feeling like a failure, and wanting the ground to swallow me up, I felt a light hand touch my shoulder. I jumped in surprise and turned quickly, to find myself looking straight into the face of another Goth. And she was smiling! At me!

"Hi," she said brightly, with a grin. "My name's Lydia. I thought you looked a bit lonely stood here all by yourself. So I thought I'd come over and say hi!"

"Hi," I replied in a choked voice, pleased and stunned that someone had come over to talk to me so quickly. Her eyes roamed over my clothes, and I instantly felt paranoid. Did she think I was fat? Obese? Monstrously massive? Was she silently laughing at me?

"I love your dress, by the way." she said eventually, still smiling, and reaching to feel the velvet. I let out a silent sigh of relief. She had been observing my dress, not my body. It was then that I knew I had found, well, more like she had found me, my very first friend at Bede College.

Lydia and I instantly clicked, and talked about a variety of things, as though we had known each other for years. Lydia was petite and very, very pretty with a slim face, enormous dark eyes and beautiful, long black hair, streaked with red. To be honest, when she told me that she went through a period of suffering with anorexia, I wasn't all that shocked. She had such a slight frame it made her appear ethereal. She actually reminded me of a little fairy, beautiful, dainty, light, and perfect. I noticed she had gathered an immense amount of admirers, as boys kept on glancing at her and pointing. I was thrilled to find that she was passionate about all the same things that I was; the same music, clothes, books, even television programmes. I was ecstatic to find she had an interest in witchcraft too. I truly couldn't believe that on a college preview I had managed to meet someone whom I felt would be my best friend for the rest of my life. I can't describe in words how unbelievably happy I felt that first morning at Bede, and anorexia played no part whatsoever in that joyous happiness.

Lydia introduced me to some of her friends, and we also instantly clicked. As we had everything in common, we had loads to talk about so there was never a dull second. If we weren't discussing Marilyn Manson's lyrics, we were discussing a horror movie, a new book or each other's shoes! (Which mostly happened to be black platform boots, Dr Martins and spiky heels.) Lydia and I stuck together like paper and glue that morning, unless we were in a different class. But when we were separated, I met other people, and made even more new friends. Not all of them were Goths. In fact, a few were just normal people into things like, ahem, pop groups, and wearing the latest fashions. But they were friendly, and we got along well. Therefore our differences didn't matter at all.

As well as enjoying the social part of the preview, I equally enjoyed the courses I had chosen, which were English Language and Literature, Media Studies, and Philosophy Theory and Ethics. I had eaten a good breakfast before I left for college, and I was making sure that I was drinking my Build Ups too, slipping outside for a quiet moment to drink them. I found that my concentration was excellent which of course helped me to make the most of the course tasters. I know my eating played an enormous part in how I was able to cope. I was able to do the work set out for us in the lessons, no problem whatsoever, which I was so relieved about, as I had been incredibly nervous that the courses would be difficult to understand and that I would struggle to keep up with all the other students.

When lunchtime came around, I managed successfully to eat in front of my new friends. However, I still found it a struggle to sit while I ate (I sat down through all my classes, and I felt that that was enough) so continued to stay standing. Some of my new friends were puzzled, and asked why I insisted on standing up. And so, with a slight struggle, I explained to them that I was recovering from an eating disorder, and I found it a struggle to sit down at some times of the day. They all appeared to fully understand, and didn't mention it again. I felt such a loser for telling them about my problem, and I felt like kicking myself for still allowing the anorexia to have that little bit of control over me. I felt a failure for not being able to ignore it, and do something so simple as sit down for a longer period of time than I normally did.

Despite my few personal let-downs, I left college that day on cloud nine. I had made more friends in one day than I had done in an entire year at Abbey Hill, all of whom appeared to fully understand about my illness and were very supportive. I had understood and thoroughly enjoyed my choice of courses, and to top it all off, I had seen plenty of gorgeous guys, who I hoped to get to know better when I started at college in September! It had all gone fantastically well, better than I could have ever imagined, and I couldn't wait to return the following day.

I felt a lot more at ease and comfortable walking into Bede the next morning. I walked into the Common Room, and spotted Lydia immediately. But to my disappointment she was standing, the centre of attention, with a group of people, talking and laughing, and I felt uncomfortable walking over there and interrupting, as I thought that she might have forgotten who I was. So I just stood where I had done the day before, and looked around miserably for other people I had met. But within a few minutes Lydia had spotted me and came over, a big smile on her face. She took my hand in hers and invited me over to the group she was stood with. I made a huge effort to be chatty and friendly, and I ended up making even more friends. I found it easier that day to talk to people, and make myself feel more at ease in my surroundings, as at that point I knew my way around Bede quite well, and felt a lot more comfortable there. I enjoyed my chosen courses just as much as the previous day. Also I was able to concentrate again, as I had made sure I had eaten breakfast. I was determined that this was going to be a new start, and that I wasn't going to cut back on my eating, and let everything spiral out of control again by losing weight, resulting in losing my concentration and social abilities. I needed to make sure I was eating well every day from then onwards, as I wanted my concentration to be one hundred per cent when I started college in September. I also wanted to look one hundred per cent better, and no longer like a walking, talking bag of bones.

When I told myself that I would have to focus hard on eating well, and gaining more weight, I did have many thoughts such as, 'But what if I gain loads of weight, and go to college in September fat? What if people think I eat too much? What if none of the boys find me attractive?'

But I was firm and told myself over and over again that not one of the things I was predicting was going to happen would. I wouldn't allow them to, and Marie had promised me that she and the Eating Disorder Team at the Rosewood Outpatients Unit would make sure that I stayed on the right track, both mentally and physically.

Before I left Bede that day, I made sure that I said goodbye to each and every one of my new friends, and we promised each other that we would stay in touch and meet up over the summer holidays. Lydia and I even planned to go out the following night! I didn't want my preview at Bede to end that day; I had enjoyed it so much. But I went home feeling just as happy and excited about everything as I had done the previous day, if not more.

When I filled my parents in with every single detail of my day, they appeared to be just as happy as I was. They were both thrilled and relieved that finally things were working out how I wanted them to, and I was now at last looking happy and not so depressed. I think they were also relieved about the fact that now I wasn't constantly worrying about my forthcoming GCSE results.

Chapter 26

The Beautiful Vision In Black

The following day went by in a flash, and before I knew it, I was getting 'Gothed up' to go out and meet Lydia. I was so excited, I couldn't remember the last time I actually had gone out somewhere with friends, and had a really good time. I made Mum take me early, to be certain that I wouldn't be late and have Lydia waiting for me. I arrived there in good time, and waited for her where we had arranged to meet. She arrived bang on time, but as I saw her getting off the bus, I noticed that there were two boys with her as well. My stomach was doing somersaults and my legs turning to jelly as they walked over towards me. This hadn't been part of the plan. What were they doing here?

"Hi Katie!" Lydia cried when she reached me, and she gave me a huge hug. "I've brought along my boyfriend Tyler and our friend Alex."

"Hi," I managed to whisper. I glanced at Tyler. He was really attractive: long, shoulder length blond hair, casual grungey/skater style, beautiful blue eyes and a cute smile. He actually reminded me a lot of Kurt Cobain.

"Hi," he said back, lifting his hand and giving a small, casual wave. He oozed coolness. Alex took my hand firmly in his and shook it.

"Hi, I'm Alex," he said with a lovely lopsided smile.

"Katie," I replied, shaking his hand back. I looked at him properly, without the curtain of my hair, and my jaw nearly touched the floor. He was absolutely gorgeous. Dressed in black jeans, black shirt and black Converse trainers, with black long hair almost to his shoulders. He smiled at me, and I nearly melted.

As we waited in the queue to enter the club, I chatted to Alex, Tyler and Lydia about all sorts of things and my nerves slowly started to fade away into the darkness that surrounded us. The more we talked together, the more comfortable I felt with them. And, as with Lydia, I felt as though I had known them for years. I was thrilled that I had made these new friends. I wasn't stood there as a loner. I was in a group! ME IN A GROUP! I was talking to cool people! I had friends, at last! Everything was going great! Brilliant! Fantastic! I was having an excellent time even before we had gone inside, just standing there with these lovely people. Anorexia played no part in this. I was being me, and people liked me. These people liked Katie.

We were just about to go on into the club, when I felt someone touch my shoulder, and feel down my arm with a large hand. I turned around quickly, and looked straight into the face of another Goth.

"You're soooo skinny!" she shouted. "How do you stay so thin? It's sooo unfair."

I glanced at Alex, Tyler and Lydia, and they were standing there waiting, watching me, waiting for a response. I felt a moment of sheer panic.

What should I say? I thought. Should I tell this complete stranger, as well as Tyler and Alex (if they didn't already know) the reason why I was, as this girl had stated, so thin? I hurriedly made the decision that it would be better if I did, as I felt that it wasn't right to lie to people who had made the effort to be my friends. They didn't deserve to be lied to.

So, I took a deep breath, and replied in a quiet, mumbling voice, "I'm a recovering anorexic. That's why I'm so, as you say, thin."

I glanced at Tyler and Alex to see what their reactions would be and they were both still smiling at me. As though I hadn't said anything out of the ordinary. It didn't bother them. Or, if it did, they didn't want to hurt my feelings by showing it. I felt Lydia slip her hand gently into mine, and give it a little squeeze. She smiled at me, and I smiled back, and a huge sense of appreciation for her welled up inside me. She knew what it was like, and I was certain she would support me.

"Oh, I'm sorry," the girl replied, and acted as if nothing had been said, which I was relieved about, as I didn't want anorexia to interfere with my night out in any way. Tonight was my night. Katie's night, and nothing was going to stop me from having the time of my life!

All too soon morning had dawned, and the night was over. I didn't want to leave as I said good-bye to Tyler and Alex, and hugged Lydia. I wanted to stay with them and dance until the sun rose. We all promised each other that we would meet up again soon.

I had been having such a fantastic time for a few days that our holiday to Kefalonia the next day had completely slipped my mind. I was really enthusiastic and looking forward to going. But now I secretly wanted to stay at home, and socialise with all of my new friends. I also wanted to see more of Alex, and find out if he liked me in the same way as I liked him. But the holiday had been paid for and there was no way that I could back out and stay at home.

I was determined that this year's holiday was not going to be a repeat performance of the previous ones we had taken. I was certain that my eating wouldn't be a problem. That I would allow myself different things all of the time, and that I wouldn't follow a strict meal and exercise plan. I wanted my family to have a fantastic time, and I didn't want to spoil it for them by letting anorexia come along. But anorexia didn't have to pay for a plane ticket, it got a free fare. And so of course, it took advantage and came along.

Thinking about Alex constantly since I had met him meant that food had hardly ever crossed my mind. Which was good in many ways, as it had been something that had dominated my thoughts for an absolute age. But in some ways it wasn't good at all. Because I was thinking about him all the time, it meant that sometimes I would forget about my breaks, and when I would remember about them, it would be too late and I wouldn't have the courage to have them at a later time. Which wasn't a good thing at all, and if continued for a long time would result in me losing weight.

I had sent a text message to Lydia about how I felt about Alex but unfortunately I had left my mobile phone behind in the rush to leave for the airport so I couldn't find out what she thought.

I reluctantly trailed behind my family as we climbed the stairs into the airplane. Mum told me that I would be able to phone Lydia from Kefalonia. But how would I be able to wait that long to find out this vital piece of information? The next day was twelve hours away. Twelve whole hours! It was going to be torture. I just knew it. Living torture.

Trying to keep myself occupied on the plane and not think of Alex was impossible. Utterly impossible. No matter what I did I just could not take my mind off him. And I knew that, text message or no text message, he was going to stay there in my mind for the rest of the holiday. I was well and truly besotted.

Chapter 27

Holiday Blues

The breakfast that faced us on our first morning was the complete opposite of what we had had on all of our previous holidays (i.e. every breakfast item available). We had booked ourselves a basic bed and breakfast holiday for the two weeks, but we never expected it to be as basic as it was.

The choices were rusks in place of toast, slices of stale bread about three inches long and, we soon found out, saved from the meals the day before, strawberry jam, boiled eggs, slices of processed cheese so thin you could see your hand through them, slices of ham that barely existed and diluted orange juice that resembled weak urine.

For the first time in a long while, and unusually so, I felt quite disappointed at the lack of variety of food on offer. There was almost nothing that I could, or would, eat, and we actually had to buy fruit, milk and cereal for me to have in the mornings. But, for the first morning there, I had to be content with two rusks spread with jam. Heaven on a plate. Not.

Immediately after we had eaten, I tried to phone Lydia on her mobile only to find when I dialled that I received no sound whatsoever. I realised that I had missed two digits off the number when I'd copied it down. I was fuming. How could I have been so damn stupid? Mum, who by this time was seriously agitated, told me to forget about the text message and wait until we were back home to get in touch with Lydia, but I knew it would be hell having to wait that long.

I continued trying to phone all through the holiday, until two days before we left, when I eventually gave up all hope that I would find out. And I was right. I never did find out, as Lydia never did reply. I had a thought that the message might not have been sent, and that she never received it in the first place, but another thought I had was that she couldn't have been bothered to reply. But that thought didn't last long at all. I couldn't think of Lydia like that. She was my new friend; she wouldn't do that to me. Would she? I would have to wait until I arrived back home to find out.

Sharing a hotel room with my younger sister had its ups and its major downs during our two weeks in Kefalonia. It had been a long, long time since we had shared a room, around three years, and we had both changed enormously in that space of time. One thing that had not changed though was the fact that I am an incredibly tidy person, and she is an incredibly untidy person: leaving a ham and cheese sandwich in your room for a week untidy! I must admit that since suffering with anorexia, I have become more obsessed with tidiness and cleanliness, but it is something that has always been there, just not as bad. I don't want to bore you going into all the arguments and fights that we had about keeping things tidy and clean, but one thing I will tell you was that there was an average of five a day!

Penny had really 'grown up' in many ways since I had been in, and come out, of hospital. She now had, at the age of fourteen the womanly figure which I used to have and had lost to anorexia. (I had lost my breasts and my hips to bones and skin.) She was a lot more concerned about her make-up and hair than I could ever remember her being, and she would spend hours in our little bathroom 'perfecting' herself. It was quite a shock to me how different she was from the last time that we had had to share a room. And I think it was during that holiday that I began to come to terms with the fact that she was no longer my 'baby' sister. I wanted innocent, small, sweet, talcum powder-smelling Penny, with the Thomas the Tank Engine wellingtons, the enormous, cow-brown cross-eyed eyes, the cheeky, lopsided smile and the blonde, soft ringlets which I used to twirl around my fingers. I wanted my 'baby' sister back. I didn't want this young woman with a mind and attitude of her own, and this perfectly formed body. I wanted Pen Wren. My little Pen Wren. But she had gone, and wasn't going to come back. However hard I wished.

I think about how I felt back then, now, and I suppose that many of my thoughts and feelings about Penny were due to the fact that I was petrified of change, not only in myself, but in my sister too. And I guess, in many ways, changes in the world as well.

I was rather upset that Penny and I didn't really talk during our two-week holiday. In the past when we had shared a room, we would always have had something to talk about. It seemed Penny didn't want to talk or discuss anything with me any more. It was strange, as she would always find something to chat to Anthony and Samuel about. They could talk for hours, like Penny and I used to be able to, about everything and anything, and it made me insanely jealous to the point where I would cry myself to sleep. Once again it seemed as though the tables had been turned on me in a matter which had always been so close to my heart.

The food in Kefalonia (except for in the hotel!) was fantastic. There wasn't an enormous range of vegetarian Greek food, but what was available was really delicious. We would visit a particular restaurant almost every single day, because of the amazing-tasting food and fantastic service. After a few visits, the staff took it into account that I had a problem with food and eating, and so they would offer to make me things that were not on the menu, and ask how I wanted my small portions served. At first, I was slightly apprehensive about this, as I didn't really want people guessing about my problems. But as they already knew, what harm could it do? So, after a short time, I became grateful for their thoughtfulness and kind service, and I basically let them take care of my needs when we visited their restaurant.

I allowed myself to try new foods almost every day, which was intensely difficult, but, as I said before, I wanted to make an effort with the holiday for everyone's sake.

I can't possibly leave this chapter without mentioning some of the foods that I managed to try, so that I can highly recommend them! Two were Stuffed Vine Leaves, (vine leaves stuffed with cooked rice and sautéed onion) and a Greek Sandwich (a toasted Baguette filled with Feta cheese, lettuce, peppers, onion and tomatoes). However, in order for me to have those foods, I still felt the need to do a certain amount of exercise to allow myself the privilege. Despite the fact that vine leaves and Greek sandwiches are everyday foods, which are not classed as something particularly special by 'normal' people who eat 'normally', I felt that for me, they were classed as a treat, and that I had to 'earn' the right to have them. It is clear now that the voice dictated the 'earning rule' to me. Although, then, it wasn't obvious in the slightest. I considered exercising to be allowed to have something to eat as normal, something everyone would do.

There were occasions my parents would buy ice cream for us all, and they would automatically ask the staff if I could have a smaller helping than everyone else. There were occasions when I would want to have a normal size helping, the same as everyone else, as I believed that I had 'earned' it with the amount of exercise that I had done during that particular day. However, I thought that if I asked to have a normal size helping, then my parents and the waitress would think that I was being greedy, and piggish, and so I stuck with my small helping, watching with envy but also pride for not choosing a larger helping, as my family dug into theirs with relish.

I now know for a fact that I could have done a lot better than I did with my eating in Kefalonia, and I really regret not speaking up when I wanted a normal sized portion, not 'letting myself go' a bit more, and trying more new and different things. But at the time, it was all far too overwhelming and scary, and the voice still too strong.

Chapter 28

Still Painfully Paranoid

We would spend most of our time at the beach and in the sea, as it was only a five minutes walk away from our hotel. The sea was a beautiful, perfect turquoise blue and always warm. I was still paranoid about showing my body in a swimming suit, but nowhere near as conscious as I had been on our previous holidays. I did still wear shorts when I went into the sea, as I was terrified of people laughing at my legs, which I still considered to be flabby.

It wasn't long before I noticed that Penny would get an astronomical amount of attention from the young men and teenagers when she sauntered around the beach and sunbathed in her itsy-bitsy bikini. I could see why, at fourteen, she had a fantastic body, and she knew just how to flaunt it. I can't say that I didn't feel jealous of Penny getting so much attention from men and boys and green-eyed looks from other women and girls, because I did feel envious. People would look at me from time to time, but their faces would show pity, disgust and shock, not lust, jealousy and want. I got more of those types of looks that Penny was getting, when I was thirteen, at a normal weight and had curves, which were better to flirt with than my skin and bones.

When we returned from Kefalonia, I met with Lydia as soon as I was able to, but to my dismay, she didn't mention a single word about the text message I had sent her. So I assumed that she didn't receive it and decided to leave my question about Alex for a while, despite the fact that it plagued me day and night, just as it had done in Kefalonia. However, I didn't want to appear to Lydia as if I was some obsessed, love-struck girl. But the thoughts I was having about him just refused to disappear, and everywhere I looked, his face was there, smiling at me, and I wanted him with a fiery hot passion.

Yet another bad reply from a publisher about my teenage novel was there to greet me on the doormat like an old enemy when we returned from holiday. But I cried my tears, had my moan, gritted my teeth and continued to keep on sending it out and hoping for the best. I had heard nothing about '*Sticks And Stones*', but continued to keep my hopes high. The fact that I had made more new friends, and had other things to occupy my mind, made the disappointment easier to cope with. Meanwhile, I continued to apply for job after job after job, but continued to be turned down again and again and again.

Disappointment continued in my efforts to find a publisher and a job but now that I had lots of new friends in my life, I was able to go out more and enjoy myself. This was one of the many things I used to find incredibly difficult to do, as it would mean breaking routines that had been set for such a long time. However, it also meant that I would often be out during mealtimes and times when I was due a 'break.' I wouldn't forget about them, as I would feel hungry, but I didn't want to say anything to anyone, as I was not, under any circumstances, going to have what I considered to be my 'stupid' eating plan get in the way of my socialising. I didn't want my new friends to know that I was meant to have certain foods at certain times of the day. I wanted to appear as a normal sixteen-year-old girl. Despite the fact that I wasn't.

My entire family was thrilled that my social life was improving in leaps and bounds, especially my parents. They were ecstatic, and were also willing to lend me money whenever I needed it so that I could go out. I honestly couldn't have asked for them to be more supportive.

One evening, when I was chatting to Lydia online (another part of my life I still had restricted access to, due to the voice's orders), I poured my heart out to her, admitting my feelings for Alex, and I consulted her as to whether I should ask him out on a date. She was slightly hesitant to answer, and when she eventually did, she said, "See how things go, as I'm not sure if you should." I was seriously disheartened when she said this, as I had been confident that she would say, "Go for it!"

Not long after our chat, I went out with Tyler and Alex. Lydia wasn't able to go because she had to work. For the first few hours we were there, I was thinking 'Should I ask him out? Shouldn't I? Should I?' However, when Alex and I sat down next to each other on the stage after a particularly gruelling head-banging session, he simply took my hand in his and held on to it, not even letting go when we stood to dance. I thought, 'Yes! Definitely! I AM going to ask him to go out with me! He must like me if he wants to hold my hand and not let go to dance! I can't be a delusional fool!'

I decided that I didn't need Lydia's permission or consent to ask him. I made a promise to myself that the following week I would ask him to go out with me. And I did.

I spent almost the entire week preparing myself for the big moment and deciding which outfit to wear. I went out, half of me confident, ready and raring to go, and the other half a shaking bag of nerves, which kept on thinking about backing out. Why would anyone as lovely and gorgeous as Alex want to go out on a date with me? I mentioned in a quiet conversation to one of my friends that I was thinking about asking Alex to go out with me, and she went ballistic and told me that I had to do it. Before I knew it, fifteen or more people who I didn't even know were telling me to ask him out. Saying that they knew for a fact that he liked me, and that we were made for each other. That we would make a perfect couple. That we were cute and sweet together. Hearing those words gave me the boost of confidence needed, and I delayed no longer.

He was standing next to the bar, chatting to Tyler, when I went up to him and asked him if I could "have a word". He walked with me to a quiet corner, and I came out with it. Well, to be honest, it was after a few erms, well, right, you see. I said, "OK Alex, I really, really like you, well, fancy you, and I was wondering if, that, well, if you feel the same way about me, erm, would you like to go out with me?"

What he said in response made me feel as though my heart had been ripped out of my chest, thrown to the floor and stamped into a mushy pulp. Then pushed back inside.

"You see Katie," he said. "I really do like you and I think you're a great girl, very pretty, intelligent and cool, but I don't think I can have a girlfriend because I know that I wouldn't be a good boyfriend at the moment. I'm really, really sorry to tell you this."

"Erm, OK then," I managed to choke out after a few moments, and I could feel my face growing red and hot underneath my face whitener. I'm positive that I must have looked like a mouldy

135

beetroot! The first thoughts that came into my mind immediately were 'Of course he was going to say no! Why did you even bother asking him? Why would anyone as gorgeous and lovely, intelligent and cool as him even consider going out with you?' I said all of this to Alex, and that I had been a stupid fool, asking him to go out with me, as I wasn't good enough for him, and I wasn't surprised that he had said no. He tried to convince me that I was totally wrong, and he told me that he wasn't good enough for me. Which of course, I didn't believe in the slightest. I didn't mention the other comments the voice had said. I was too humiliated to. 'You're an ugly fat cow with no life,' was one.

'You're a pathetic loser who no one in the world likes,' was another. 'You aren't good for or at anything in the world. Crawl into a black hole and die die die! It's all you deserve to do. Fat people shouldn't live.'

Those comments, along with countless other comments of self-hate, filled my ears and echoed around my brain again and again and again. The music didn't exist any longer. Only the voice was sounding in my head.

Being rejected yet again meant that I was upset for a long time afterwards, and it took a lot of people, including my mum and Marie, to convince me that it wasn't because I was fat, stupid, ugly, boring and an embarrassment to be seen with, that he had said no. I did continue to see Alex on occasions, but things were never ever the same as they had been before. The atmosphere was always tense and awkward, and that's how it stayed, no matter how hard I tried to act normally as though nothing had happened. I couldn't forget it. Alex remained in my heart, thoughts, dreams and longings for months afterwards.

Chapter 29

The Poisoned Papers

The time to receive my anxiously awaited GCSE results was looming ever closer, and I was getting more and more anxious and praying every day that they were going to be good, as I needed a serious boost to my crumbling confidence after the many various rejections in all aspects of my life. I also wanted my to make my family proud. I wanted to prove to them all that I was a hard worker, and could achieve things in my life other than losing weight and obeying what I was told to do by a voice in my mind.

On the morning that I collected my results, I was unable to keep my clammy hands from shaking while opening the envelope. I felt my stomach turn, and my eyes starting to burn and sting with hot tears as I quickly scanned the small piece of paper again and again and again, in disbelief at what was printed on it. The teacher who was standing next to me at the time told me that I had done extraordinarily well with my grades considering what I had been through, and the length of time that I had been back in school for. But I felt the complete opposite. I had an E for maths, which I had half expected anyway as it was my worst subject and I was terrible at it, an E for science, which was expected too, because I hated that. An E for General Studies, a C for Art, which I was quite pleased with. But my favorite subject, English, I managed to get a C and a B with speaking and listening. I had been positive that I was going to get an A or even an A*. In IT I managed to get Merits, Distinctions and Passes. My parents acted as though I had won the Olympics, and gripped the piece of paper as though it were a precious gold medal.

"They're fantastic!" they both cried enthusiastically. "Well done! We're so, so proud of you!"

"But they're not as good as I wanted them to be," I managed to eventually stammer.

My parents tried to make me feel better by telling me they were brilliant considering everything I'd been through, and when they told me just how proud they were of what I had managed to achieve, it made my disappointment fade slightly, and I stopped

137

putting myself down so much. However, I still felt a failure, deep inside, and I was embarrassed to tell my friends and other members of my family about how I had done. I had thoughts that even though my parent and teachers were saying that they were proud of me, that they really felt as though I hadn't worked hard enough to get the best results I could have managed. I tried to reassure myself that it wasn't the end of the world as I had been promised a place at Bede, no matter what the results of my GCSEs were, which made me feel better. I know it was the anorexia's fault. If I hadn't become anorexic, I would have exceeded my expectations. Being restricted from doing as well as I could have done is one thing that I will curse anorexia for until the day I die.

It was only a matter of days after I had received my results that I had to enroll at Bede for the courses, which were due to start in September. I was full of determination and enthusiasm to increase my food intake, and slowly gain weight. Before now, starting college had been, well, a dream that I wasn't positive was ever going to happen, but going to enrol made it real and true. It really was happening to me! I was really going to start at college! I was determined that my new life in education was not going to start with me being drastically underweight and skeletal, still living my life by a set routine, day in day out. I knew change needed to happen. I needed to become a teenager and live my teenage years to the full, before they slipped through my fingers forever like grains of sand.

On enrolment day, I was the only person at home, as the rest of my family had gone to visit friends, and were only due back the following day. I went to Bede with my results, feeling nervous and excited, but also alone and angry, as I had wanted my parents to be there to support me, help me with my nerves and give encouragement. But I had to do it myself. My parents had spoken to me briefly on the phone, but it wasn't the same. I had to give myself the push that I needed, which was a very hard thing to do.

I smiled my largest, brightest smile as I sat in front of the results inspector, and handed him my results, and the papers containing the information about which courses I wanted to start doing in September. He looked at my results, and the courses, jotted down a few notes, handed them back to me with a smile, cheerfully told me to enjoy my time at Bede, and sent me off to see my interviewer. I waltzed off, happy as Larry, thinking, 'Gosh, isn't everything going so damn smoothly! This is fantastic! At last, things are going well for me!'

I sat down at a table with my interviewer, and he already had a copy of my results and papers of the courses I wanted to do, but his face was grave and serious. I felt my smile falter slightly at his expression, but then thought, 'Hey, he might look like that all the time. Poor bloke. How depressing.'

"So, these are the courses you want to do, Katie?" he asked slowly.

"Yes," I replied brightly. "They are indeed!"

"So, would you mind telling me exactly what it is you hope to have as a career?"

I practically bit off his last word with my answer. "I hope to be a best-selling author or be in a rock band playing electric guitar. And, with the money that I make with either of those careers, I would like to train to be a chef and open a vegetarian restaurant."

He chuckled to himself and glanced at my grades yet again, with an expression that I didn't like in the slightest.

"It's all very well being an author, Katie," he said, in a high and mighty tone, as though he was an all-knowing bestseller. "However, whether any one will buy your books is another matter altogether of course. And those other career options, well, to put it simply, they're very difficult things to get right, you know."

I flinched at his snidy, cruel comment. This man was supposed to be encouraging me, not shooting me down in flames. While I was aware that my career pathways would be tough to travel upon, I was someone who worked hard and was willing to do anything to reach my goals.

"I have high hopes and aspirations," I told him, determined not to feel put down or hurt by what he had just said, despite the fact that I was mortified beyond belief inside.

He continued to ask me a few questions about what I would do if none of those careers worked out for me, why had I chosen to come to Bede and what other colleges had I looked at. I answered his questions as best I could, and felt everything was going all right, other than his rudeness earlier.

"OK Katie, could you possibly explain to me why your grades are," he sighed heavily, "well, as they are."

'A pile of nonsense,' I expected him to be thinking. I felt my entire body tense up, and the thoughts that everything was going all right vanished instantly. I thought that all of the teachers at Bede had been informed about me and my circumstances, and that I wouldn't have to explain about them all over again. However, as it appeared to be a necessity that he knew, I explained to him, feeling embarrassed, that I was a recovering anorexic, about being in hospital and about missing a year and a half of school and not coping well in exam situations, thus explaining my grade situation. I asked him if he had been told any of what I had just said by the headmistress, and he said no, as she had recently left Bede to work at a secondary school down south. I was shocked into silence when he told me this, as she had made it perfectly clear that she would be there in September when I started college, to support and guide me if I needed her to. And if that wasn't bad enough for me to hear, he then went on to tell me that my grades were not of a high enough standard to be able to do any of the courses that I wanted to do. That's right. I wouldn't be able to do ANY. I don't know how I managed to speak, but, by a miracle, I managed to find the power of speech.

"But... but when I was interviewed and told the headmistress about everything, she told me that whatever my grades were, I would be able to do the courses that I wanted to do. She promised me. Why has that changed? Please, please tell me."

"Well I'm sorry, but there must have been a misunderstanding somewhere along the line. We just cannot let you do the courses. It's a simple fact. Your grades are simply not good enough."

I couldn't prevent the tears, and I cursed myself for not having bought a tissue with me.

"But she promised," I choked, wiping the tears away with the back of my hand. "She told me that my grades didn't matter. She promised."

"I understand this must be hard for you to hear," he replied, with absolutely no emotion or understanding whatsoever. "But there is nothing that I can possibly do. You can of course do re-sits at a different college, and then maybe come back to us next year with presumably better grades."

I had a sudden case of déjà vu. I definitely did not want to do that. I wanted to start at college to get away from school lessons, not to go back to them.

"Please, please let me try the courses," I begged. Literally. "I can promise you that I will work really, really hard. I can prove to you that I can get good grades. Please let me try. Look, I did two years worth of GCSE course work in less than one year. I'm sure that I can cope with A levels."

He shook his head and a sort of snorted chuckle came from his pursed lips, before he replied. "It doesn't matter if you can promise anything to us, Katie. I am sorry, but there is no way that rules can be changed. They are there for a reason. Now, we can offer three courses to you in September, which are, Health and Social Care, Business Studies, and Key Skills. And if you manage to get some good results with those, then there may be a possibility of you doing some of the courses of your choice next year."

He looked at me expectantly, and I stared back at him blankly, before loudly cursing anorexia and the education system. None of the options he had suggested appealed to me in the slightest, and had absolutely no relevance to what I wanted to do as a career. I knew for a certainty that I could do more than what he was offering, and told him immediately that I wasn't interested in any of those options at all. I think he became very uncomfortable with the situation at this point, and he scuttled off, muttering, "I'll quickly discuss this with some of the other members of staff, and see what they say about it all."

And I was left alone, sobbing my heart out, snot mingled with tears running down my face, surrounded by other students, who were laughing and chatting and joking with their interviewers, everything going smoothly for them, and bumpy as a ploughed field for me. I caught a few students and teachers glancing over at me, from time to time, as I waited for my interviewer to return, and I felt so embarrassed and ashamed. I didn't blame them for looking, though. I guess that they only wondered why I was crying. But I couldn't stop. No matter how hard I tried, I couldn't stop the tears from cascading down my burning red cheeks.

He returned after a few minutes, shaking his head and repeated the same options as before, except that there could be a small possibility of me being able to do English Literature. But I didn't just want a small possibility for one subject. I wanted THE possibility to do all of the courses that I wanted to, and that I had been promised. He went on to say that I didn't have to make a final choice about what I wanted to do there and then. I still had a few days left to make my decision whether I wanted to have a look at some other colleges again or do the things that they offered me at Bede. Panic washed over me like a tidal wave. We were late into August, and college was due to start in early September. I am the sort of person who likes to have everything organised and ready well in advance, and I thought I had done really well, until now. I couldn't believe that this was happening. I was basically being told that I had to completely rethink my plans and all of my ideas. The plans and ideas that had been set in stone for months. Exactly how I liked them to be.

I was in such shock that I could barely respond when he talked to me. I felt numb all over, and I think it affected my speech. I did eventually manage to tell him that I would come back the next day with my mum after she had returned from Surrey and hopefully have everything sorted out then. He apologised for the misunderstanding, and let me leave. I stumbled out of Bede, barely seeing for tears, feeling deflated, lost, confused, upset, humiliated and angry. And I needed a hug. Around me, gaggles of giggling, grinning girls chatted excitedly about their brilliant GCSE results and starting college, and I wished to be one of them. I needed to be wrapped up in someone's arms and made to feel human again. But there was no one there. I was alone to wallow in my sadness and despair.

Chapter 30

Mother The Miracle Maker

After a few hours, when I had had time to calm myself down a little bit, I rang Mum and explained to her what had happened. I couldn't help but start to sob again on the phone. The reason mostly being because I wanted my mum with me, holding me, telling me everything was going to be fine, and not four hundred miles away, on the other end of a phone line. Mum went ballistic when I had finished relaying the scene to her. She knew for a fact that they had accepted me, as she had been in the room herself when the headmistress had said so. She couldn't understand how this had happened. OK, so the headmistress had left, but that was no reason to uproot plans that had been formed, for the sake of a few measly exam results, which proved nothing about my true capabilities.

Mum promised that they would leave Surrey as soon as possible the next day, so she could come to Bede with me and sort this enormous mess out. She was adamant that she would be able to put things right, and that I would be able to do the courses. The power in her voice made me believe that she would be able to do so, and some of the panic and disappointment I felt amazingly melted away. My mum had managed to give me new hope. My mum the miracle maker.

The moment my family returned, Mum grabbed me and we made our way back to Bede. She walked with a fierce determination in her stride, and gave me the strength and guts needed to show my face there again. She asked at reception to see the interviewer whom I had spoken to the previous day, but we were told he was not available. We were asked if we minded talking to someone else. I said that it didn't matter at all, however Mum was fuming. She wanted to talk to the man who had spoken to me and give him a piece of her mind, and quite possibly her fists had the chance been available.

Once an interviewer had been allocated, and we had all sat down, Mum calmly asked why this had all happened, and why we had both been lied to about my position at Bede. I felt safe and

143

positive that things would turn out well for me with Mum sat by my side, radiating courage and confidence. She slowly explained everything about what had happened during the past four years, but the look on my new interviewer's face said it all even before he had opened his mouth, and my sense of safeness and security vanished. Along with all new hope.

"I am sorry, both of you, but after hearing what happened, I am afraid that you were told right. There is nothing that can be done. Katie will not be able to start these courses in September. It's simply not possible. We cannot have one rule for hundreds of students, and another for one student alone."

"But what about the promise that was made to her?" Mum bellowed, causing heads to turn in the process. But she didn't care. The man raised his hands and shrugged.

"I'm sorry," was all he had to say.

All three of us were silent for a few moments, before Mum, with a face like thunder, stood up, and reached for my arm. She thanked the man, through gritted teeth, for his time, and we made our way quickly out of the college. I was once again crying. Once again making a fool out of myself. Once again feeling embarrassed, angry and devastated. And once again wishing that anorexia had never chosen me as its victim.

When we arrived back home, I cried for all I was worth. I couldn't believe it. I really could not believe what had happened, and neither could my mum, and she showed that by crying herself, as she held me in her arms. When I had cried myself dry, I just sat in mute shock on the stairs, exhausted, my lips dry, my eyes red and sore, my hands clenched into fists, while Mum explained to my dad what had happened. He was just as furious, and couldn't understand the mess-up. When I eventually found the power of speech again, after about half an hour, all the panic that had welled up inside me flowed out.

"What the hell am I going to do now?" I choked to Mum. "The college term starts in a few days' time and I don't have a college to go to. I don't have courses to study. I don't have the right bloody grades! I don't have the right life."

My mum thought for a while before answering my question. "Are you sure that you don't want to do re-sits, Katie?" she asked me. "That was a possibility, you know."

"I know it is, Mum, and I'm sure that I don't want to do them."

"You know, you could always take a year out. Not everyone starts at college as soon as they leave school."

This was a new idea. Taking a year out would give me time to work on my writing and getting a part-time job, but it wouldn't do a lot for my social life, and I wouldn't get any qualifications by doing it either. After a short time thinking about it, I decided not to. I was determined to go to college and continue with my education. I wanted to be like a normal sixteen-year-old, studying the things I enjoy studying, and being with people who liked me. Mum then reminded me of Middlesbrough College. We had been to an Open Evening a few months previously about the catering course, which had been an option that I had considered doing, before deciding to go to Bede. Mum suggested that we ring Middlesbrough College and talk to them about enrolling there. I agreed almost immediately, as I was desperate to prove to myself, to my parents, to Bede and to the world that I was ready and able to make a brand new start with my life. So Mum rang up and we both talked to the main tutors of the catering course. We were told that enrolment at Middlesbrough was happening that very day! And so I mopped my tears up, slapped a smile back on my miserable face, and stepped back out into the cruel, mean, hard world, to show it that Katie was making a comeback.

It was an enormous challenge not to cry as Mum and I drove to Middlesbrough College. I tried to be light-hearted and positive, but it was incredibly difficult. By the time we arrived, I was in such a state that Mum asked me if it really was a good idea to go inside and face another interview. I told her that I was fine, wiped my face for the hundredth time, and forced a smile back on to my lips. I told her that I was going to 'show Bede' that I could make something of myself, and that they would regret not taking me on.

Enrolment took under half an hour, and the two tutors whom I spoke to were absolutely fantastic. It was quite difficult repeating once again what I had been through, and often my eyes threatened to give way to yet more tears, but the tutors were kind and understanding, and said they were very impressed with my grades. They said that I appeared to be a very promising young lady with a lot of talent. Hearing someone say this to me after all the crap that

I had been through that day was like being presented with a prize. It was also an enormous relief.

Doing a catering course to become a chef had been the alternative to studying English Language and Literature at college. But I had thought that I could have studied English and then done a catering course at night school or later on in my life. However, now that it appeared to be the only thing that I was able to do, other than re-sits or staying at home, I decided that I would grab the opportunity with both hands, and make the very best of it. Fortunately, my course started late in September, so I had more time to get prepared. I had my chef's whites and waiter's uniform to order, as well as my knife kit, something that I would never have imagined myself owning, and something that, one year earlier, could have been my ticket to suicide.

Mum and I left Middlesbrough College, with me feeling positive about my future again. Although I was still furious with Bede for what they had done, and deep inside I was furious with the anorexia and myself, I was going to show the world that I was a strong person, and could make something of myself.

After the bedlam had subsided, I found, to my complete dismay that I had lost a large amount of weight, and was close to the weight I had been while on bed rest in hospital. Bed-rest weight meant no activity whatsoever, and I was currently running around like something possessed. I knew the reason for my weight loss was all the stress, panic and tension that I had been facing, but it was difficult to explain this to my family. They assumed that whenever I lost weight it was because I thought that I wasn't thin enough and was listening to the voice telling me not to eat. It wasn't at all. I'd like to get that straight immediately. It's a fact that if you are stressed out and have a lot of things happening to you, you will lose weight or gain weight.

Unfortunately for me, at this particular time, it meant that I lost weight. I wasn't pleased, happy or proud about it, and to me it just felt as though it was yet another hurdle to get over. However, I was fiercely determined that I would manage to leap over it and gain again, as I wanted to be able to start college at a stable weight.

I continued to apply for part-time jobs to help keep my focus on gaining weight, but still had no luck. It was the same old story with

146

publishers too. It appeared as if no one wanted to know. But still I persisted. I wasn't going to give up under any circumstances. I knew what my goals were and knew that I was going to achieve them. Nobody was going to stand in my way now. Even if I had to go through every single publisher in the United Kingdom, the USA and the world if needs be, with a fine-toothed comb, I didn't care. I was going to find a publisher to take on my book. I was going to find a part-time job. I was going to gain weight. I was going to get to where I wanted to be. I was going to reach my goals. I was going to win.

Chapter 31

Seventeen On A Sour Note

Before I knew it, the summer holidays were almost over. The long, warm days were becoming colder, the darkness settled earlier, signifying the beginning of autumn. I was close to reaching the grand old age of seventeen, which I found hard to believe, as it only seemed like yesterday that I had turned sixteen.

On the day of my birthday, we had planned to go to Whitby for the day as a family. It was what I really wanted to do, as I adore Whitby with a passion, and I wanted to spend a lovely day there with my family. There is also a wonderful vegetarian restaurant, which I wanted to go to for my birthday lunch. I had planned to have my favourite sandwich: egg mayonnaise and cress, to prove to my siblings that I could eat what I wanted, when I wanted, as they doubted that I could, and thought that I still only ate what 'the voice' told me to eat.

When the day of my seventeenth birthday arrived, it ended up being only Mum and me going to Whitby. My dad had to work, and my siblings decided that they couldn't be bothered to go. They would rather spend the day on the Playstation, watching TV and playing on the computer. I became really upset, and felt as though I didn't matter to them in the slightest. It was yet another occasion when I felt invisible.

I tried to cheer up during the day, smile and laugh and enjoy the time that I had to spend alone with Mum. As well as trying to accept the fact that my siblings were just being typical teenagers.

The day after my birthday, college started. I was seriously nervous at first because I didn't know a single person there. I kept my eyes on stalks for anyone who looked even slightly Gothic or alternative, but didn't see a soul. Not one Goth. Not one alternative person. I won't deny that I do enjoy being an individual and being different to other people, but it's nice if there are one or two people who share the same interests and styles as you. It means someone to talk to, and it makes you feel more comfortable in your surroundings. I was quite surprised to find that I was the oldest student on my course, as a lot of the other girls looked years older than me. They had the bodies of young women, with curves in all the right places. Part of me felt envious of them; why couldn't I look like they did and be content and happy? Why did I think that I had to keep the body of a little girl? A body of innocence. I was envious that they were able to have 'normal' bodies, and not think twice about it. It became a natural sight to walk into college and see perfectly slim, beautiful girls, chomping away on chocolate bars and crisps and drinking cans of Coke and being admired by the male students. I would be amazed and jealous that they were able to eat like that, and keep their perfect figures, nails and hair. I was positive that if I had a chocolate bar or a can of Coke on a daily basis I would blow up like a helium balloon.

Despite the fact that nobody on my course had the same interests as me, other than the love of cooking and working under pressure in a kitchen, I did manage to socialise and mingle with the other students, and make some new friends. A number of students, some who were on my course, and some who didn't even know me, asked me straight out if I was anorexic. I was quite embarrassed to tell them that I was, but made it clear to them that I was recovering from the illness. A part of me felt weak and pathetic for telling people about my illness, as I had wanted college to be a completely new start, away from anorexia, away from my abnormality. However, I soon found that it wasn't going to be as easy as I had thought and hoped it would be. I had written a book all about my illness, so I was going to have to get used to people knowing all about my life and my personal problems. If I wanted to be famous and known for my writing, then I was going to have to take the rough with the smooth, the good with the bad. When I would explain to people about what subject I was studying at college, almost every single person seemed puzzled and confused. I don't think they could understand why a recovering anorexic was studying catering. A lot of the people I know were aware of the fact that I loved cooking and was a passionate vegetarian, but they never thought I would have studied catering, as becoming an author had always been my ideal career path!

Over the first few weeks at college, I lost weight. Not purposely, but my life was so much more hectic and busy than it had ever been before. I had to get up at 6am to catch the bus at 7.45am, which I had to walk half a mile to get to. I then started college at 9am and sometimes didn't get home until 8.30 - 9pm at night. Every day we had a different finishing time. Some days we'd get finished at 1pm, some days 9pm. However, every day was the same, always busy, always tiring, but fun and exciting too. Well, most of the time, anyway! Of course, it could be a drag too sometimes. I promised my family, Marie and myself that I would try my hardest to gain the weight again.

I tried my best to keep in touch with the friends that I had made at Bede during Preview, but only managed with a couple. I tried especially hard to keep in touch with Lydia, however, to my surprise and disappointment, she didn't make the same effort. Yet I should have known all along that was going to happen. I should have known that she was only being my friend because she felt sorry for me, and then realised that, actually, I was too much of an embarrassment to be seen with. She was smarter, prettier, funnier and in general a better person than I was. The 'fat thoughts' that had stopped plaguing me, now returned with a vengeance. The rolls of blubber around my neck multiplied, as did the flab on my thighs, stomach and forearms.

It didn't help that my brothers returned to their old habits of calling me offensive names. Although they probably weren't as horrible as I thought. I was incredibly sensitive, and they were most likely names that any sibling would holler. I once again became withdrawn and depressed at home, spending hours alone in my room, or out on my bike, attempting to escape my feelings of fatness and, at the same time, the constant demands from the voice. However, at college I put on a bright happy mask and attempted to become the opposite of the depressed soul I was at home. I didn't want my home situation to interfere with my life at college at all. I didn't want people worrying about me. I wanted to appear as though I was handling my life perfectly, both inside and outside of college. I wanted to appear as a strong and able person. A person who had come out of hospital and was making up for lost time. A teenager who was coping with life as any other normal teenager would. But I wasn't doing that. I was achieving the opposite.

Receiving two positive emails from publishers about my book inspired me to ignore the 'fat thoughts,' forget (almost) about my failed friendships, and block out my brothers' words of venom. I once again needed to dig myself out of the rut of depression and self-hatred. So '*Sticks And Stones*' was sent off once again, and I had new, positive visions, and high hopes in my heart.

I managed to cope with the rejections better than ever before, as I had my book to think about and college to concentrate on. Talking about college, it was going from strength to strength, as I was managing to keep myself in a positive and happy frame of mind. Most days I would come home exhausted, but happy.

Chapter 32

The Day My Wish Was Granted

I know that taking part in a mind exercise with my tutor in college during an individual tutorial helped me to achieve what happened in the next few days of my life. The exercise involved concentrating on where you wanted to be in the future, and what you wanted to be happening. I concentrated intensely hard on managing to get my book published and it being a bestseller. I was so overjoyed about getting replies from publishers that I found it simple to imagine this really happening.

About a week after sending my book away to one of the publishers, I received an email from a small publishing company called Crystal Publishing. The publisher, Edith Collier was impressed with the sample chapters I had sent her, and wanted to see the rest of my manuscript! I was ecstatic, and sent it away immediately. My fingers must have been on fire as they pushed the pages into the envelope!

A matter of days later, I received an email from another publisher who was also interested. Things were going from strength to strength! Having these fantastic things happen made it so much easier for me to eat well, as I had other things to think about than exercise, food and calories. College was improving by the day, as my mood and concentration shot up. Another week later, I received an email from Edith, saying that she thought the story was fantastic, and would love to take it on and publish it! She also said that there would be a chance of TV and radio coverage as well! I could not believe my eyes, and had to read and re-read the email several times. I was actually sitting in the public library at the time, and I almost jumped out of my seat and ran around the place screaming, before remembering where I was. I was grinning from ear to ear as I went to the library desk and told them I had finished using the computer. I was desperate to tell them what had just happened, but managed to contain myself, and sprinted to where Mum was patiently waiting for me in the car.

"You won't believe what's happened to me," I said to her, as calmly and as collectively as I could manage.

"What?" she asked half-heartedly, expecting me to say that the new book I wanted was in stock.

"I've only got a bloody publisher for my book!" I shouted, unable to contain my excitement.

At first, Mum was speechless, and her face was a picture of undiluted shock. Sort of like a goldfish when it can't remember how to close its mouth! But then a huge smile broke out, and she hugged me tightly over the handbrake.

"Oh Katie, that's fantastic! I can't believe it!" she cried. "I'm so, so happy for you! And proud beyond words."

I felt as though I was floating in a dream for the rest of the day. It had happened. It really, really had happened to me. I had worked so very hard, and was now eventually getting what I wanted most in the entire world. I was having my story published, and I was going to be famous! ME! KATIE METCALFE! The plump one at school, who couldn't jump the gym hurdles, or get herself a boyfriend, was going to be a star!

The following day after receiving my fantastic news, I was checking my emails at college, to find that I'd received one from Edith about appearing on GMTV. Yes, G-M-T-V! NATIONAL MORNING TELEVISION! Apparently, she had contacted them about my story, and they replied, stating that they would love to have me on the show that coming Friday! They explained that they would provide me, and one other person, with transport down to London, accommodation and transport while we were there too. I couldn't believe it! It felt as thought my life had been flipped around and transformed into something amazing!

I rang Mum immediately to tell her the brilliant news about GMTV, and, at first, she thought it was a joke, but when I read the email to her over the phone, she believed me, and was as ecstatic as I was. As soon as I arrived home from college, the phone didn't stop ringing for hours, as I had people from GMTV needing to speak with me, Edith wanting to keep track of everything that was going on, and of course friends and family desperate to know every precise detail. It was probably the most hectic day of my entire life so far! I kept in close contact with Edith and the people at GMTV over the following days, even though being at college full-time did make it awkward, to say the least, as often they would need to contact me during lesson times, when my mobile would be switched off. However, some of my teachers were lenient about the situation, and would allow me to make and accept calls, but there were the odd few who were difficult.

It was the following Wednesday when everything was finally arranged and officially confirmed. I called as many of my friends and family as I could, before we had to leave, and told them the fantastic news. I tried to sound calm and as though it was an 'everyday thing' but boy, was it a hard thing to do! As it was in fact the least 'everyday thing' to have ever happened to me.

I still couldn't believe what was happening when Mum and I were sitting on the train whizzing our way down to London. I already felt like a star, and we hadn't even arrived in London yet! I rehearsed what I was going to talk about on the show over and over and over again. I had so much to say, but I knew I would only have a very limited amount of time to talk. I had planned ahead to try and cram in as much information as possible.

We had a phone call while we were on the train from the producer at GMTV, asking if it would be feasible to do some filming as soon as we arrived at our hotel, for the show in the morning. It was going to be late when we arrived at the hotel, and I hadn't really prepared to do any filming that evening, but I agreed immediately. Who was I to disagree?

I attempted to relax for the remaining hours of the train journey, and not think of the filming that was going to take place. But it was virtually impossible. I was erupting with excitement and nerves, and there was no way I could keep cool, calm and collected!

The train journey was over before I knew it, and we were out of the train and into a Mercedes that took us to our hotel in Drury Lane. We told the receptionist that we were there for GMTV, she immediately knew who we were, and we were shown to our room with a smile.

The room was lovely, comfortable and well-sized and out of the window you could see lots of the sights of London. We had only been in the hotel for a matter of minutes when there was a knock on the door, and we let in the lady who would be directing the short 'film.' My stomach was filled with butterflies and I could barely speak as we discussed what was going to happen, but as Joanna (the director) asked me questions and the filming began, I was able to relax. She asked me if I would mind reading out parts from my personal diary, and I said that I didn't mind at all, as I wanted people to hear the real, raw truth about my illness and all of the factors surrounding it.

It was a rather emotional experience for both Mum and me, reading through my old diary again, as it brought back so many memories, a lot of which I would have preferred to completely forget. I must admit that both of us had to wipe away tears a number of times while I read. We spent about an hour and a half on the 'film' before Joanna and the cameraman were content with the footage. They took some photos away, that I had brought with me from home, photos of me at my lowest weight in Tenerife and when I was on bed rest in hospital, to add to the 'film' for the following day. We were then left to our own devices.

Before Joanna left, she told us that a car would pick us up at 6.10am, and we would appear on the show at 6.50am with John Stapleton and Penny Smith. I guess it was only when she told us that, that it began to sink in what was happening.

After Joanna and the cameraman had left, we decided to go and get something to eat. We were seated immediately and handed menus. I automatically scanned the menu for the meal lowest in calories and fat, and found it, tomato and basil soup. It was actually a starter, but I planned to have it for a main meal, despite the fact that I yearned for the delicious sounding wild mushroom, pea and shaved parmesan risotto. Mum chose a feta cheese and sesame seed salad. She also chose the mushroom risotto for her main course. She told me that we could share the risotto, but I muttered to her that I only wanted the soup. Mum's face, which had previously been glowing with happiness, fell slightly.

"But you adore mushroom risotto, love." I struggled to look her in the eyes and stared down into my lap. "Come on, Katie," she said, and squeezed my hand. "You can have some risotto as well. The soup is only meant for a starter. Come on. I thought this New Year was a new start for you, and look, we're almost at the end of it now. Come on. Let's show this bloody anorexia who's boss! Plus, you don't want to look starving on GMTV tomorrow. Do you? And imagine if your stomach rumbles on air. Now that would be embarrassing, wouldn't it? Katie, you're supposed to be showing the world that you're recovering from this illness."

Mum's encouragement persuaded me to change my mind, and I decided to attempt to eat some risotto as well as the soup.

"OK then. I'll try," I replied.

Mum's glowing smile returned, and she squeezed my hand again. I immediately started to feel nervous and afraid about my enormous decision, but was determined not to let it show.

When the soup arrived, the thick, steaming, deep red, sweet smelling liquid had an offensive swirl of astonishing white cream on the top as a garnish. Which of course was scooped straight out. Automatic reaction. The soup was delicious, and I ate it slowly, relishing each spoonful, but secretly praying that none of the cream had managed to dissolve before I had had the chance to remove it. Mum offered me a taste of her salad, and at first I declined, but then, remembering my 'new start', I accepted a tiny taste. That too was delicious. It was amazing having so many different flavours and sensations exploding on my tongue, as my palate had endured the same foods for months on end.

When I placed my soup spoon down, roughly half still remained in the bowl, but Mum didn't say a word. I suppose that she wanted to avoid starting an argument as one would have surely arisen had she even muttered anything about the amount I had eaten. The risotto arrived moments after our starters had been cleared away, and it looked and smelt divine; the creamy rice was packed with large slices of mushrooms, plump bright green peas and topped with shavings of parmesan cheese. I slowly spooned a small amount on to my side plate, and with a deep breath started to eat. Tears actually welled in my eyes as the taste was so delicious. I can't actually describe on paper the feelings of pleasure and warmth that I felt as I let the food be absorbed into me. Thoughts of how many calories my mouthful contained spiralled around and around in my head, and guilty feelings were starting to bubble and boil inside me, but I did my best to ignore them and enjoy the sensational food that I was allowing myself to taste. At last.

After I had consumed a few small forkfuls, the thoughts of calorie content and guilt had almost vanished completely, and I was able to think about how much I was enjoying this food, and why on earth had I deprived myself for such a long time of the things that I enjoy and which fill me with so much pleasure. When I had finished my small side plate of risotto, I found, to my astonishment, that I was still hungry. My stomach was still growling, the pangs still present, and I found myself wanting more. I wanted more of the delicious, amazing pleasure. I also wanted to be rid of this empty, hollow feeling inside, of hunger. The year before, I would have wanted the hunger to be there. It would have given me the needed sign that I was managing to successfully deprive myself of food and not swallow the calories and fat, which I had been convinced I didn't need. But now, most of me, not all, wanted it to vanish. And so I found myself forking into the plateful, and allowing myself to have some more. I didn't bother with my side plate; I just ate it straight off the large plate. A tiny mouthful at a time. Mum didn't say anything. She just smiled at me, and helped herself to some more too.

Mum and I went for a walk after finishing our meal, which I must admit I was glad about. My stomach felt comfortable, not quite stuffed, but warm and satisfied. A feeling I had not experienced in a very long time. Even though I had not stuffed myself by any stretch of the imagination, some of the guilt came back, and I felt that it was necessary to do some exercise. Mum and I eventually fell into bed at 1am, with our alarm set for 5.30am. Mum managed to fall asleep immediately, but I couldn't, as I was so excited about the following morning, and kept on rehearsing what I was going to say. It was 3.30am when sleep finally encased me in its embrace.

Chapter 33

Images Of Me All Over The Country

I woke up five minutes before our alarm sounded, and was surprisingly awake, for the short amount of rest that I had had. I dressed quickly, had a large cup of tea but was unable to eat anything. Part of the reason I didn't want to eat just before the show was because I had a stupid thought that it would put weight immediately on my features. And also, my stomach was so knotted that I don't think it could have held anything anyway.

The car came for us at exactly 6.10 am, and drove us straight to the GMTV Studio. As Mum and I sat side by side on the plush leather seats, I secretly hoped that she was proud. When we arrived, I tried my best to control my shakes, and act as cool, calm and collected as possible. We handed our luggage to the receptionist at the desk and were hurriedly introduced to the producer who showed us to the Green Room. As we walked along the plush carpeted corridors, past all the photographs of presenters and celebrities, we were told about the kind of questions John and Penny would be asking us, and, to me, they sounded perfectly acceptable. I was fully prepared to tell them anything that they wanted to know. There did seem to be fewer questions than I'd imagined there would be, but that's television for you, I suppose. You can't always have your own way.

Once in the Green Room, we were told to take a seat for a few minutes before having our make-up done. I sat down, and received the shock of my life, as next to me was Doctor Hilary Jones! I couldn't believe it. I was sitting next to Doctor Hilary Jones! The most renowned doctor on television! He smiled at me, said hello and went back to reading his newspaper. I think Mum was slightly in awe too, by the gobsmacked expression on her face.

After a few minutes, we were rushed into the make-up room, where I had my coat whipped off and was sat down in front of a large light bulb-lit mirror. I felt like a movie star! Surrounding me were the various presenters of GMTV walking about, sipping drinks and sitting having make-up applied, and I can tell you one thing now, not all of them are as happy or cheerful as they appear to be on screen! It took the make-up artist a matter of minutes to apply my make-up, and before I knew it, Mum and I were being whisked off again, being told we were about to appear in exactly two minutes! I still couldn't really believe that in a matter of moments, people across the nation were going to know who I was!

The first thing I noticed about the set was that it was a lot smaller than it appears to be on TV. Everything's cramped in together; there was Lorraine's small set in one corner, the weather set in another corner and, slap-bang next to that, the news desk and the sofa where we were going to sit. All the other space was taken up with cameramen and electrical equipment. It was so packed you could hardly move without standing on someone or an appliance of some description. People were rushing around, banging into each other and tripping over wires. It really was quite hectic!

We had to be completely silent as we waited for our cue to sit on the sofa, and when I heard John Stapleton saying my name, I thought I was going to faint.

"And after the break, we are going to be talking to a very brave young woman; seventeen-year-old Katie Metcalfe, who has battled with anorexia, and who will be sharing her story with us."

As soon as the break started, Mum and I were ushered to the sofas, where we were 'positioned into place'. John shook my hand warmly and asked me if I was all right, and Penny did the same. They were both very nice and really friendly, and told us just to relax and enjoy our time on national television. They both complimented me, saying that they thought I was very, very brave doing what I was doing. Before I knew it, the adverts had ended, and the cameras were focused on us. John introduced Mum and I to the nation, and the film that had been produced the previous night by Jo rolled. I stared at the enormous screen showing it, shocked to hear my own voice, and see myself on television! It did feel incredibly surreal. I found myself cringing, and my throat tightening, when the photos of me as a small, happy child came into focus, followed closely by the horrific images taken when I was on bed rest in hospital; my eyes staring but unseeing, my forehead high as I had pulled out most of the hair at the front of my head, making me look as if I was bald, my skin pale, almost translucent, stretched tightly over my cheekbones, and my collar bones so protruding that it reminded me that I used to be a living skeleton. The film was over almost as soon as it had begun, and the focus was on the sofa. John started with the questions immediately. Not one second was wasted, as we only had seven minutes. However, there was a slight hitch. The questions John was asking were not the questions the producer had told us we were going to be asked. Inside, I panicked, but tried to stay calm and collected, and to answer the questions as best I could. Before I knew it our time was up, and I had barely said a word of what I had wanted and needed to say, and what I had been rehearsing for hours. Mum, well, she had been able to speak about one sentence, maximum, which was "Yes, it was unbelievably difficult for all of us." The last words I managed to say, I actually had to interrupt John to speak them, and they were; "Whatever you do, do not listen to the voice in your mind." That warning might not have meant anything to most of the audience, but I knew it would mean something to quite a lot of people, and not only people with eating disorders, but other mental illnesses as well.

John and Penny told Mum and I that we had been fantastic, but I was still in slight shock that it had all been so short, and was only able to grin and say "thanks". We were ushered off set as quickly as we had been ushered on, our microphones were hurriedly removed and passed on to the next guests, and we were brought back to the Green Room. I felt as though I was just another piece of plastic on a production line.

"How do you think it went?" The producer asked me as we hovered around the door to the Green Room.

"Oh, great," I replied, with an enormous grin, but in my heart of hearts I knew that was not what I really felt, and that I was actually incredibly disappointed that there hadn't been a chance to say the things that needed to be said, which included thanking Edith for agreeing to publish my book. All of the presenters and other guests who had watched it on the plasma television in the Green Room told Mum and I what a great job we had done, and that I was an incredibly brave young woman for agreeing to share my story with so many people. I was still in such a stupor, despite my disappointment, about being on national television, and watched by thousand and thousands of people, that I just grinned and accepted the compliments. Mum and I said goodbye to all the people whom we had hurriedly met, including Dr. Hilary, and were ushered, along with our luggage, out of the studio, into a car and away. The driver asked us if we wanted to go back to the hotel, as it was only 7am. But we wanted to be getting off home soon, so we asked him to take us to Camden Town. Camden was close to the station where we needed to catch the train, so it made sense. He dropped us off there, and we went off in search of an open café. One minute stars of the screen, the next, luggage carriers looking for a bite to eat!

As we wandered down the street, we shared our opinions about our appearance on GMTV. At first, I don't think that either of us wanted to admit that it hadn't gone nearly as well as we had imagined it would. I was trying to be as positive as possible, but couldn't help feeling slightly – well – very, disappointed. As most mothers can, Mum was able to see my distress, and assured me that the film we had done the previous night had been great, and at least we had been on national television! But even though I had been on television, on a show broadcast across the UK and Europe, I still felt frustrated that I hadn't managed to say everything that I had wanted to. I had been desperate to let the nation know about how anorexia wrecks lives and what a dangerous, devastating illness it is to have. It is not possible to discuss a subject such as anorexia and get across all the major points in around eight minutes. I also wanted to speak about my book, and how I was hoping to help people recover by having written it and having it published, as well as mentioning something about the state of facilities available for people with eating disorders, and the fact that my family and I have found aromatherapy and alternative healing work wonders in the recovery process. Everything the nation needed to hear about took up far more time than had been allocated. I think that a week's slot would have been about enough to explain everything... or maybe not.

Mum and I eventually found an open café, and went inside to find that GMTV was on on an enormous television mounted on the wall. Several of the people in the café looked at Mum and I as we ordered our drinks and sat down. It was peculiar knowing that, only a few moments ago, these people had been watching us on that exact television. But I found that I enjoyed this. I enjoyed the fact that people knew who I was. However, I was slightly uncomfortable about the fact that they knew what was wrong with me and the reason I had been on GMTV. Although I knew that I was going to have to get used to it, if I wanted fame and fortune!

Before I knew it, Mum and I were on the train homebound. I couldn't believe that it was all over and we were trooping back home. It seemed as though everything had happened in a complete blur. The further we travelled away from London, the more upset and annoyed I became that I hadn't managed to say everything that I had rehearsed. In some ways, I felt as though I had let the entire nation down, by not properly informing them about how anorexia tears lives apart, and not only the lives of the anorexic, but also the lives of the families and friends. Of, basically, everyone involved. I felt annoyed that I had not informed them that there is hope as well. Hope of recovery and happiness and new beginnings. Hope of a life after anorexia. Mum and I were not given a chance to speak about the lack of facilities for people with eating disorders in the north-east, a point we both wanted to get across very strongly. Mum could see how distraught I was becoming, and began to brainstorm other ways in which we could get our views and points across to the public. We both then came up with the idea of a newspaper article, which would be able to mention all three; about my book, how anorexia affects lives, and the lack of facilities available. We decided to try our local newspaper, The Evening Gazette, as it was read widely across the whole of the north-east of England. This brightened my mood considerably, and I spent the rest of the journey home thinking about it.

Almost as soon as we set foot inside the house, Mum was on the phone to a journalist from the Evening Gazette. She was speaking on the phone for almost an hour, describing my story and situation. The journalist, fortunately, was eager to hear all that she had to say and was more than willing to do an article, and it was arranged that she would come and interview Mum and I in three days time! I was ecstatic that I was going to be given the chance to tell the newspaper everything that I hadn't had the chance to say on GMTV. It was going to be fantastic, of that I was sure!

Back at college the following day, I had hordes of people coming up to me and asking if I was the girl who had been on GMTV and what it had been like to appear on television. All of my teachers said I had done fantastically well, and agreed that far more time should have been allocated for the slot. Many people at college just looked at me with curiosity, not saying a word, but whispering with their friends. They made me feel rather uncomfortable, as I conjured up various thoughts in my mind about what they were thinking and saying about me.

I remained in a fantastic mood all though the weekend, as I had my interview to look forward to and was determined that it was going to be a success. Feeling great and happy made my eating situation a lot easier. I was managing to eat well and not think about it all the time and feel guilty, as I had so many other things on my mind that were far more important. But every so often, I'd get little thoughts popping into my mind. Thoughts such as 'you don't want to try too hard with your food, Katie, you'll end up looking fat on your photo for the newspaper.' But I'd battle with them, and argue that I wouldn't look fat, I'd look healthier. I'd look better. More prettier, more sexy, more photogenic. More human.

Monday came, and I was ready and raring to be interviewed. Once again, I'd prepared all that I wanted to say and was determined to say everything and get my point across properly. The journalist who came to our house was called Alice, and she was really lovely, friendly and genuinely interested in everything that Mum and I had to say. Mum, the photographer, Alice and I all sat in the living room, and the interview began. I felt really comfortable with answering all the questions, and answered each one as honestly and as well as I possibly could. I think having the experience on GMTV helped me a great deal with my nerves and knowing how to answer questions. Alice asked me such questions as 'how did it all start' through to 'what is your weight now?' and about why I thought the facilities in the north-east are so bad for people with eating disorders. We also managed to talk about my book, which really pleased me. Alice also asked Mum various questions about how she and Dad had handled the situation and how they, and the rest of the family, were coping now. Mum managed to answer them all, although it was quite hard to hear some of what she had to say, as there are still various things which I find difficult to admit to. The interview lasted for about an hour and a half, and afterwards I was asked to go outside as the photo shoot needed to be done! Another hour was spent outside in the garden and on the street, with me holding my diary and posing for the camera. At first, I was quite nervous, but after a short time I began to relax, and found that I actually enjoyed having my photograph taken.

Alice took some copies of photographs of me before I became ill back to her office, to put in the article along with the new photos. I felt confident, when she and the photographer had left, that it was going to be a fantastic article. And I was over the moon that I had managed to talk about everything that I had wanted to.

The next few days went by as if I was living in a fantasy world. My family and I were getting on superbly, college was going great; I was getting good marks in everything I did, and my eating, as a result, was better than ever before. The thoughts and feelings about being fat, lazy and greedy when I ate what I was supposed to, or when I treated myself, didn't exist. My mind was so full of happiness, achievement, excitement and anticipation that there really wasn't space for negative thoughts. Only when I was alone, and not doing anything for a short time, did the negativity try and worm its sly, sneaky way back into my mind.

On the day that the article was published, I was in college, and on a buzz the entire time I was there, unable to concentrate on anything other than seeing the article.

Mum and Dad collected me immediately after college had finished, and we went straight to the newsagents'. It was when I saw the two massive piles of Evening Gazettes that the nerves set in, and the butterflies in my stomach started to go berserk. My face, my story, was in every single one of those papers. Every single one. I could hardly believe it. We bought three copies, and I was physically shaking when I eventually managed to manoeuvre my fingers. The article was on the third page, and was enormous! Much bigger than any of us had expected it to be. It covered the entire page, and it was a broadsheet page too! My picture covered more than half of the page, and was surrounded by masses of writing. There was also a smaller picture of me when I was five years old, looking well and happy, wearing one of my dad's old motorbike T-shirts as a nightgown, with shining blond hair, gleaming blue eyes and an enormous grin, proudly displaying the gaps where my two front teeth had fallen out. I remember the photo was taken the day after they had come out and I had received my fifty pence from the tooth fairy! I had to read the article three times, to absorb every word, as my eyes kept on skipping sentences. It was everything I had wanted it to be. It was perfect, and had a mention of all the things that I had wanted to speak about on GMTV. It was a peculiar feeling knowing that hundreds and hundreds of people would be looking at my picture and reading my story. It was even more peculiar knowing that there was a possibility people would recognise me when I walked past them in the street. And I loved it! I loved the fact that I was going to be known. But I wanted more. I hoped that this was just the beginning of my 'fame' and that it would expand beyond my belief. I was hungry for it now, as these two events proved to me that it was what I was destined for, and what I really, really wanted, more than anything else in the world (other than to get well): to be known. To be famous. To have people recognise me when I walked past them in the street, for something I have achieved. For helping people to rid themselves of their demons. I hoped and prayed that this was just the beginning of something huge...

Chapter 34

The Fear Of Death

The hype about GMTV, the Evening Gazette, and the future publication of my book soon died down, and became just a memory lingering in the back of people's minds. However, I was determined that I was going to keep pushing myself forward in my recovery, as we were now in November, almost at the end of yet another year, and my weight was still far away from my short-term aim of seven and a half stone. My sessions with Marie were becoming more focused on moving forward at a quicker pace, rather than just creeping, one baby step at a time. We would focus on death and dying too, something that I was thinking about quite a lot and have actually now become very scared about. (Odd, I know, being a Goth and wanting a hearse!) I was having frequent dreams about dying and people around me passing away, and they would plague me, often for days. Some of them were incredibly horrifying, leading to me breaking down in tears, thinking that my mum was going to be killed in a car accident, or that my dad would be shot. In some cases, I would even attempt to prevent Mum and Dad leaving the house.

I often found it difficult when we had very intense, focused sessions, as a lot of what we would talk about was my future, and the actions I would have to take to be able to do what I wanted to do, and to have the future that I wanted to have. There was a huge part of me which wanted to push ahead quickly, and gain weight faster than I was. But there was also a part of me that was still very, very scared about change unless it was tiny and creeping. I was scared to let go completely of anorexia, which I was convinced would definitely happen if I charged ahead at full speed. I didn't want to lose complete control. I kept on having repeated visions of myself eating and not being able to stop, and growing into an obese beached whale overnight, unable to move without aid. Both professionals and others constantly reassured me that that would never, ever happen, because I was, and always had been, a strong and determined person and I wouldn't allow myself to become overweight. One fact about all anorexics is that every single one is a determined person, in one way or another. That's how I managed to become anorexic and stay anorexic for such a long time, because I am determined. I was continually reassured that if I was able to stay determined to continue being anorexic, then it was possible for me to be just as determined not to allow myself to over-eat and become fat or obese. This helped take a load off my mind, and also helped me to try to continue to plough forward in my recovery.

I continued to apply for part-time jobs, but still had no luck. However, I managed to change the disappointment from all of the rejections into positive concentrated focus for my college course, as well as continuing to eat as well as I could manage. My focus obviously paid off, as I managed to achieve two distinctions at college for practical work; one for bread-making and the other for pastry-making.

My parents and siblings were thrilled about my progress at college, which made me feel fantastic in turn. But it didn't last long. Before I knew it, things had returned to how they were before, if not worse. My siblings' support entirely disappeared, and the feelings of bleak aloneness started to envelop me once again. Along with the lack of support came the struggle with trying to eat everything I was supposed to. I started to feel as though my parents were not giving me the amount of support that I craved, and still desperately needed. I was just about able to handle the lack of support from my siblings at that particular time, but I needed it from my parents and I wasn't really able to handle not having it from them.

A few weeks after I started developing the feelings that the support in my household had basically stopped dead, I opened up to Marie about the problem, and what I thought was happening. She asked me if I had told either of my parents that I felt as if they were not providing me with enough support, and that I needed it. I told her that I hadn't. She made it clear to me that neither Mum nor Dad are mind-readers and they wouldn't know what I wanted and needed unless I asked for it. I guess, in a way, I thought that they should know when I needed support, or a little bit of extra attention to help get through or manage certain things such as having different foods or watching a video. (Two of the normal things that

167

I still greatly struggled with.) I thought it was something all parents did naturally; recognise when their child needed something, without them having to ask for it. I imagined that all parents were able to see their children's problems with their eyes closed. Unfortunately, though, that was not and is not the case. Therefore I tried what Marie recommended I do. When some extra support or attention was needed, I asked them for it. It was incredibly difficult at first to do so, but it became easier each time. On occasions, though, I was unable to find the strength inside to ask. I would think that if they hadn't given support to me already, then I didn't need it, and should be able to manage and cope well without it.

I started to notice that, on days when my eating was a success (in other words when I managed everything I was supposed to eat), even though I still struggled greatly with the guilty feelings that came along with trying hard, I was able to concentrate a lot better, and the good, positive feelings were eventually levelling out with the bad, negative ones.

Chapter 35

Pleasure From A Little Piece Of Paper

In mid-November, I received the contract for my book '*Sticks and Stones*'! It was so exciting actually having the evidence in my hands that I was having my book published. I felt immensely proud to be able to say "I am being published!" It was quite unbelievable how fantastic these few pieces of paper and a tiny signature could make me feel about myself, that I had managed to achieve something I had been working so hard at, and that I had wanted all my life. I was going to be a published author! I knew that this was IT. I had to gain weight, and a significant amount at that. I could not have a book published, stating in my author profile that I was a recovering anorexic, while I was still struggling to maintain a weight over forty kilograms. I wanted to look better, feel better and be happy and healthy by the time my book was on the shelves in bookshops nationwide and I was asked to do signings and television appearances. Now, it wasn't only myself I needed to gain weight for; I had to gain it for other people too. I had to be strong for all the other sufferers out there, who would be reading my book, and looking for reassurance and hope in their days of darkness. I had to show them that there is a light at the end of the bleak, dark tunnel, and that you can beat the voice, and be happy and healthy at a safe, normal weight.

For reasons unknown, thoughts about death and dying grew all the more frequent in my everyday life. I released that I was terrified about dying and not having conquered anorexia. Having those thoughts would help me in useful ways though, for example I would automatically drink my Build Up milkshake or eat a little bit extra. At first I didn't talk to anyone about them, as I guess I was afraid to, and I didn't want people to tell me that it really does happen that we all do grow old and eventually die. But one afternoon when I was having a session with Marie, all of the fear that I was holding inside flooded out, and I told her exactly how I was feeling about every single thing. It was a struggle discussing death in even more detail and depth than we had been doing previously, but I guess that it did me some good. I know that hearing about old age from somebody else encouraged me to fight even harder, and banish the voice from my head once and for all so that I was able to start living again. I knew for a fact that I didn't want to be on my deathbed worrying about having had an extra 50ml of milk on my cereal, and being terrified that it would make me a fat and greedy person.

December was upon me before I knew it, and once again out came the hat, gloves, woollen jumpers and extra socks. Tights were still something I wore every day, so no change there. My weight hadn't altered much over the past month, as I thought it would have done with my slightly improved eating.

December is the busiest time for the students on the catering course in college, as we start serving Christmas dinners at the beginning of the month, and they are incredibly popular with the public. The customer capacity in the restaurant doubles, at least, which means extra food has to be prepared, meaning extra hard work. I knew in my heart that I was going to have to really make an enormous effort and eat more to keep my energy levels up during this busy and hectic time, but I still found it difficult to accept that I had to actually add things into my meal plan, not take things out and change them with something else, unless they were of a higher calorie content of course. It didn't make it any easier when I would go into college and see my friends eating what they did on a daily basis. I would think to myself, 'now, why do I have to eat more, and not them?' I know now that was the anorexia thinking and not me.

Discussing this with Marie, and also mentioning how I felt in our family sessions, helped my parents to realise where and when they needed to give me extra support. And the extra support both my parents started to give to me from then on, gave me that bit of extra confidence to manage to eat more, and think about myself, and what I needed to have, and not what other people did and didn't have in their diets and daily lives.

I was determined that, this year, Christmas was going to be perfect in every way possible. Well, as perfect as I could make it. I wanted it to be traditional, with everything done the right and proper way. In my eyes, the right and proper way was the

170

traditional way. I was also determined that I would be able to eat what I wanted to on Christmas Day, and not what the voice dictated.

In the weeks leading up to Christmas, I made an enormous effort to get into the festival spirit, as well as getting the entire family involved too. But getting them to do the things that we had done all the years previously was proving to be a mission impossible. Nobody (with the exception of me) wanted to bake mince pies and Christmas cake, make cards and paper stars, open calendars or sing carols in the car when we went out on a journey. It made me really upset and annoyed, as I felt I was the only one making the effort to make the Christmas period a happy and festive occasion. I secretly wished to myself that it would all change on Christmas Day, and that everyone would want to be festive, jolly and creative, and that I wouldn't be left to do that all on my own.

Christmas Day did go well, but not as well as I had hoped. I managed to eat some chocolate, sit with the family at lunchtime around the table, eat a reasonably-sized portion of Christmas dinner, and allow myself to watch television at times when I wouldn't have done normally. I was proud and pleased that I had succeeded and had done these things, although there were some guilty feelings and thoughts too. The day wasn't as traditional and as perfect as I had wanted it to be. I had wanted the entire day to be just how it had been when I was younger, and before I became ill, when all the family would be together. When my siblings and I would get up at an unspeakably early time in the morning, and rush downstairs to see what was under the tree, after having opened stockings and bounced on our parents' bed to get them up. I wanted to be able to eat some of the chocolate that I had been given like I used to, without feeling guilty. I wanted to potter around in my pyjamas all day and watch the Christmas TV shows, like I used to. I wanted to stuff myself silly with delicious Christmas food. I didn't want to have to worry about my normal routine, or what I was going to eat at breakfast, lunchtime or tea. But those were wishes, not realities that I was strong enough to make happen. Another reason why my Christmas wasn't perfect was because Nanna, Granddad, my auntie and cousin were all in Scotland, where they had moved, and my other grandparents were not with us either. It didn't feel right, them not being there. I didn't like it that our once a year routine had been completely disrupted. As much as I missed seeing the rest of my family, I tried to enjoy the company of the family who were around, Mum, Dad and my siblings. It was difficult sometimes during the day to keep a cool head, and stay calm and collected when Anthony, Samuel and Penny became disruptive, argumentative and annoying. But I tried my hardest not to get stressed out at them, or overreact when they did something that I didn't like.

I spared a thought and some tears for my friends whom I knew would be in hospital still, surrounded by nurses and doctors, eating food from silver containers, and watching the world go by through their locked windows.

A few days after Christmas, my family from Scotland came for a short fly-by visit, which was fantastic. It was almost like when we were all younger; all of us crammed into a tiny living room, ripping open presents, drinking mugs of tea, eating (some of us) slabs of Christmas cake, and laughing with each other.

Almost as soon as Christmas was over, I was back into the same old routine once again. I tried to stay in the festive spirit, as we still had New Year's Eve to come, the house was still flamboyantly decorated, Christmas programmes continued to show on the television, special foods were still filling the kitchen cupboards, and the holidays were not yet over. My family, on the other hand, could not be bothered to make the same effort, and slipped back into their normal routines, taking me down with them.

Unlike most normal teenagers with full and busy lives, I had no plans whatsoever for New Year's Eve. Not one of my friends had been in contact to let me know if there were any parties happening. Which made me feel miserable and alone, as I knew there was bound to be at least one somewhere. This proved the perfect opportunity for the voice to leap in, and shatter any self-confidence I had built up.

'Why would anyone want you at a party? Your blubber would suffocate everyone. No, you're better off alone.' This is just one example of the heart-wrenching comments which would burn in my brain.

I was preparing myself for an evening staying in at home, writing resolutions, and planning how I was going to battle and

172

beat anorexia in the new year of 2004, as I had obviously not managed it in 2003, as wrongly predicted. However, a day before New Year's Eve, I received a phone call from Nanna in Scotland, asking if I would like to spend New Year's Eve with her! To my astonishment, I had mixed feelings about it. I wasn't sure any more about leaving the rest of my family. But hearing the excitement in Nanna's voice as she told me how much they would all love to see me and have me to stay and how my visit could be just like the old times, persuaded me to change my mind again, and I decided to go.

On the journey to Scotland, I couldn't help but think about what I was going to do without my bike rides, Build-Ups and all the other things that happened in my daily routine. I had wanted to change everything so desperately; get out of my fixed and set way of life, but I was scared to alter anything and take the risks, in case they made things worse. But now the time had come when I had to face up to those fears, and experience what would happen when I took the risks that I had to. I kept on telling myself, as I came closer and closer to the land of haggis and Hogmanay, that I was going to be absolutely fine with the change of scene and routine, but the voice always managed to bite savagely back, saying that I would have to find ways to replace the things that I wasn't able to do like at home. It was yet another back and forth, back and forth battle between the two of us.

When I arrived in Scotland, and found my grandparents huddled waiting for me on the platform in the pouring rain, my fears about how I was going to be able to exercise etc. vanished from my mind. All that mattered now was that I was going to have a fantastic time with the people I loved and who loved me too. That I was going to have fun and enjoy myself. The other things would have to wait for now. They would have to come second in my list of 'things the voice wanted me to do'. Or so I hoped. But of course, things don't always work out as we hope.

When we arrived at my grandparents' new bungalow, smack bang in the centre of the smallest village imaginable, my first impression was 'this is really beautiful, but where is the house?' I honestly thought that we had parked outside the wrong house, and that their old house would suddenly appear, despite the fact that we were in a completely different country altogether! It was incredibly bizarre as they proudly took me on the tour, seeing all of my grandparents' possessions in a different setting. When they had finished showing me around, I wanted to close my eyes, count to three, open them again, and be in their old house, in Ripon. In the place which I was familiar with. In the place which I loved. In the place which I had always known. I liked their new home, and the surrounding countryside, but I preferred their Ripon home. This bungalow, which I was standing in, didn't really feel like it was my grandparents' house. It felt more like it was a holiday home, and they were living there temporarily, and it felt like that for the rest of my visit. Like we were going to pack up any minute, end the holiday and go back to Ripon. Back to the real world. Well, what I had in my mind as being the real world anyway. But I guess, I'm not certain, that it was the anorexia that was making me have those feelings. Making me have the feelings that it all wasn't right. That they didn't belong in Scotland in this miniature village and bungalow. The part of me that still listened to some of what the anorexia had to say, didn't want change. Didn't want change with any aspect of life at all. It wanted everything to stay the same. Stay how it had always been since I was a small child. It was not only my body that I wanted to remain untouched by time, but also life around me, and other people's lives too. However, I wasn't able to prevent change from happening in other people's lives, and deep down I knew that.

I managed to eventually come to terms, on the day before I left to go home, with the fact that Scotland was now the new home of my grandparents, my auntie and my cousin, no matter how much I didn't want that to be. No matter how much I wanted everything to go back to what I considered to be 'normal', it simply wasn't going to happen. There was nothing that I could do about it other than move on and away and get on with my life and the changes that had happened in it.

It was now another new year, and I couldn't remain stuck in the past. I couldn't keep hoping and praying that everything would eventually return to how it had been when I was small, innocent and unaware of the difficulties the world throws at you. I had to move forward with the times. I had to pull myself up and out of my rut, face the world and catch whatever it decided to hurl at me.

Chapter 36

It's Just Another New Year's Thursday

I didn't do it. Yet again I was unsuccessful in my attempts to banish anorexia from my body and soul. I was unable to understand how I hadn't managed to win my battle with the voice. Unable to win my battle with anorexia and its control over me. How had I not managed to turn my life around? I had been fighting for such a long time...

But my determination was present. More than ever before. It was just putting it into action that was the hard part. Here is some of the evidence of just how determined I was to get anorexia out of my life once and for all. It is an extract taken from my personal diary on the 1st January 2004.

HAPPY NEW YEAR!
I am SO determined and focused on making this a good year. I am going to be focused on getting anorexia out of my life once and for all.

And here is an extract taken from my diary on the 2nd January 2004, showing just how hard it was for me to put the determination in my mind into actions.

Guilt is still here.
Trying my best to ignore it.
I have to gain weight.
It's as simple as that.
But why is it so damn hard to accept?
Especially when I have so many things to look forward to in my life.

Despite the fact that members of my family were constantly around me in Scotland, I still felt incredibly alone in many ways; alone fighting the voice. Alone in giving myself support, as no one else was able to. I suppose that my grandparents and auntie were slightly apprehensive about saying anything by way of support, as they didn't want to upset me or make me angry. But I would often wish that they would say something along the lines of, "Come on, Katie love, you've got to try really hard at lunchtime to have a bit more to eat than you normally do. You've really got to kick this thing where it hurts and throw it out of your life once and for all. And don't forget, we are here with you all the way, to give you all the support you need and want." However, they remained wishes and hopes, and I ended up saying those encouraging words to myself, which is a great thing to be able to do, but to have someone say it to you as well is always better. It makes things easier.

I think that if I'd had been at home during New Year, things might have been different, as my parents would have known when I needed that extra bit of support and encouragement. I know that it was not my grandparents' and auntie's fault; they didn't know when I needed support because they had not lived with me all the time that I had had anorexia.

When it was time for me to leave Scotland and go back home, part of me wanted to – to see my parents, to be able to go on my bike rides again, to regain some of the support that I was missing by not seeing Mum every day. However, there was also a part of me that really did not want to go back. The part that was enjoying being away from my siblings and the constant arguments that we would have, the enjoyment of the peacefulness inside the house and outside in the garden and the surrounding countryside which I missed so much from living in Margrove Park, my old home, and the part of me which was enjoying being with the members of my family whom I loved dearly and really didn't want to part with.

As it was the beginning of another new year, I needed to go for a general check up with my local GP. I also had to have blood taken and have my weight checked. I was shocked, amazed and seriously frustrated when I stepped on the scales to find that I had lost weight and was below the weight that I should have been to be off bed rest! I weighed 38.1 kg. The anorexia attempted to make me feel happy and proud that I had lost weight, especially as it had been Christmas and I had had to change my routine when I visited Scotland. However, I refused to feel proud and happy. There was no way that I was going to give in to the feelings that it wanted me to have. But the scales were different scales than the ones that I was normally weighed on, so I was slightly dubious that what they read was actually my real weight.

Even though I was unsure about my 'official' weight, I still tried to be focused about gaining. My routine at college had started up again, and I was busy, busy, busy all of the time. I knew that I had to add more calories into my day, I was told often enough by my dietician, and I would often manage to. However, it would never last. I would manage to increase during one day and then think that because I had managed to eat more, or things of a higher calorie value on one occasion, that I would be able to have a 'day off' the next day and eat like normal, and then maybe try hard again the day after that, or maybe the next, or the next. I thought that by doing this: by increasing my intake every so often, it would help me to gradually gain weight at a steady pace. It didn't. Marie and my dietician would tell me time and time again that I couldn't do that; I couldn't just try extra hard with my eating every other day. It had to be every single day to have a positive effect on my weight. I would agree with them to a point, but after a while, I would think, 'Hey, wait a minute; this is my body. They don't really know what I need to eat and what I don't. They don't really know how many calories I need to consume in a single day to be able to gain weight.' But they did know, of course. They knew exactly what it was that I needed. They were professionals in the field of my disorder, and they were trying to lead me in the right direction, and all I did was pull away and venture the other way. It was the voice that would tell me that they didn't know what they were talking about, and that would tell me to ignore them, block them out, pretend that they didn't exist. Not me. I knew, deep down that they were right, and that I did need to do what they advised, but I would nearly always give in to what the voice said to me. It seemed easier to handle that way. It felt better doing what I knew I felt comfortable with, instead of something that was scary and unfamiliar.

Chapter 37

Breaking The Exercise Obsession

I had a gruelling routine for college, which would more often than not leave me exhausted by the end of the day. Even though I had long days at college where I would often be on my feet and active 95% of the time, I still felt obliged to get on my bike when I arrived home, and go out for a ride. It was proving to be a very difficult obsession to break. I thought I had cracked it at one point, but I only lasted one and half days before I was peddling again, and making up for lost exercise.

Eventually, I discussed the bike ride obsession with Marie and we dissected it piece by piece, talking about why I felt the need to cycle every day, why I felt I had to obey the voice with its orders as, often, I would be saying to myself that I didn't need to go. Six hours cooking in a restaurant, and a mile walk to catch the bus was enough exercise. I agreed, after much discussion, to experiment, and see how well I would be able to cope without going on a bike ride. It was incredibly difficult to walk past the bike in the garden, and ignore the whiny voice nagging at me to get on it, and the first time I failed miserably. The temptation was too strong, the voice too overpowering, convincing me that riding it would do me good. Convincing me that it was the best thing to do. The second attempt was successful though. I managed to overpower the whiny but powerful voice and walk away from the bike, convincing myself that I didn't need to get on it and go for a ride. I didn't need to burn essential calories that it was necessary to have in my body. The voice nagged and nagged at me, eventually begging and pleading with me to go out, but within an hour it had almost faded completely. I had managed to ignore it! I had managed to overcome its demands! I felt immensely proud and strong, and refused to feel guilty. To many people, not going on a bike ride may seem a tiny baby step, but to me, it was an enormous achievement, and yet another move forward in my recovery. Another step in the right direction.

It proved difficult to stick to my new routine of not going for a bike ride every day, but being weighed numerous times after I had cut down on my rides, and finding that I hadn't gained loads of weight like I had feared, but only small amounts like planned, made it much easier to continue with.

The weeks were flying by, and slowly, slowly I was making progress with my weight. Before I knew it, we were in February, and Valentine's Day approached. I knew that I wouldn't receive anything, as did everyone else in my family, but in my heart of hearts I wished that there was one person, just one, who liked me enough to send a card. The previous year, I would have taken out my upset and anger on my body, by not eating, over-exercising, and by listening to the anorexia when it told me that I wasn't thin enough for any boy to fancy or even like me. Now it was the complete opposite. I was listening to my own voice, and to the voices of all the people around me who were constantly telling me that to look better, feel better, and be better in all senses, I had to gain more weight, and have more flesh on my skeletal figure and face.

Even though I was managing to very slowly gain weight, my thoughts would still often be completely preoccupied with food and exercise. This seriously confused me, and made me incredibly angry, as those thoughts were supposed to disappear when I managed to gain weight, not increase. I mentioned this in my sessions with Marie, and she explained to me that the more weight I managed to gain, the fewer the thoughts would become. I obviously wasn't gaining enough weight for them to begin to fade away just yet. Another sign to my conscience that I needed to work even harder than I already was.

Life at home was ever-changing. One minute, all would be all hunky-dory, the next, hell on earth. The days when I managed to successfully eat a significant amount of calories, I found that I could cope better under stress than when I didn't. Although my mind, more often than not, would be in an enormous battle to cope with the guilt, I was able to handle bad situations with my family. But some were too difficult to cope with, despite having eaten more. For example, I had an argument with my youngest brother about something incredibly petty and he told me that he thought Penny's ex-boyfriend, Jason, who still came to the house a lot, was more of a member of the family than I ever had been and ever would be. That small comment broke my heart, and very, very nearly sent me into a downward spiral, losing all the weight that I had managed to gain over the past months. What prevented that from happening was reminding myself continually about the future publication of my book *Sticks And Stones*. I knew that I had to remain focused and ignore all the nasty comments my siblings would spit at me; otherwise I would end up back at square one and possibly beyond, on a drip feed. I had to build up an imaginary barrier around myself, defending me from nasty comments, so that I was able to move forward and progress more and more each day, so that when *Sticks And Stones* was in print, I would be fit, healthy and strong in mind, body and spirit.

I not only had my book release to focus on, but the trip to the USA which I was planning to take in the summer, to stay with the family of my dad's friend, Les, who sadly had died from cancer.

I had to change my routines if I wanted good changes to happen in my life.

I was constantly on the lookout for new methods and tactics to help in the struggle to ignore the voice when it would become strong in my mind, and to stop the guilty feelings.

Marie told me it was important that I started to focus much more on myself, rather than being so concerned about other people and their welfare. I told her that I wasn't aware in the slightest that I was doing any such thing. I thought that I was already spending far too much time on myself. She explained that if I were spending time on myself, then I would be gaining substantial amounts of weight at a steady pace. Realising that this was true, I made the decision to look at how much time I did spend focusing on myself and getting better, and it wasn't actually nearly as much time as I thought it would be. I couldn't live my life constantly thinking about the well-being of all the people around me, otherwise where would I end up eventually? Nowhere. I had to focus on me, and get me better. No one else would be able to do that for me. I had to learn to accept that other people were capable of sorting out their own problems and I didn't always have to try and do it for them. When I was better, helping other people with their problems could be a priority, but for the time being I needed to focus on my problems, as I had certainly had some to sort out!

The main problem to sort out of course was the demon voice. I began to experiment with all sorts of ways in which I would be able to challenge it and ignore what it was trying to make me do, think and feel. One of the ways in which I did that was to write down the exact details of what it was telling me to do, and write my argument and decision next to it. For example, it would say to me;

"Don't eat that egg mayonnaise sandwich. You don't need it. It's got far more calories and grams of fat than you need in your body." And I would write a reply saying;

"I will eat it! I do need it! I AM going to ignore you and have it." Writing it down on paper, and seeing the argument in front of my eyes, made things a lot easier to deal with. Creating these new methods of coping and blocking out the voice helped me to gain the weight I seriously needed.

Extracts taken from my personal diary;

19th January 2004.
    Voice: Don't eat that sandwich, it contains too many calories.
    Me: I will eat it. I need more calories to gain weight.
20th January 2004.
    Voice: Don't have that piece of cake. It contains too many calories and you don't need them.
    Me: I want some cake. I also have not had all three of my Build Ups. I need the cake.
21st January 2004.
    Voice: Don't sit and read. Do something constructive.
    Me: I have the time. I want to read. I will read.
22nd January 2004.
    Voice: Don't sit and eat. Stand.
    Me: I will sit and eat. I've been on my feet nearly all day.
24th January 2004.
    Voice: You've sat too much. Stand.
    Me: No I haven't. I will sit if I want to.
27th January 2004.
    Voice: Don't have that extra bit of milk.
    Me: I am thirsty. I want it. I need it.
3rd February 2004.

Voice: Go on a longer ride.

Me: No. It's cold, late, windy. I don't want to.

4th February 2004.

Voice: You're never going to be rich and famous.

Me: Yes I will! I will do anything and everything to get what I want!

7th February 2004.

Voice: Don't have three Build Up drinks.

Me: Oh fuck off! I've had enough of you now.

As my weight increased week by week, I became panicky that I was taking things too quickly, and the temptation to 'slow down', not try new things, and not try and do less exercise, was enormous. What helped me to resist those temptations was the pride I would feel about actually moving forward in my recovery and not staying put in the rut I had been in for such a long time. The praise I would receive from my parents would also really help. My brothers and sister would never ask me about my weight, or anything to do with my illness to be honest. But I guess the main reason why they didn't bother was because they were being typical teenagers. They were living their teenage years, most of which I missed out on. They had far more important things to be worrying about in their lives than my illness.

As I gained weight, I managed to get myself into a train of thought that I would be able to push myself to work harder in everything I did. Unfortunately, it didn't quite work like that. As I was still at a low weight, energy continued to be burned off quickly, which meant I should have still been taking it easy with everyday life, and not trying to cram enormous amounts of activity into one day, every day, as I was doing.

I could feel myself becoming run down over a matter of days, but I ignored it, and carried on as normal, convincing myself that, as I was managing to gain weight, the sickness would pass as quickly as it had pounced on me. However, it didn't. It gradually became worse, but still I would drag myself out of bed every day to attend college. I refused point blank to take any time out whatsoever. Well, more like the anorexia refused to.

On the 10th of March, I visited my GP. I had lost weight, and she carried out tests on my heart and blood. I attempted to convince her that I only had a flu bug, and that I would be perfectly fine in a matter of days, like any normal person would be. She admitted me into North Tees Hospital despite my protests, insisting that the doctors there carried out more advanced tests on me in case there was something seriously wrong.

It was awful being back in hospital, wired up to a heart monitor. It brought back all the horrible memories from the time before, when I was admitted because of my heart problems. Never once had I thought that I'd end up back in a public hospital ward as a consequence of my weight loss.

I was only kept on the ward for one night, but it felt like a week. I was still convinced that absolutely nothing was wrong with me, other than a simple flu bug. Although I must admit a small part of me was petrified in case they did find something wrong. Fortunately, they didn't; I wasn't going to have a heart attack and die or anything along those lines. My pulse and white blood cell count were both low, meaning I was prone to infection. But I knew that anyway.

I was released back out into the world, told to take care and keep fighting my battle to gain weight and beat the anorexic voice. I knew the hospital admittance had been a wake-up call in an attempt to slow me down a bit, and so I tried, with all my might, I honestly did, even though I was still slightly doubtful that I needed to. I now know though that it was the anorexic voice which was making me doubtful. Katie knew I had to slow down, take things easier. But the battle was still continuing, and at times the voice still won me over. This was one of those times.

Chapter 38

The Stunning Girl In The Photograph

At the beginning of May, Marie announced that she was pregnant and would be leaving the service to take maternity leave. Therefore, my sessions with her would cease. I was overjoyed about the baby, but panicky and shocked about having to end my therapy with her, and start with someone new. I had thought and hoped that she would see me through to the very end of my illness. We had already come so, so far together and I wanted it to continue, as I was getting better, and our sessions were becoming more positive on every occasion.

But as before, it was necessary for me to be able to accept changes and move on from my past.

At one of our few remaining sessions, Marie asked me if I would mind bringing in some photographs of myself before I became ill; when I was healthy, well and happy. We only had four sessions left together, and both she and I wanted them to be dedicated to focusing on my future, instead of all the crap that was happening in the present and that had happened in the past. She suggested that I bring photos of myself to the session, not to dwell on the past, but to look to the future. By looking at the photos I would be able to see what I had looked like at a healthy, normal weight. As a healthy happy person. As an anorexia-free being.

I was reluctant to bring them at first, and on purpose forgot twice, as the nagging voice convinced me that Marie would think I was an obese elephant.

Eventually I did, on my next to last session. I handed them over to her, and grimaced as she slowly looked through each one, studying them intently. I was convinced she would be thinking 'look at all that fat! How could someone at such a young age be so enormous?' However, there was no need to grimace or be afraid or think those thoughts, as Marie looked up at me, smiling, and said;

"Katie, in these photographs you look absolutely stunning. You can look like this again you know, and better, because you're older now, and your body is more mature." It was incredibly hard to accept what she said, but I knew Marie had never lied to me before, so why would she start now? I knew I had to believe what she was saying. I had to believe that I had been stunning and could be stunning again.

I repeated to my mum what Marie had said to me about the photographs, and some of the specific words such as 'stunning' and 'look like that again'. Mum told me that she agreed completely, and that was all the reassurance I needed to make yet more changes. I knew that I could believe my mum. The times when I thought everything she said to me about my body was lies had passed.

And so I increased my food intake. Thirty grams of cereal became forty, two tablespoons of dried fruit became three, cottage cheese was replaced with peanut butter, etc. I noticed that the hard work I put into eating more paid off when I went into college. My concentration would improve enormously and I'd manage to do things in half the time it would have taken me before, and I wouldn't feel so exhausted after a day's hard work either.

I was entered for a competition at college, to create a vegetarian meal for two people, and I was ecstatic. I was convinced that the teachers at college must have seen that my work was improving all the more. Why else would they have entered me for it? And so my determination and focus continued. There was absolutely no way that anorexia was going to rip away these opportunities from my fingers, however much it wanted to.

Not long after the announcement about the competition, I received news that was to make my writing dreams come alive in a different form altogether. A project at college called Aim Higher, whose purpose is to support students who are gifted or have special talents (although I need to note that I personally do not believe what I am able to do in the way of writing is a special talent. I believe it is what I was born to do. My purpose in life, so to speak!) gave me three hundred pounds towards a laptop computer. I only had to contribute one hundred pounds of my own money. They also went ahead to provide me with funds for books about creative writing, a university two-day English conference and creative writing workshops.

All the positive things that were now happening to me helped to keep my mind off calories, exercise, and my weight. I had far more exciting and fantastic things to be thinking about now! All I had to do was keep on increasing my weight so that things would keep on going fantastically well. Or so I hoped.

On the day of the competition, I was quietly confident that I'd do a fantastic job. (I was making a goat's cheese and red onion marmalade tart garnished with rocket salad, balsamic vinegar and lavender oil dressing and tomato flowers.) The tart was simple to make, and I would have been able to prepare it with my eyes closed. However, the tomato flowers were proving to be a disastrous nightmare, and I had been up until midnight practicing how to make them. Mum must have spent at least five pounds on cherry tomatoes! The competition was being held at St James's Park in Newcastle, and was being attended by all the catering colleges in the north-east of England. I had to wait and watch other competitors for five hours before it was finally my turn. I was determined to do a brilliant job and make my dish appear and taste out of this world. But when I saw what the other competitors were creating, my heart sank. Their dishes were all exotic and unusual, with ingredients from all four corners of the globe, making mine look and sound dull and unexciting. As I stood waiting for the judge to announce that we could begin, the voice whispered to me "You may as well walk away now. You've lost already. Your ingredients are pathetic and crap compared to theirs, and your skills are non-existent. You can't do anything right. You'll mess up big style. Go on, waddle away, take off your hat, your chef's whites and apron and leave the best to win. They deserve to. You're a mound of fat with no talent." I focused with all my might on ignoring its taunts, and gritted my teeth. I knew my teammates were counting on me and I was counting on myself. Not letting myself down was the most important thing. I was going to do the competition no matter what the voice called me or demanded I do.

Before I knew it, the whistle had been blown and we were all rolling, sautéing, pricking, dicing, baking, and lining. The voice vanished unexpectedly, and I allowed my mind to focus on getting my dish correct and perfect.

Unfortunately, I didn't win, but I didn't allow myself to become upset and annoyed. I had done it at least, and had fought my demon and not backed down when it had told me to. In my own mind I had won my own competition. Katie 1 Anorexia 0, and winning first place in that tournament was far more important than any other.

After months and months and months of rejected application forms, I had a successful interview! The job was for a canteen worker in a KP Crisps factory kitchen, cooking and serving breakfasts on a Saturday and Sunday morning from 7am till 11am. Fortunately, I'm a morning person, so I knew that it wouldn't be a problem dragging myself out of bed. Unfortunately, it was half of my weekend taken up. The wage I thought was very reasonable though: £5.75 an hour, therefore that made up for the excruciatingly early mornings!

Before I went into my interview, I had something substantial to eat and drink, and went in all smiles and brimming with confidence, not even thinking about food or exercise, just about giving a fantastic first impression. I was determined that this was going to be the one. I was going to have an impact on the boss, one that he wouldn't forget, and I was going to get this damn job! I had tried for long enough.

I already had all the correct qualifications, which were stated on the job description, so that made answering all his questions simple. I knew all the qualities needed for interviews: smile, keep eye contact, look smart, don't fidget, be enthusiastic, etc. I even managed not to rock my legs for the entire interview! I had managed to build up my confidence at college over the past year, and it paid off! My enthusiasm, smile, and self-confidence must have shone through, as I managed to get the job there and then. I knew that my weight would have had something to do with how well my interview had gone. I knew that when I had lost weight in the past I would have found it impossible to keep eye contact, smile or not fidget. Everything was happening for the best now that I was eating better and gaining weight. There was no reason at all to start losing it again.

Penny and I went out to a nightclub to celebrate my achievement, and I was gobsmacked to see how much she had changed since I'd last been out with her. All made up she looked amazing, sexy, seductive, beautiful, twice her age even! When we stood next to the mirror together, I felt like crying. I looked like a tiny child compared to her. My bony bird hands poked out from my velvet dress sleeves, my chest looked like two tiny molehills only just nudging the material of my dress, and my neck looked like an ostrich's; my dog collar hanging from it, too big too fit snuggly around, as it should have done. I resembled an underweight, ill, seven-year-old, dressing up in her older sister's clothing. While Penny, on the other hand, had an ample chest, which swelled above her corset top, a perfectly photogenic face, slim hands and resembled a twenty-year-old woman ready for fun. This time, no voice squirmed its way into my mind. As I stood there with my sister, I heard no nasty whisper, no horrible taunts, nothing. There was complete silence. I knew then, at that point, when I eventually realised that I looked younger than my baby sister, my baby sister with the lopsided smile and blond ringlets, Thomas the Tank Engine wellies and chocolate-stained face, that my efforts to gain weight were not enough. Gaining two hundred of four hundred grams a week was not sufficient. It wasn't enough progress. I couldn't keep on believing that I was increasing my food enough, as I wasn't. I couldn't allow myself to be content with that. My life could not continue inside the body of a child.

The amount of attention Penny received when we went out together was astonishing. She turned heads everywhere we went. I felt pleased that people found her so attractive, but I was also insanely jealous. No one would look at me the same way as they looked at Penny. What did they have to look at anyway? Nothing. I was one of the living dead.

To help keep my focus on gaining weight, I looked for all the incentives I could find, which ranged from regaining my periods and having children, to going out with friends for meals and having a dessert. One of my main incentives was being able to wear the Laura Ashley ballgown, which I had bought for my book launch, without having to use safety pins to make it fit. I wanted to look like a princess on my special night. A princess who had been granted all her wishes.

Chapter 39

My Mind, My Body, My Life

Before I had time to blink, exams were upon me once again. It only seemed like yesterday that I had been sitting, squirming uncomfortably in my seat at Abbey Hill. As the exam dates loomed closer, I tried to remain calm, and do my revision in an orderly, sensible manner, unlike the previous year when I had panicked and crammed. But of course things didn't work out orderly and sensible. Do things ever? I was reading up the classifications of root vegetables, and the type of extinguisher you use on an electrical fire right up to the very point where we had to leave our bags at the front of the examination hall, and choose seats.

To my surprise, I was feeling reasonably calm and confident. I knew that if I had panicked and not eaten a thing beforehand, my mind would have been focused on food, calories and exercise and I wouldn't have been able to even look at the exam paper, let alone answer the questions. I knew that because I had fuelled my brain, (with complex carbohydrates, essential fatty acids, vitamins and minerals) I would be able to cope. I made sure I did exactly the same for my following two exams, and they too went fine. My concentration was great, my mind focused and my stomach wasn't growling with hunger! I had gained weight before my first exam and weighed 42kg (6st 8lb), and so I was already on a happy high. It's peculiar, because there was no way that, a year before, I would have been happy about having gained weight, or happy about having eaten my fill and not feeling hungry. A year before, when the voice was in control, hunger was a feeling of strength. Hunger was a feeling of achievement. Hunger was a feeling that I was thin and in control. Now, however, it was the opposite. Hunger was knowing that I needed something more to eat. Hunger was knowing that I had to push myself that little bit further, and so I did.

With exams over, my first year at college came to a close too. I found it hard to believe that a whole year had passed so quickly, and I had come so far and achieved so much. Not only in college, not only with my writing, but with my battle against anorexia as well. I was finding a whole new me. I had found a job, conquered my fear of trying new foods, made new friends, lost many old routines, appeared in a newspaper, sat on the GMTV sofa, and was having a book published! To top it all off, I was on my way to the land of my dreams, America, where I would discover new people, new opportunities, and new ways of life.

I had battled with the voice and had strength and power over it. I no longer obeyed the voice; the voice obeyed me. I had the strength to decide what I wanted to do with my life, my body and my mind.

Now that college was finished for the year, I was able to prepare for my trip to America. I had managed to clinch a fantastic deal with my tickets, and my accommodation was already done and dusted. I was to be staying with the wife of Les, my dad's friend who had died from cancer. I would work while I was there, and get a real taste of American life. What I was looking forward to most of all was visiting New York. The City, which I had fantasised about going to ever since I was a tiny child. I put all my savings towards the trip, as I was confident that it was going to be the best two weeks of my entire life. With more spare time, I now had the opportunity to strive for my short-term weight of seven stone. I introduced new foods into my diet, and slowly cut back on my exercise. Despite having so many incentives to gain weight, change was still often incredibly difficult for me. You'll probably think that because of all the changes I had made so far, more would have been simple. But they were not. Easier, maybe, depending on the change, of course, but not simple as in 'you do it and never think about it again.' However, I knew from past experiences that it's no good putting things off again and again, as they just get harder and harder. It's easier to do them there and then, despite your feelings. I also knew from experience that once changes were made, there could be no going back to the old routine. Changes had to be consistent and that was what I was striving for.

As my trip to the USA was coming so close that I was almost able to smell the freshly baked bagels and fried pirogues, I decided to go clothes shopping. I weighed myself beforehand, to find I had almost managed to reach my target weight of seven stone for my trip. I was only a few pounds off. I felt incredibly disappointed that I hadn't managed to reach my target, but I wasn't going to allow it to get me down. I knew I'd be able to get there; only it would take slightly longer than I had hoped and expected. I spent a lot of money buying new clothes, hair dye and jewellery. I wanted to go to America with a completely clean slate. Even though most of the clothes I bought barely clung to my still frail frame, and had to be held in place with safety pins, I refused to allow it depress me. I knew it would only be a matter of time before the safety pins could be discarded. Forever.

It wasn't until I was walking down the gangway to board the plane to Washington, and my frantically waving, grinning, crying mother vanished out of eyesight, that what I was doing actually hit home. I was travelling, all alone, to the United States. I was taking complete control of my life. I was getting on a plane and leaving my past behind me. I could feel it inside, along with the nerves and excitement, that this trip was going to change me for the better. I wasn't going to think about my weight, worry about calories, or consider exercising obsessively. Those days were past and gone. There was no way I was going to deny myself anything while there. I was going to buy a hot, salted pretzel from a stand in Central Park and eat it all, I was going to shop until I dropped in the malls and the streets of New York City, buying things that I wanted to buy, I was going to forget all about the routines of my past, I was going to meet new people, make new friends, experience a new way of life. Experience a new way of living as me. I was leaving anorexia behind, to wither away into a place of nothingness. A place where it belonged. I knew that in this new land of hopes and dreams, wishes and aspirations, I was going to be me, I was finally going to be Katie.

Central Park was unusually quiet for such a swelteringly hot day in New York City. Erica and I wandered around the wide footpaths, stopping every now and then to allow a jogger to pass, or look at the artists with their berets and trailing scarves, proudly displaying their work on the freshly mown grass.

"I'm hungry," Erica cried suddenly. "I want a pretzel!" I looked where her arm was pointing, and spotted the moored pretzel wagon. A bead of sweat trickled down my forehead, and I am certain to this day it was not because of the heat. My throat became dry, and I struggled to swallow. Erica hurried ahead, and handed over \$1.50 for an enormous, magnificent, freshly baked, traditional NYC pretzel, wrapped in a white napkin, its criss-cross deep brown top dotted with white specks of salt, peeping out. My stomach was growling, it was noon, and I hadn't eaten since seven, when we'd had breakfast. Twice I moved towards the wagon, and twice I moved away. However, on the third attempt, I stayed and handed over my money. With the pretzel between my fingers I knew it was now or never. And so I took my first bite. The pleasure was immeasurable. The taste so out of this world. So with a smile, I took another...

Part 2

Chapter 40

The Family's Story

Generally, people assume that the illness anorexia affects only one person – the person with the symptoms. The person they can see is emaciated, physically ill, not eating and suffering immeasurably. It doesn't, anorexia has a terrible effect on the friends and family of the anorexic as well, causing unimaginable torment, anger, upset, and heartache.

Anorexia can affect any person and family, anywhere and at any time. It is important to stress that it is not an illness that affects only a certain type. It doesn't matter whether you are rich or poor, a large family or small, a family that gets on well with each other or a family that despises one another. It's unimportant whether you live in Australia or England. If anorexia is given the opportunity, it will slip into your lives and your home and not leave without a fight. Another factor we want to make very clear is that anorexia is *not* only about the desire to be 'supermodel' thin. It goes far deeper than that, with many more factors than just those surrounding weight.

Anorexia affects people who have a constant want for perfection and order in their lives, and who do not want to change.

This book delves deep into the core of one family. Our family. Who have *all* suffered over six long years! The six years that have been dominated by the illness anorexia. Dominated by a demon who one day just decided to move in and who almost destroyed an affectionate family

We all sincerely hope that we will have helped answer a number of the questions that you may wish to know about this horrible illness and the devastating effects it has on the sufferer, their families and friends. Creating this book has been fantastic therapy for all concerned, and we hope with our hearts that it will help others.

Rosemary, Tony, Katie, Penny, and Samuel Metcalfe

(Anthony decided for personal reasons that he wouldn't participate in the making of this part of the book).

A Letter To Anorexia

Dear Voice in Katie's head,

For the first time in my life there is something that I hate, and that is you. I can't find one thing about you that is good. You are sick, twisted and bad. I hate you for all that you are. I know you are there for a while so we as a family will have to show you we are strong and we will show you how to change and form yourself into a voice that is a bright light full of love and good. So the choice is yours. Stay and change.

Yours,

Rosemary

(Katie's Mum)

Why Our Little Girl?

When we found out that I was having a baby, Tony and I were both so thrilled. When I was pregnant with Katie it was a bit scary like it is with all pregnancies, but at eight to nine weeks I had a threatened miscarriage. Luckily the rest of the pregnancy was lovely and after a quite easy labour, I gave birth to a beautiful 9lb 13oz baby. I thought I had never seen anything so amazing and she was ours. The immediate love you feel for a baby is so special you don't think you can ever feel that way for anything or anyone else (but with the subsequent babies you realise that you can). When Katie was six months old, I went back to work, and Katie stayed with a child minder called Sylvia, who she adored. Katie was a really contented baby; there were only a few sleepless nights. She did suffer terribly with ear infections and at seventeen months old was taken into hospital having febrile convulsions. These were quite severe, but once Katie's temperature was under control the convulsions stopped. In May of 1988 we had another baby, Penny, and Katie was thrilled to bits to have a little sister. I stopped work then as Penny was not an easy baby and wouldn't settle with the child minder. Soon, we settled into a routine with the girls and everything was rosy. When Anthony was born on Katie's third birthday we think she was happy although she wanted a slide.

We moved in February of 1990 to Thornaby, which I think the children were OK with. That was when Katie stopped sucking her dummy as we had left it in Ripon and couldn't buy one that night. She didn't really bother with one after that. Katie was always very bright and able to converse from an early age and at about four and a half began to really develop her own mind and opinions and could sometimes be a bit rude, saying what she really thought!

When Sam was born in July of 1991 our family was complete and what a lovely little family we were. We did lots of walks and going places, and actually it was a great time and the kids were well behaved really and they all played beautifully together. They always did things together as a foursome. Katie was at school and Penny at nursery when we thought about sending them to a Steiner School. The curriculum, founded by Rudolf Steiner, is based upon a pedagogical philosophy, which places emphasis on the whole development of the child, including their spiritual, physical and moral wellbeing, as well as their academic progress. The only one close was in Botton Village, some thirty miles away. The amazing surroundings, the wholesome education and the whole package we thought would suit us all. It was hard work getting up so early (six every morning) and travelling all that way, but the children coped very well. Often, we would have picnics on the way home and make a day of it. Katie settled in really well, enjoying the space, the school and her friends. Katie's teacher, Erna, became a firm family friend and Katie would often stay at her house in Botton with Annie and Martin, Erna's children. Altogether, family life was very pleasant.

We were a normal everyday family. Mum, Dad, kids, hardly any sibling rivalry. Not many holidays, Dad working a lot, days out usually just involved Mum and the kids. The kids were growing up and becoming more opinionated and testing boundaries, wanting to explore the benefits of being a little bit older.

We moved to Margrove Park in 1994, a tiny hamlet in the middle of the countryside, surrounded by moorland and forests. It seemed the ideal place to bring up small children, a village green, community life, and not so far to travel to school. Quite soon we realised that we were not accepted by a few of the people who lived there, and it was quite a shock to discover how narrow-minded and bigoted some people can be. Some local children picked on our children, and it became horrible. There were two particular families who made our lives hell. We received poison pen letters, had things stolen from the garden, our children were called names and even spat at by an adult! (When Katie became ill, and her hair was very thin so that her scalp showed through, the mother of one of the village children called her 'Baldie'.)

All the children were at Botton School by now and thoroughly enjoying it. Katie was a normal teenager, growing up, testing boundaries, caring, funny, asking questions about life, boys, looking forward to growing up and being able to go out, get a boyfriend, a job, travelling, etc. Katie was always trying to please people, anxious not to upset anyone. Katie was in love with life and really enjoyed discovering new things.

When Katie reached thirteen she went to Israel with her school, and had an amazing time. When she came back from Israel, she became a vegetarian and very aware of problems with the world. At this time her teacher of seven years was leaving the school, and it was decided that there would be no Class 8. Katie was distraught at the thought of leaving Botton. At the same time, we decided to move to be nearer Tony's work and so that the children would not have to go to a school in Guisborough with the same kids that we lived near. Katie really did not want to move and made it quite obvious. Also, Anthony was having problems at school, and suddenly things were not quite so rosy in the garden. Tony and I were also having arguments and finding life really tough.

In January 2001, I noticed that Katie began to get very fussy and even more tidy than usual. She was still vegetarian, and her interest in food increased as well as a desire to exercise, come hell or high water. I had also begun to exercise and lose weight. Almost overnight Katie's periods stopped; she wouldn't let you in the bathroom or bedroom if she was getting changed. Because she was getting older we respected this, but I began to think there was another reason. I walked in when she was getting changed and was horrified at what I saw. My beautiful daughter had lost weight, so that her bones shone through her skin and her little body was covered in hair.

She was exercising every day come rain, sun or snow. At school it was tough, as they had decided to go up to Class 8. So there was Katie and three boys. It was not easy for any of them, and we asked Katie to leave but she was adamant that she would finish Class 8. Katie became the target for their teenage jokes and pranks and remarks that are usual in school but as she was the only girl it was so hard for her. She would react, often quite aggressively. She thought no one was on her side, although they were. It could sometimes get so bad she would end up in tears but still refused to leave. I made an appointment for her to see the Doctor. I already knew she was ill before the doctor said so and when she was diagnosed as anorexic it came as no surprise. We had no idea though of all that it entailed. Katie became hysterical a lot of the time, finding fault and being critical. It became harder to find the real Katie as anorexia took a hard hold of her. The other children found it confusing and hurtful and asked, "What the hell is going on?" As a family it tore us apart.

We felt so helpless, not knowing what to do. Our daughter was in pain, physical and emotional, and there was nothing we could do. The voice had taken over.

By now we had moved to Billingham, a small industrial town, and that compounded everything. Katie had started at Billingham Campus and tried so hard to fit in, but it was getting harder for her as anorexia was well and truly part of our family. After a few weeks she began to get physically ill and had to go to hospital for monitoring. I have to say this was the most devastating time of our life. I felt as if my entire world had turned upside down and did not know what to do. Katie's friends by now had all disappeared, not knowing how to cope with her moods, attitudes and appearance. Because of that, she felt even more isolated and more dependent on the voice. Katie had been going to the Roseberry Centre, getting weighed and seeing a counsellor. I felt no one understood, or did enough or actually really cared. I am sure that this wasn't the case but that is what it felt like. When Katie was taken into hospital she was just like a toddler – that is what it feels like sometimes, a toddler that looks eighteen but in a body of an eleven-year old. *What to eat, what to wear, why are you doing this, why are you talking like this, what a mess, don't swear, don't fart, don't drink, I hate you, please help me, no piss off, I should have been an only child. No one cares, don't tell me what to do, go away, come back, don't leave me, I love you.*

When Katie was little, she had to go into hospital with an ear infection and that we could make better, but this illness, how do you make it better? Can you make it better? What do you do? We visited Katie every available opportunity. The kids found it so hard because we would just sit there, in this room, Katie on total bed rest not speaking, not listening, just rocking her legs and staring into space. If they did not go, Katie would go mad, and if they did go they almost always ended up arguing. Teenage years are tough enough for them but when they have a sister that changed so radically in such a short time it must be heartbreaking. I know as their mum it broke me to see them and hear them, the nastiness and confusion.

I don't know what we expected from the hospital, really. They were great and we will be forever thankful, but we did feel that they could have done more alternative things like meditation, relaxation, massage and the like. We were having family sessions with Dr. Steven Harrison, a ward nurse called Jackie, and Dr. Stephen Westgarth. It was so bizarre, Dr Westgarth and Jackie looked as if they had just left school and were not old enough to be in the kind of job that they were. Katie was on observation and had to have accompanied showers. Often, I would leave her crying and when I got into the car I would break down myself. Her weight was up and down and once she had tried so hard to put some weight on but then got a tummy bug and lost it all. Back on bed rest, it seemed so unfair. My mum was also sending her things every day, which at first was great but the others felt left out and when it stopped Katie felt so sad. I think we lived in limbo every day, not sure how it would be.

After a year, Katie was discharged. I really felt that it was too early, and we were not ready for her to come home. I had to say to the doctors, in front of Katie, that we did not feel ready for her to come home and we also felt that Katie was not ready to come home. No one listened, and indeed Katie was discharged.

We went on holiday to Tenerife and had a lovely time, but Katie would spend as much time as she could swimming up and down not for pleasure but for the exercise – she looked so, so thin. When Katie did come home, hysterical outbursts became the norm and not just from Katie but from all of us. We were walking on glass, worried about what we said, what we did, continually coming under criticism. It became a vicious circle; a pattern had been set that we could not seem to break out of. The boys and Penny said such hurtful things to Katie, and she to them. It was such a negative atmosphere; I didn't know how it could continue. For things to thrive they need light, warmth, water, love and it is just so bloody hard. The support you need and want is so hard to get because you don't know where to get it, how to get it, and what it is that you actually need. You need someone to listen to you, someone to take them away for a few days, someone to make it all better. I know it will get better, but when? What Katie, Penny, Anthony and Samuel should know is that we love them, but not unconditionally. We might be Mum and Dad, but we are human; we have flaws, bad days and good days.

Rosemary – I'm sure that this illness has changed me, but I don't know how. I really don't know how I would be if it had never happened.

Tony – Well, personally I believe it has contributed towards me experiencing bouts of depression. However, overall it has torn our family to shreds, making life so much harder for everyone involved and it has changed relationships for ever.

Katie went to Abbey Hill School – a unit for anxious pupils – and they were fantastic there. She worked phenomenally hard and got her exams, applied to Bede College, was told she could go and then went on her own for the entrance interview (we were visiting friends in London) and was told that her exam results, the ones she had worked so very hard for, weren't good enough for the course she wanted to do. Katie felt as if her world had ended there and then. When we got back from London, we went to Bede and sorted out the confusion. For the courses Katie wanted to do she had to have As, or Bs and the level of exam Katie took she couldn't get better than Ds or Cs (except for English in which she got a B). She then enrolled at Kirby College to do catering. Many people with eating disorders go into catering.

I think that anorexia is a control thing, but to constantly deny yourself something can't be good for you. We all know that to survive you need food and water, and to deprive yourself of this could kill you, so how can they do it to themselves?

Now Katie finds it difficult to relax, trying to take charge of everything, acting as a parent not a sister. Katie also clings to the past, good and bad, and finds it oh so difficult to forgive and forget. We often talk about what we did when she was younger, stories we would read, songs we would sing, etc. and this she hankers for. She does not want to grow up and get older. Sometimes Katie can be horribly selfish, demanding time and attention, and woe betide if you say no. Also, she acts as if no one else matters to her and therefore should not matter to you. She can also be caring and thoughtful but often to those not connected to the family.

At the moment Katie is doing very well at college, our life feels like it's on hold, and the kids are being teenagers, but with a difference. Sometimes, I will look at this child and wonder what in God's name I did to deserve this, when they are shouting at you, swearing at you, telling you how worthless and lazy you are. It is themselves they are angry with, but it is so hard to remember that. They can bring you down so low and you get so tired but you must take time out for yourself and take whatever help is made available to you.

Looking to the future, we can see that things are now progressing well with Katie's recovery. Katie's positive attitude and determination to get well is beginning to reap benefits. The professional help Katie and our family is receiving has helped enormously but we would have appreciated more. As Katie is getting better she is more able to believe that the love and support given by her family is genuine.

We both imagine health and happiness in Katie's future and Katie enjoying her life, achieving her goals and ambitions, meeting a partner, having her own children and finding fulfilment in her life.

We both wish health and happiness for all our family, for everyone to feel happy and peaceful within themselves, with their family, friends and environment

Penny's story

I'm Penny Sophia 'Wren' Metcalfe, Katie's little sister, and this is to be my story too. This chapter is my chance to explain about what our family has been through in the years of Katie's anorexia. Also, for me to explain about how I think our family has suffered and changed.

It was the year 2001, and Katie had decided that her New Year's resolution would be to get slim. I'm still now not quite sure why she decided upon this, as she was a beautiful young woman with a perfect figure. At the time, I couldn't have even imagined how 'slim' she would actually get with this New Year's resolution.

Our family was a nice, 'normal' family. We had our differences amongst ourselves, but we got on because we loved and cared for one another. We (Katie, Sam, Tony and I) used to play football, play at the park and generally hang out and have fun. We'd go out to places with Mum and Dad, when he could get the day off work! We were kids enjoying our childhood, and a family enjoying life together

Katie first started just eating healthily, cutting out foods that had that little bit too much fat in them, but still treating herself to sweets and desserts every so often. It was strange seeing Katie stop eating things she enjoyed, as she had always been a great cook and loved creating recipes for herself and for us all to try. It was one of her ambitions in life to have the best vegetarian restaurant in Britain and to be a best-selling author.

I first noticed Katie was ill when she started eating less, and leaving food on her plate, even if the food was healthy, for example, salad or pasta.

She started doing a phenomenal amount of exercise, and I noticed she was losing weight pretty dramatically. She went for bike rides and walks every day, either on her own, or with myself or another member of the family. We would sometimes take picnics, but Katie would only have a piece of fruit and some water. I remember one time, Katie staring at me eating a piece of cake for my dessert, and I wondered what was wrong with her. Why wasn't she eating cake? Why was she staring at me as though I was eating a maggot-infested apple?

I noticed Katie eating less and less throughout the spring and summer, and became rather worried as she was losing a lot of weight. She was going on eight-mile bike rides each day and barely eating enough to get her up a steep hill. I decided to tell our mum that I was worried Katie might be developing an eating disorder and she was getting too slim to be healthy. She said she was sure Katie was fine and she did not have an eating disorder. I was not convinced.

She started acting differently too. She would keep everything overly tidy, neat and clean. Katie had always been tidy but she became obsessive. She would argue about the pettiest things and call me and our two brothers 'fat' and 'lazy', which none of us were. She acted so differently before her illness. She was friendly and approachable. She wasn't obsessed with food and what everyone eats. She was more open-minded, and more caring of the people around her. She wasn't selfish and at the same time self-hating as she can be now.

As the year went on, Katie lost more and more weight. She was eating much less and doing gradually more exercise. Her backbones and ribs were becoming visible, and she had lost a lot of natural body weight and fat.

I was worried, concerned and angered. I was worried because obviously I didn't want my sister to have an eating disorder, she could die, and I loved and cared for her, and I didn't want anything to happen to her. I was concerned for the same reasons. I was angry at Katie for letting herself get the way she was. I was angry at the family and myself because I thought we weren't a good enough family to prevent this.

When Katie was becoming increasingly ill, our family wasn't used to her new ways of 'living life'. Life was particularly strained at home, and the strain was hard on all of us. It was forcing us to grow up faster, and forcing us to leave our own childhood behind. Although I think it was only Katie and I who actually did it!

Everything changed. The way everyone acted around each other, and Katie, the way we lived in the house, the things we ate, the way we treated each other. Everything.

Katie went into hospital for almost a year. She has had numerous ups and downs. I have lost the sister I once had. I have lost my sister who I used to look up to and respect and get along with. I have lost our 'girly' chats and days out. Nothing good has come out of Katie's suffering. Out of these changes.

A week ago, I didn't see any progress. But this week, there seems to have been a change in everyone's attitude towards each other. Katie seems to have had some sort of revelation, and be progressing better than before.

I hope our family becomes like it was before. I just want my family to get back to 'normal'. I want us to be happy again. I want my sister back.

I am confident that Katie will, in time, get better, with the help of her family, her friends, and of course she will have to put a lot of work into it herself. Katie is a remarkable girl, and I know she can overcome it with the help of her family and friends. I hope for Katie to become what she wants to become, and to do what she wants to do. I hope for her not to be tied down by her illness any more. I hope for Katie, to be Katie. I wish Katie the best of luck and she has all of my support and love.

Well done, Katie.

I'm Samuel James Metcalfe, but most people just call me Sam, and I am the youngest in the family. I am fourteen and I was eight years old when all of this stuff started to happen. I now have different views about it all than what I had back then, because I am older now and I know a lot more, and I have gained loads more knowledge and understanding about it all.

Before she became ill Katie was important to me because she would stick up for me whenever I was in trouble. She used to be really strong and was a fast runner too. But sometimes the bullies would catch her when she was trying to run away, which wasn't nice as they used to hurt her with planks of wood and things like that. We used to ride bikes and go for picnics in the woods and make dens, which was wicked. But sometimes we would get lost. Katie would lead us off the path because she wanted to explore places that we had never been to before. It was scary sometimes, but mostly it was fun. Katie wasn't able to stick up for me any more after she became ill. She was too thin and weak and had no strength.

She started getting angry easily, and her emotions changed, if that's the way in which you describe it. Her writing changed. It became neater, more Gothic, and less colourful. She became tidier, a bit of a control freak about mess, if you know what I mean. She didn't feel like my sister any more. She was getting weird.

Before she wouldn't be so self-conscious about her food, and she wouldn't mind a bit of mess around the house. Now, she is much more concerned about mess, cleanliness, things like that. She now likes to know what people eat. She is always cooking for the family, but doesn't always eat what she makes. She will do sometimes, but not all the time. When she does, it makes me pleased.

Katie changed so much, and I want the old Katie back. But I don't think that will ever happen. No, I know it will never happen. Ever. But things are progressing well. Katie is doing better than before. She is eating better, which I am really pleased about.

I want our family to be normal. Like we were before all this started. I want Katie to be like she was before she got this illness. I want her to be happy and famous with her book and to have a restaurant. I believe Katie can get better. I believe in her.

Now Whole

by Katie Metcalfe

Mother
Father
Listen
Please
To my heartfelt apology.
I never
Not once
Meant to hurt you
I never
Not once
Meant to make you cry.
You have
To me
Been like statues of stability
Rays of sunlight in the bleak black
Anorexia had torn us apart
Limb from limb
Soul from soul
But together
We have battled.
Forever
Will we stand.
So Please,
Both of you,
Wait,
Listen,
Take heed,
To the voice calling to you from the depth of my heart
From the centre of my soul.
Mother
Father
We are now whole.

Part 3

Chapter 41

Introduction

I hope the first two parts of this book will have helped you understand what anorexia is, how it gains control and the effect it has on people.

This part is intended to help people who may be suffering from anorexia, and their families. I'm not a medical expert, if you are suffering from anorexia, then of course you need expert help but I do know that you can't leave it all to experts, ultimately it's what you, and your family, do which will be decisive in your battle against the disease.

So I've tried to put together all the things that I wish *I* had known during my struggles with the voice.

Firstly there is a section on *The Lies and Truths Surrounding Anorexia*. I hope this will help the sufferer resist the siren call of the voice and will help sufferers' families to understand when it is the voice talking, and not the person.

Then there is a section *What You Can Do To Help* which gives practical suggestions as to how the family can help and how sufferers can help themselves.

Next, for helping recovery, there is a section *A Helping Hand With Weight Gain*.

I have also suggested some complementary therapies that can be helpful and some ways of coping with stress.

Finally I have listed some books that are worth having a look at and some useful contact details

But, first (in case you don't get round to reading all this part!), I'd like to share with you... the most important things I have learned...!

DON'T DIET!

Don't waste time fretting about what you look like. Life is too precious.

Shrug off what other people think of you. What you think about yourself is what really matters the most.

Eat what you want, when you want. Life is for living.

Treat your family with the love and respect they truly deserve, and listen to all the advice and encouragement, even if you do not use it.

Never turn your back on your family and friends. Remember that life is more than difficult for them too.

When you want to talk to someone about anything, anytime, talk. Don't keep things to yourself as they build up and may erupt with dire consequences.

Ignore and walk away from people who disrespect you and call you names. They are not even worth looking at.

If you don't want to talk, but want to express how you are feeling, write it down in any way you feel is best. That could include song lyrics, poetry or a short story.

Keep a diary to record your personal thoughts and feelings. You can even use it as a special friend to whom you can tell all your secrets. It will never tell a soul.

When you need to cry, cry. Never hold back tears, it's the worst thing to do. They block up within you, creating bad energy and they eventually erupt into something far worse.

If you need a hug, tell someone you need to be hugged, and never feel stupid for doing so. Everyone needs to be hugged sometime.

Live life to the full every day. You're a long time dead.

Never listen to the voice inside your head.

Only listen to your own voice.

It's your life – your voice, your body, your rules.

Chapter 42

The Lies And Truths Surrounding Anorexia

This is a list of things, which the voice may say to people suffering from anorexia regularly to try to stop them from battling against it. Do they look familiar to you? If they do, it is vital that you ignore these lies that the voice says to you, if you wish to become well again. Truths that will be hard for you to believe, but they are honestly one hundred per cent THE TRUTH.

That is how I managed to beat my demon; by ignoring the lie and focusing only on the truth. It took me a very long time, but I managed it in the end! I promise you that the more you ignore the voice, the easier it will become not to believe the things that it is saying to you. Are you doubtful? Well, try it for yourself! It will be very difficult to begin with; I can't tell you that it will be easy. But be reassured that it will get easier. Go on give it a go! Listen to your own voice, and listen to what *you* truly believe.

Lies And Truth For The Sufferer

Your bum looks huge in that skirt / trousers, you need to do more exercise to make it small again – Of course, your bum doesn't look big! The demon is only saying that because it wants to satisfy its appetite for excessive, unnecessary exercise. It wants you to feel bad about yourself so that you listen to it and act, as only it wants you to. Only when you do as it wants, does it gives you praise. (Have you noticed this? Whenever you disobey the voice, it gives you hell and grief, and when you obey it praises your actions.) But what the demon is giving you isn't praise at all; it is negative feedback in the real world. Feedback that you're slipping, slipping into its grasp again and its ways of doing things.

You can't have that sandwich for your tea, you can't change your daily meal routine – Of course, you can have a sandwich! Who has the right to say that you can't? Who has the right to say that you can't change your routine, except you? If you want the sandwich, you can have one. You make the rules of what you do and don't eat. NO ONE should dictate to you other than yourself. Only YOU have the right to decide.

You can't watch TV, you don't deserve to – Who is to say that you don't deserve to watch TV! You deserve to do anything that you want to do. And you don't *need* to deserve to watch TV anyway. Watching TV is a NORMAL thing to do. You don't have to do anything to gain the right to be able to sit down and watch a favourite programme.

You can't watch TV / read a book, you have more constructive, important things to do – If you have free time, and watching TV or reading a book is what you like to do, then do it! Only YOU can say whether you have more important things to be doing. You are the one who really knows and who can make the correct decision.

You can't spend longer than five/ten minutes in the bath – Of course, you can! Unless it has something to do with a family situation or rota, then spend longer. Spend as long as you want! (Of course you shouldn't spend too long though, or you'll end up looking like a shrivelled prune! As everybody does.)

You can't have a lie in bed under any circumstances. As soon as you are awake you must get up – If there is no need for you to get up, say on a weekend or a holiday, then lie in for a while longer. Nothing will happen to you if you do. You will probably feel more refreshed and awake if you get up after having an hour or so more sleep than normal, especially if you had gone to bed late the previous evening.

That headache/stomach ache isn't real. Carry on as normal. Don't stop for help or get medicine – If you feel ill, depending on how bad you feel, you need to REST, see a doctor and/or get medicine. It's as simple as that. NO ONE can carry on as normal if they are ill. EVERYBODY needs rest if they are not well. Why should you be an exception? You're not an exception. YOU have the same rights as everyone else has. Remember that next time you're feeling under the weather.

You must do the exact amount of exercise every day otherwise you'll blow up like a balloon – Ha! What a joke. That is all it is, a massive joke. There is no way on this earth that you would blow up like a balloon if you didn't do the exercise that the demon instructed you to do. It's NOT possible. If you don't believe me, try it for yourself. I tried it. I altered my exercise routine and did not blow up into a balloon at all! (I'm sure you would have heard if I had done though, as it would have probably made it on to a national news programme!)

You can't have anything extra to eat. Not one mouthful. You will get instantly fat – This is yet another NO-WAY-that-would-happen-one. Having a little something extra is the beginning of normalising your eating habits. If you don't have anything extra to eat then you don't gain weight, if you don't gain weight, the demon is still in charge, if the demon is still in charge, you don't get better. Ever. It's as simple as that. Unquestionably. You WILL have to force yourself to eat more, as YOU ARE the only one who can. Once you have managed to eat extra, you MUST, MUST, MUST keep it up. There is NO point in eating extra one day, and then thinking 'OK, I've eaten extra today; I can go back to 'normal' tomorrow. Things will improve from now on.' They won't. You have to be consistent and dedicated to sticking to your new changes. It took me an absolute age to realise that I had to be consistent with my changes. That I couldn't do it one day and then not the next. I eventually realised this after months of continuing to hover around the same weight and not making any real progress at all. You must make changes if you are to improve. There are no ifs or buts about it. And don't be thinking, 'Oh, I can't do it. It's not possible,' because IT IS. IT IS possible. I am living proof that it is possible to make changes and stick to them. So come on! Join me in proving that IT IS possible. Prove to yourself. Prove to your family. Prove to everybody. Prove the anorexia demon wrong.

Lies And Truths For Parents

This list has been created to reassure parents about comments that their child may make. They are not true, and are actually voiced from the anorexic demon.

I hate you! – Let's get one thing straight immediately. Your child does NOT hate you. 'I hate you' is often said when you are trying to encourage them to make changes. It's what the anorexia demon is telling them to say to you, as it hates any changes being made, unless, of course, they are made in its favour. The anorexia demon hopes that by getting your child to say that they hate you, you will back off and leave them to do what they want. Well, what the demon wants.

Leave me alone. I don't want anyone near me – Your child WILL need someone near him or her, in their own heart. But, the demon will not allow it. When your child says this, you must try to let him or her know that it is all right not to be alone. You need to reiterate that it is perfectly acceptable and normal to be with and near people.

You're a crap parent – They don't mean this at all. If you are trying to encourage your child to eat / not exercise, etc. you will be told that you are a crap parent, or often worse. There is no doubt about it. However, you need to remember that it is NOT your child who is speaking, but the demon voice, the anorexia. Constantly keep in mind that when your child has recovered, he or she will apologise profusely for years to come for calling you a crap parent!

I can battle this all by myself I don't need any help – Anorexic people have to battle the demon inside their minds by themselves by refusing to do as it says, but they will need help in their battle in other forms such as gaining weight. Whether it is from a doctor, sibling, parent or friend, they will need unconditional support, love and encouragement along the way. How you decide to help them in their battle will ultimately be your decision, whether it is sitting with them while they eat, assisting them to occupy their mind, or in a severe case, admitting them into hospital.

"I can battle this all by myself" is one thing that cannot, under any circumstances, be agreed with.

Chapter 43

What You Can Do To Help

To cut out lots of tedious *he / she* and *him / her* constructions in this chapter, I have used *she* and *her* in the singular case; of course lots of anorexics are male, (sorry, boys!).

Parents

It is notoriously difficult to know what you should say to your anorexic child and when to say it. It's equally, if not more, difficult to know what to do when your child is on the road to recovery. I hope this chapter will provide some basic advice on what you can do to help your child on her journey and, ultimately, on your journey as well.

Although each journey is different, as we are all individuals with separate lives, the same applies, generally, to all anorexics in the love, attention and support that they need.

Tell them that you love them and care:
Ensure that you tell your child that you love her every single day. You can tell her more if needs be. Even if she is abusive to you, nasty and horrible, you must still tell her. Try to remember that IT IS NOT HER that is being abusive, nasty and horrible. Ignoring the abuse and nastiness is an unbelievably difficult thing to do, but it needs to be done if you want to get through to your child, and make your message heard over the voice's domineering orders. Telling her that you love her and that you care about her doesn't have to be done face to face. It can be done by text message, email, telephone, a letter or even a simple note left on her bed. It doesn't matter how you express it; it's just important that you do. It will mean just as much to her, any way that it is done. During her recovery the anorexic needs to feel and know that she is loved by you.

Show affection:

If you can tell that your child needs to be hugged and soothed, do not wait for her to ask. It is common for anorexics to feel as though they do not have the right to ask for a hug, and they don't deserve one. You can gently either ask whether she would like a hug, or just give her one without asking if she needs one or not. Ninety-nine per cent of the time, she will accept your comfort. While you are hugging her, it helps to mention the fact that everybody needs to be hugged sometimes, and everybody deserves to be hugged.

Supporting changes:

If your child decides that she wants to try something new in her diet, encourage and give her praise for deciding to. Changing eating habits is one of the main and hardest parts of the recovery, and is a long and tediously slow process. (You need to be prepared for the time it will take. There is no set time for how long it will be before your child's eating habits resemble anything like the norm.) If, for example, she decides in the morning that she is going to have a cheddar cheese sandwich instead of a cottage cheese sandwich for her tea because she wants to be brave and challenge the demon, but when the time comes for her to have it, she says that she has changed her mind, and wants the cottage cheese she has every day, encourage her as much as possible to stick with what she had originally planned to have: the cheddar cheese sandwich. DO NOT immediately agree with her, and say "All right then, it's OK for you to have the cottage cheese instead." Try gentle persuasion, and be persistent. Often, when anorexics first start to make changes in their lives, they feel that they need to have someone else saying to them that they can have the different choice. They need to be reassured that it is OK to have something different. Maybe offer to have the same as her. You too could have a cheddar cheese sandwich for your tea and show that it really is all right for anyone to have what he or she wants to eat.

Keep calm under stress:

Try to not get angry, upset, and frustrated or stressed when your child flies into a rage or has a violent mood swing. It is easier said than done, and will be difficult, but try and remember that your child still has a different being inside them, an anorexic voice. How well your child may be recovering rests on how big a space the anorexia occupies inside your child. Remember that IT IS NOT your child who is acting this way but the anorexia. There are a few options available regarding what you could do in a situation where your child is being abusive. You could walk away from the situation, remaining calm and telling your child that you are there for her when she has calmed down. Or you could ask straightaway if she would like to talk or needs a hug. It is often at times like this when hugs and kind, soothing words are required most. Walking away and not reacting isn't an easy thing to do at any time, but sometimes it honestly is the best thing to do. And remember, it is not your child who you are walking away from and ignoring, but the demon inside her.

Other options:

If your child is trying to gain weight, but wishes to exercise every day, attempt to distract her from feeling the need to. Suggest that she does something else, such as painting. Something which involves movement and activity to a certain degree, but nothing as strenuous as going for a bike ride or swimming. If your child is managing to gain weight, you may wish to do some 'gentle exercise' with her, such as going for a short walk, for example.

Help them to socialise:

Try and avoid having your child spending too much time alone. It is really important that she tries to socialise and gets involved with things that involve more than one participant. If your child is left alone for long periods of time, to mull over her thoughts by herself, the anorexia will try and take complete control again. If your child is with other people, and taking part in activities that have nothing to do with her illness, it makes it easier for her to block out the demon voice, as she will have many other things to think about apart from food, exercise, her weight and satisfying anorexia's demands.

Simple suggestions for a smile:

Every now and then buy a nice card or, even better, make one and write a meaningful quote or verse inside it. Leave it on your child's pillow maybe with a flower picked from the garden.

Organise a family event, such as an outing to the cinema, bowling or a video/games night.

Ask for assistance in preparing a meal, and listen to music while cooking together. Encourage your child to eat what you have both prepared. Lay the table with napkins and nice crockery, light a candle, and make it a special event.

Take a trip to the beach or nearby countryside and talk about the nature around you while you stroll. Discuss the ways in which nature naturally changes and evolves. This may have some effect on the way in which your child thinks about changes in her own life.

Prepare a food item that your child remembers and loves from her early childhood such as flapjack or shortbread and gently persuade her to sit with you and have some.

Brothers and Sisters

Try not to react:

If your sibling gets into a terrible mood with you, becomes aggressive, angry, or abusive, calls you names and says the most horrible things to you for no apparent reason at all, try as best you can to let it go straight over your head. Ignore it and try not to react at all. The anorexia demon inside the person close to you wants you to rise to the bait. Its aim is to see you losing your temper and calling her horrible names and getting your own back on her for being nasty to you. Because it wants to see your sibling suffer. Every time that you can tell your sibling is going to 'erupt', leave the room quietly, or if that's not possible, try and shut off from it completely. Constantly remember that it is not your sibling saying or doing those things, but the anorexia demon.

Spend time together:

Try and spend time with your sibling when you are able to, doing things that you both enjoy, or used to enjoy doing before she became ill. If she is having problems with her social network, allow her to sometimes be a part of yours. For example, if you are going out to the cinema with a few friends, and she would be at home with nothing to do, ask her if she would like to join you. Do not get angry if she refuses your invitation at first. Remember that it has probably been some time since she has been able to participate in such an event. Try a little gentle persuasion saying that it would be good fun, but don't try and force her. It is important that she makes the decision to change her ways herself. If she does not give in to gentle persuasion, back down, suggesting 'maybe next time'.

Show encouragement when the time is right:

If your sibling would like to try something new, be enthusiastic about it and encourage her. Even if it is something which you might think of as minuscule, such as another slice of bread at teatime, or going out somewhere when otherwise she would be hidden away in her room. Remember, don't try and force her, as it has to be her own individual choice, but show real, honest enthusiasm about any change. If she tells you about it, for example she says 'tonight I'm going to have a drink of hot chocolate instead of a cup of tea' it most likely means that she wants and would really like and appreciate some moral support, reassurance, and, in some cases, permission. But if you notice her doing something different, for the better, such as making herself a different drink, and she hasn't said anything to you about doing it, it's often best not to say anything at all to her. Just smile and leave her to it.

The Sufferer: How To Help Yourself

Trying new things:

If you want to try anything new in your life, such as a different food, a change in your daily routine, anything at all. DO IT! If the demon says not to, do not listen. Do not give in. YOU CAN BE the more powerful voice. If you want to recover. If you want your own life back again. If you no longer wish to share everything with the anorexia demon, ignoring what it tells you to do is a very, very important part of the recovery process. Change has to happen if you want to get well again. If there is no change in your life, for example, if you eat the same foods day after day, if you exercise the same day after day, if you have the same attitude day after day, you WILL remain the same until you die. Not a nice thought, is it? Having the demon with you until you draw your last breath. And it would most likely tell you how to draw that last breath too! It doesn't matter if the changes you make at first are tiny ones, all that matters is that they are made and that they continue. That you keep them up and they happen more and more as time goes by. Make sure that when you make a change, you do not revert to your old habits after a day or two, as that would be allowing the anorexia to win. If it is saying to you, "If you have something more / different to eat you'll get fat", DO NOT LISTEN. It is lying to you. To prove it, experiment – have something extra or different, and see that it doesn't make you fat. I did it and it proved it to me.

Gaining weight:

Gaining weight is a very scary thought, and an even scarier thing to actually start to do, but it is what you are going to have to do if you are to get well and have your life back again.

You can gain weight at whatever rate you want to, but remember that the longer you take, the longer the demon will remain with you. Whatever rate you decide on, it is going to be uncomfortable, unpleasant and difficult. There is no escaping that fact, but you have to go though all the unpleasant and difficult times to be able to come out the other end of the tunnel, triumphant and well. Research has shown that anorexics who ponder and take a long time to gain a little bit of weight are usually the people who are unable to have children, and who end up suffering from osteoporosis, as well as other problems when they eventually do reach a healthy weight, more so than the people who gain weight faster, and reach their healthy body weight in a shorter space of time.

Talk if you want to:

If a member of your family or a friend asks whether you would like to talk, and you have many things on your mind that you are desperate to discuss and get out of your system, accept the offer. You deserve to be able to talk about your problems as much as, if not more than, anyone else. If you think that they are only asking you because they feel as though it's their duty, well, that's wrong. They're asking you if you would like to talk because they care for you. They genuinely want to know if you are struggling and need someone to talk to. If the demon says to you that it can talk to you instead, that it can provide you with all the support you need, DO NOT LISTEN. How can something that has caused so much pain and heartache, grief and sadness really give you support and be something that you can talk to about your problems? After all, it is the demon who caused them in the first place! The demon only wants what's best for it. NOT WHAT IS BEST FOR YOU! It is a selfish, ignorant, cunning, manipulative thing, which will only stay with you for AS LONG AS YOU LET IT.

You don't have to:

If it is raining or snowing and cold and miserable outside, but the demon voice is ordering you to go out and exercise, saying that if you don't then you will become an elephant, that the fat will just pile on you, IGNORE IT. I know it's not easy, remember, I've been there, too. However, it is possible. If you miss out one day of routine exercise you obviously will not become an elephant. Fat will not pile itself on to you immediately. That's just what the demon wants you to believe. It's not the truth and it's far, *far* from it. Try, and you will see. It will be hard, but it will prove yet another point, which the demon is wrong about. It is normal for people not to bother with a certain amount of exercise when they don't feel like it, or if the weather is terrible. And it's all right for you not to bother too. It's your life. If you don't want to exercise in the rain, wind or snow, and every single day, then don't! Dig your heels in and refuse to do what it wants you to do. DO WHAT YOU WANT TO DO. I disobeyed the voice eventually, and didn't go outside and exercise when I didn't want to, and I never ended up fat or looking like an elephant because of it. I admit that I felt like one, at first. However, I stuck with my determination to do what I wanted, and eventually overcame my false fears.

Accepting encouragement:

If your family and friends are trying to give you encouragement and support when you are attempting to make changes, you may not see it as support and encouragement, but be reassured that it is. You may think that they just want to see you fat. BUT THEY DON'T. HONESTLY. THEY WANT TO SEE YOU WIN. They want to see you healthy, happy and well again. Your family and friends want to see you being able to make your own decisions again, without the demon voice interfering 24/7. For example, if your mother smiles and says things such as "Go on, it's OK" when you are eating something new, she is smiling and telling you it's OK because she is happy for you and thrilled that you are progressing with your recovery.

Reassuring and explaining:

There will be arguments, misunderstandings, shouting matches, etc. as you make your way down the rocky road to recovery, there is no doubt about that, and there will be no way of avoiding them. Unless, of course, your family is abnormally perfect, which is extremely unlikely. Arguments, and shouting matches, etc. will usually occur at times when you are saying things to your family or friends that you know are not what you intended to say. Things that you know are what the demon is making you say out loud. It is at times like this that is it very important to reassure your parents/siblings/friends, that it is not you who is saying these things.

Writing down targets:

Often, it can be a great help and support to see specific tasks set out in writing and in an orderly format, e.g. a bar chart, as it makes the task a lot more real instead of just being thoughts swimming around in your mind. Plus, as an anorexic, it is not uncommon to forget. Therefore, it can help to write down the specific tasks or goals you want to achieve. Put down the date you set the target and, when you achieve it, put in the date when it was achieved and tick it off. Keep the sheets as a reminder and as a record of what you've achieved.

Socialising:

This is a major factor to take into consideration when you are recovering. If your siblings ask you if you'd like to go out with them, for example going out on a shopping trip, but the demon voice is telling you not to go, saying that you don't deserve to go, that you could be doing better things with your time than enjoying yourself, although you are bored and have nothing to do – say to it, out loud if needs be, that you DO deserve to go out. You do deserve to enjoy yourself as much as any other person does. You do have the right to spend time with people whom you care about and who care about you too. Tell the demon that you do not need its orders any more. It will be a very difficult thing to do, but you, with will power and determination, CAN DO IT! I have, and I will tell no lie; it was difficult beyond belief. There were even moments when I considered surrendering and allowing the demon to take control over me and make everything easier. However, I persisted and I won. And if I can manage it, anyone can. ANYONE. Also, everyone in the entire world has the right to socialise. Socialising is a very important part of life. It is a very important part of living. And, don't forget, it is a vital part of the recovery process.

Reading this list of incentives!:

Remind yourself that when you are well again and the anorexia demon has been finally kicked out once and for all, the doors will be wide open. Here are a few (of course, there are many, many more) of the main advantages of getting yourself well and free from the demon that is anorexia nervosa:

• You will be able to go swimming, cycling or to the gym for pure fun and enjoyment.
• You will be able to exercise when you want, where you want and why YOU want to.
• Eating can again become a pleasurable activity which you enjoy doing with others.
• Making decisions normally, and on the spot, e.g. agreeing to go out with friends at the last minute, will be much easier to do.
• Doing normal pastimes which you enjoy, e.g. reading, watching television, will be seen as something you can do in your free time once again.
• You will begin to notice the opposite sex through different eyes!
• If you are a female, your chances of conceiving healthy children will increase.
• If you are a male, you will feel significantly more sexually active (of course this applies to the ladies too!).
• Having a close relationship with someone will be easier as you will not feel self-conscious, uneasy or hesitant.
• You will not be overly concerned about insignificant things in your daily life.

- Eating in public will be a normal thing to do again, and you will not have constant fears about what people think about what you are or are not eating.
- The relationship that you have with your family will greatly improve, as you will not get as easily annoyed by them.
- Missing a meal will not be a big deal as you can have something at another time.
- Your family will not have to worry about you every day.
- Your concentration and focus will be set on other aspects of your life, other than food, calories, weight and exercise. Your thoughts will be free to roam wherever they please! Some of which will include relationships, pleasurable activities, work, school, college, and university, whatever!
- You will be able to handle *any* situation that occurs one hundred per cent better, e.g. complications at work, school, college, etc.
- Any type of change will be easier for you to handle, from the tiny things such as having a different sandwich filling to moving house! As your body and mind evolve and change, so will your ability to cope with anything. It works hand in hand.
- You will not have to stick to a strict daily routine, which may or may not have rotated around your meals. You will be freer to alter your day how you wish to.
- You will be able to wear clothes that compliment or show off your fantastic figure, and don't swamp it. You will feel good about your figure and your body, and so you should!
- Outings with family or friends will be a pleasurable event, not a military operation as before.
- Your nails will grow stronger.
- Your skin will not be as dry, and will not bleed or crack.
- The cold will not affect you in the way that it did.
- Your hair will cease thinning.
- Chances of developing osteoporosis will be lowered or halted.
- You will feel more confident and out-going.
- People will see you as being more approachable.
- Your pain threshold will be higher, e.g. having your legs waxed.
- You will be more flexible with your sleeping hours.
- If you are making food and wish or need to taste it, you will be able to.

• In fact, everything in life will be better without the anorexia demon there!

Chapter 44

A Helping Hand With Weight Gain

This chapter is focused on giving a helping hand with the eating and weight gain part of the recovery process. Although being primarily aimed at the sufferer, it is a chapter written with parents in mind as well, and fundamentally all those who are involved in the recovery and the life of the sufferer beyond anorexia. Most of all, the foods that are mentioned in this chapter are healthy with the odd treat thrown in here and there. It is important to remember that treats are healthy too! Just as long as you don't have them 24/7. Although you will find that, if you are trying to gain weight, having more treats than a person who is at a healthy weight is perfectly acceptable. It is important to remember that the needs of an undernourished, underweight person are different from those of a well-nourished person at a healthy weight.

The mention of calories and fat has deliberately been avoided, as it's important while you are recovering that those two things do not continue to control your thinking as they have previously done. Although at first it may be necessary sometimes to have a guide to how much you are managing to consume in a day, so that you can be sure you're getting enough.

You can alter the suggestions for food listed in this chapter, to suit your personal taste. (Your tastes, and not the anorexia's, remember!) They are not written in stone. However, make sure that it's not all low calorie/fat things that you change them to! You are most likely to find that to gain weight, eating three meals a day and three snacks will be required as a minimum. It is important to get a good balance of protein, carbohydrates, fat, vitamins and minerals with every meal so that what you are eating is providing you with everything you need in order for your body to function properly and to gain weight successfully. Now is the time to stop denying yourself nice, good food. You need to allow yourself to be creative; ignore that voice ordering you what to eat and when. We all need to eat, it's a fact of life. Simple. So break those set routines. Live for the moment. Live for you. Carpe Diem!

If you are a recovering anorexic and are trying to gain weight, I really hope that this chapter provides you with a good insight into what can help you to reach your goal weight and a healthy, happy lifestyle.

As an anorexic, you are probably used to eating alone, away in a different room from your family. Now is the time to quit that routine! Bring yourself back to the normality of eating with and around people. It's a proven fact that families who eat together regularly get along with each other better than those who don't. Bear that thought in mind. It won't be an easy move to make, but it is possible. You can do it with determination.

Mealtimes aren't only about eating and getting it finished; they're also about socialising with your family, talking about your day, what everyone has done, discussing future plans, and having a joke and a laugh with one another. Mealtimes are supposed to be pleasurable times, where you take time over your food and enjoy what you are eating, as well as enjoying the company you are in. It is advisable, if possible, not to sit in front of a television or read while you are eating, as you should enjoy consuming your food. You should try to experience the smells, taste and texture of your meal. Doing this makes eating a more pleasurable experience. It is important to remember to make sure that when you are eating you are sitting down. This might sound stupid, but many anorexics (and non-anorexics) stand when they are eating – either out of pure habit or because they feel they would be lazy or fat if they sat down.

(If you find that you can eat better by watching television or reading, then by all means do so. When you are in the first stages of recovery, any distraction that helps you to eat is acceptable. However, as you progress, ease yourself away from this routine until you can cope without it.)

It is a good thing to remember that, after eating a meal, it is important to try to relax for at least half an hour. Read a book, paint or listen to some music. The reason for relaxing is so that you can reserve some of the energy you have just consumed, if you try to participate in vigorous activities too soon after you have eaten, you will find you will have heartburn, or simply not feel too good.

It's perfectly understandable that breaking routines, and eating with and around others will be an enormous step to take, but it is something that has to be done as a stage of the recovery process. And you can't say that for the rest of your life you want to eat alone. Can you?

Take it one step at a time. Begin with one meal a day, or a snack, and work your way up. Organise what you will be eating, and at what time, in advance, if you feel anxious. I am positive that your family will be only too happy to accommodate your needs. (The need to organise your mealtimes will decrease as you manage to gain more weight, and eating will become something that does not need so much thought and planning.)

The same applies with friends. Is it your dream to be able to go and see a film at the cinema and join in the 'passing of the popcorn' or the 'sharing of the sweets'? Going to a café and ordering a cappuccino and a piece of cake while laughing and chatting with friends? Make your dreams a reality. Do it today. Don't wait until next week, or next month. Before you know it, it will be next year… and then where will you be? I think, and hope, you get the picture now.

You might just want to invite one friend over to your house, and eat something in front of them while watching TV or doing homework. That's fine. As with the family mealtimes, start small and work your way up. I started small, and it worked for me. It can work for you too

Vitamins – Vitamins and minerals are essential nutrients, just like carbohydrates, fats and protein. We need to consume them regularly and in the correct quantity to become and stay healthy. They play an enormous role in building and maintaining the body's bones, tissues, fluids and organs.

Vitamins help to balance hormones, provide energy, boost the immune system, keep skin healthy, protect arteries and ensure the brain and nervous system work properly. (And you always wondered why your parents and teachers harped on at you!) Minerals build strong teeth and bones. They allow oxygen to be carried within our blood, control blood sugar levels and help to repair cuts or bruises.

The key to getting the right balance is a healthy mix of foods, fruit, vegetables, meat, fish, eggs, and dairy products. Nuts and seeds are great too, as they provide a fantastic source of many minerals.

Salt – Anorexics tend to use vast quantities of salt, and it does enormous harm to the body. Not only can it cause high blood pressure, which triples the risks of developing heart disease, but overusing can also lead to strokes and kidney failure, whatever your age. Overusing salt also promotes fluid retention, which results in swollen ankles. A high salt intake also promotes an increase in calcium excretion and may exacerbate osteoporosis. You can easily cut back on salt that you use on your food by substituting it with fresh and dried herbs and spices.

Chocolate – Chocolate will most likely be something that has been out of your diet for a very long time. However, despite all the bad publicity this 'food of the Gods' receives, there are many positives to balance this out. So go on, break those anorexia rules and live. Have some chocolate today!

Chocolate contains more antioxidants (substances that help to prevent cancer) than red wine and green tea.

A single bar of milk chocolate contains ten times the calcium that is in a medium sized apple.

There is more caffeine in a cup of decaffeinated coffee than in a medium sized bar of chocolate.

So, how many more reasons do you need to enjoy some chocolate?

Breakfast – Breakfast is *the most* important meal of the day. *Always* make sure that you have it. Eating breakfast starts up your digestive system after its long period of rest and fuels you up for the day ahead. It's really important that a balanced meal is eaten at breakfast, consisting of protein, carbohydrate, fat, vitamins and minerals. Here are two examples of meals, which include a balance of all:

(I must stress that these are only guidelines for mealtimes. Some people may need more, others less. Make sure you accommodate your needs with the food you eat.)

If you eat meat: grilled bacon, tomatoes, one poached egg and a slice of toast, followed by a hot drink, tea/coffee/Horlicks with milk and sugar, or pure fruit juice or a smoothie.

If you are vegetarian: a bowl of Cornflakes with one chopped banana and milk, one slice of toast spread with butter and jam/marmite followed by a hot drink, tea/coffee/Horlicks with milk and sugar, or pure fruit juice or a smoothie.

Lunch – Once again it's important to get a good balance of all the necessities for keeping your body in functioning order and of course for being able to gain weight. It's up to you whether you eat a main meal in the middle of the day or in the evening. I personally prefer my main meal at lunchtime, as it sets me up for serious brainwork in the afternoon!

Below are two examples for both vegetarians and meat eaters.

If you eat meat: a jacket potato split and spread with butter, and filled with tuna mayonnaise served with a salad and followed with a piece of flapjack.

If you are a vegetarian: mushroom and cheese omelette served with a salad and followed by a slice of banana loaf/cake.

Dessert – Round off your lunch and evening meal with a delicious dessert or pudding. If you struggle to allow yourself something sweet, remember that you are in charge. YOU choose what you can and can't have and not some stupid voice. Also remember that treats are allowed.

Dinner – Once again, aim to include protein, carbohydrates, vitamins, minerals and fat into your last meal of the day.

If you eat meat: toad-in-the-hole served with boiled carrots, cabbage, mashed potato and gravy, followed by a portion of apple crumble and custard.

If you are vegetarian: spaghetti bolognaise made with quorn mince, served with a lettuce salad and grated cheese, followed by a portion of vanilla ice cream topped with mixed nuts.

Snacks – Ideal times for snacks are mid-morning, mid-afternoon and just before bedtime. Including snacks in your daily diet is important if you aim to gain weight.

Drinks – Keeping your body hydrated is exceptionally important. As you increase the amount you drink, you will be certain to find that your skin improves, becoming less dry, sore and prone to bleeding. (Thus saving a fortune on hand cream in the long run!) Headaches will also decrease. Remember to drink *before* you are thirsty. (And not only water!) Aim to have a milky drink with each of your snacks, and fruit juice and water in between.

Chapter 45

Complementary Therapies And Dealing With Stress

This chapter focuses on making you aware of the many aspects of help that are available outside the NHS for anorexics and their carers and on ways of dealing with stress.

Complementary Therapies

Unfortunately, complementary therapies are almost unused by the NHS in the anorexic recovery process and for many other mental illnesses too; however, the therapies are out there and available. Be assured that if you do have to pay for the therapies, you will not be disappointed by what you receive. Complementary therapies have helped so very many people with their recoveries, and we are a family who recommend them to everyone we meet.

As the name suggests these are complementary and can work alongside allopathic medicines to aid in the recovery process. Homeopathy, massage and reflexology are non-invasive treatments that can be performed anywhere and fully clothed, which is helpful if you are a sufferer who is still learning to love your body, and who is still apprehensive about strangers seeing you partly undressed.

However, you may find that, after some time, you can feel comfortable with fewer clothes on. Just taking time out for yourself can be relaxing, especially if you are being treated with essential oils that can benefit many conditions, physical and emotional.

As a carer you may be under an enormous amount of stress, which can result in emotions running high, an inability to think straight, headaches, feelings of guilt, an aching body, all these can be helped by having regular treatments.

Massage is a great liberator of emotions which when suppressed can cause damage.

Complementary therapies are available in many varied forms: art therapy, visualisation, dance and music through to yoga, massage, acupuncture, reiki, reflexology and the use of herbal medicines.

Many techniques are used based on systems practised for thousands of years. All complementary healing practices have one aspect in common and this is that rather than treating a specific symptom or symptoms, they treat the person as a whole. Treating patients at their physical, mental and emotional levels. All three of which are affected by anorexia.

Art therapy, dance, and music can all help in the recovery. It may take some time to settle into a treatment, but once you do you will feel the difference and reap the benefits. Painting helped me enormously. We were fortunate that a friend is an art therapist, and she worked with me using a technique called 'veil painting'. Working with tactile materials often helps with stress, and you may discover a skill you never knew you had.

Foot reflexology – A natural healing art that deals with the principle that there are reflex areas in the feet which correspond to all the glands, organs and parts of the body when stimulated by using a unique thumb and finger walking technique.

It helps to relax and calm, balance the body, and improve blood, nerves and blood supply.

The therapist asks for a full client consultation, followed by an examination of the feet. The treatment would normally last for about forty-five minutes, with the therapist working on both feet. Some people find that after the treatment they feel relaxed and sleepy for some time. Many others feel relaxed and soon after feel energised and motivated. Some people find that they have a runny nose, increased perspiration and shivering, but this is a sign that the treatment is working, and that toxins are being successfully removed from the body. Reflexology is not a painful treatment, nor is it ticklish as one might expect. However, if there are reflexes with energy blockages, they can be slightly uncomfortable until they have been properly worked with and balanced.

Indian head massage – Having an Indian head massage can promote relaxation, help concentration, relieve tension and headaches and aid work performance. Based on an ancient Indian healing system, it is a massage to the face, shoulders, head and neck.

It is said to rebalance the body's energies and banish negativity, promote relaxation and relieve tension.

The massage can be done with or without oils and is normally performed in a quiet room, with the recipient sitting straight in a chair with both feet on the ground. Before the treatment, the therapist will do an initial consultation where the client will be asked about their medical history, health and lifestyle. Treatment begins with the therapist and recipient taking deep breaths to relax. The therapist begins by using a combination of deep, rhythmic kneading movements working over the top of the upper back, neck, shoulders and then on to the head. The head is then worked. The scalp and muscles in the head are squeezed, rubbed, pinched and tapped. The face and head are worked using pressure point techniques. People may find that after the treatment they feel tired, but very relaxed. Hair might be slightly greasy, but it's nothing that a wash won't sort out.

Body massage – This form of therapy involves using the hands to perform movements on the skin to promote well-being, relaxation and healing. The main techniques involve rubbing, pressing, kneading and stroking. Aromatherapy massages uses essential oils derived from flowers, leaves, stalks, plants and the roots of certain trees.

When the body is touched, receptors in the skin send messages to the brain causing the release of chemicals such as endorphins. These produce a sense of relaxation and well-being, and can relieve pain. Massage also improves the flow of blood and lymph fluid, helps to eliminate waste products from the body, relaxes the muscles and can stimulate the immune system. Massage is used to treat specific ailments also, such as depression, neck and back pain and insomnia.

Before the treatment begins, the therapist will give a full consultation about health and lifestyle. For a full body massage, all clothing is normally removed, with towels covering the parts of the body which are not to be massaged. However, clothes can be kept on if the recipient is uncomfortable. The recipient will lie on a massage table in a quiet room. The massage will normally start at the feet, and the therapist will work methodically around the body. The treatment will take forty-five minutes to an hour. After the treatment, it is common to feel tired, but incredibly relaxed and de-stressed.

Art therapy – Art therapy offers the opportunity to explore intense or painful thoughts in a caring, supportive environment using art materials in the presence of a trained art therapist. No skills are needed as the art therapist offers guidance and support as well as the opportunity to explore issues of concern using art materials.

The overall aim of art therapy is to enable a client to effect change and growth on a personal level with art materials.

Before a session can take place, an initial consultation is taken to determine general health, medical treatment and lifestyle details. Art therapy can take form in many ways, for example creating batik, painting, collages, clay work and masks. Depending on the therapist, their place and method of work, art therapy can be done one to one or in a group.

Coping With Stress And Handling Your Emotions

Having anorexia creates astronomical amounts of stress, both for sufferers and their entire families. And the road to recovery will not make that stress go away! However, as the sufferer gains weight and gets better, it will naturally decrease. At the beginning of recovery, stress will most likely increase. But, hold tight, push your way through, learn to cope with the stress and you can be assured that it will gradually become less. The previous section contained some very good ideas for a number of stress-relieving therapies. This section gives examples of how as a family we coped with stress during this difficult time, and advice on what you and *your* family can do to reduce stress levels. This part also gives examples and advice on how to handle your emotions, which will be, no doubt, all over the place. As were ours.

Not all stress is bad. Strange to hear but true. A certain amount of stress is necessary to motivate you, and without pressures life would soon become boring and without much purpose. The trick is learning how to handle your stress in a positive and practical way.

How you as an individual react to stress depends on whether you see yourself as being in control of a situation or overwhelmed by it.

You don't need vast amounts of time to reduce stress, just try some of these
Smile!
Pet a friendly dog or cat.
Don't know all the answers to every single thing.
Look for the silver lining in something you feel has gone wrong.
Say something nice to someone.
Stop saying negative things to yourself.
Ask a friend for a hug.
Say hello to a stranger.
Buy yourself a flower.
Look at a work of art.

It's a fact of life; we are all extremely busy human beings leading chaotic lives one way or another. However, it is vital, as a human being, to allow time to yourself every single day. Whether it's five minutes or an hour, you need to make it happen; time just for you. Here are various ways of relieving stress and spending time on you, varying from five minutes to a couple of hours. You'll be pleasantly surprised what you can do to help yourself in such a short time.

Here are some techniques to use if you have a spare five minutes. They can be used by anyone at any time, in school, at the office or at home. They have all been tried and tested and proven to work! There are also suggestions for twenty minutes, an hour and longer, if you can provide yourself with that time.

Five minute stress-busters

- Massage the palm of your hand using circular movements.
- Rub your temples and ears using your thumb and first two fingers.
- Rub your scalp and run your fingers through your hair.

This helps relieve tension.

- Eat a piece of chocolate.
- Read a short poem.
- Sing.
- Listen to a relaxing piece of music.

Twenty minute stress-busters

- Sit in a really comfortable chair, put your feet up, have a nice warm / cool drink by your side and read a chapter from your favourite book, or an article from a magazine or newspaper.
- Make a phone call to a friend who you know will make you laugh and smile. Talking and laughing are both fantastic stress busters.
- Sit in a comfortable chair and close your eyes. Focus on the rhythm of your breathing. Allow your whole body to become limp and loose. Imagine a relaxing scene, it could be a beach with waves lapping gently at the sandy shore, a field filled with beautiful flowers on a sunny day, a woodland glade with sunlight streaming through the green leaves on the trees.
- Take your time making a delicious coffee or hot chocolate. Sit in a comfortable chair and drink it from your favourite mug, maybe with a biscuit or two.
- Put the radio on. There's a good chance you'll find a radio show to make you laugh, or one with a song on that you love and want to sing along to.

One hour and more stress-busters

- Run a warm bath, add some lovely oils or bubble bath and soak your stress away.
- Have a full body massage.
- Attend a yoga class.
- Watch a good television programme or film.
- Take a nap.
- Go for a short walk (NOT a jog or a run. Just a relaxing stroll).
- Write a short story, poem or an article.

- Do a watercolour painting.
- Sketch.
- Meditate.
- Go shopping for something really special.

Here are some other creative ways to relax and de-stress

Keeping A Scrapbook

We all have at least one interest or passion in life and what better way to illustrate them than by putting together a scrapbook? You might idolise a football star or know everything about a television show or book. Whatever you feel passionately about, you can keep a scrapbook about it. You don't need to spend much money on this pastime, as all you need is a large grey page scrapbook or a blank notebook, some glue and scissors. Anything that you collect, stick it in. You could even keep one of your own life and chart your progress. Fill it with photos, poems and drawings. It would be a fantastic heirloom to pass down to your children's children.

Writing In A Journal

A journal is a record that you keep of impressions, feelings, emotions and responses over a long time. It is different from a diary, as it doesn't have to be filled in every day. You can add something to it once a week, or month if you wish. In it you record what experiences have happened to you during that time. As years go by, you will see patterns and notice changes and progress.

Logging your life experiences in a journal is a great way of looking back and seeing how far you have come and how much you have managed to change. A journal is also a fantastic thing to pour your heart out to. You can ramble all you like, and it will not complain! Remember, your journal is yours and yours only. Display it only if you want to.

Here are some ideas of things you could put in your journal
How things happened to you on a particular day.
What was the reason for them happening?
How you felt inside when they happened.
What your response was.

How you felt about it afterwards.

What steps you took to recover the situation or celebrate it.

How you feel about such events ever happening again and how you believe you would handle them.

Of course, it is your journal and in it you can write whatever you want to. There are no rules. Follow your creative mind.

Keeping a reading journal

For this pastime it is important to have an interest in reading! You'll need a notebook, pen and a heap of books. (I adore reading, so invested in a beautiful velvet notebook, and a fountain pen to record the books I'd read.) Keeping a reading journal is a really good way of recording your reading habits and the styles of the authors you read. Note the book you read, who wrote it, why you read it, and what you thought of it overall. You will most likely discover that you will begin to read far more widely after keeping a reading journal for a few months. You will wish to investigate characters, the setting and the atmosphere created. The characters within the books you read may well provide you with solutionsto specific questions you subconsciously need to know the answers to, through the ways in which they handle situations within themselves and with other people and the world around them

Writing your life story in 50 words or less

I learnt this activity from a creative writing teacher and found that it worked brilliantly. It's a fantastic way to combine creativity with confronting your life, and the various changes that you need to make to it. Think for about five minutes about your life so far. Then put your thoughts and feelings into simple and direct words, they don't even need to be put into sentences if you don't want them to be. This technique helps you to think about who you are as a person, and where you have come in your life. You will find that the real truths of your life will stand out. You will hopefully then be able to take steps to make any changes or improvements to your life that are needed.

Example:

Born. Grew. Badly treated. Lost. Found. Picked myself up. Learnt to love. Learnt to forgive. Devastation. Found salvation. Happy at last.

(21 words)

Creating a family newsletter

This is a brilliant way to bring your family closer together, and is also a fantastic 'rainy day' or 'boring weekend' satisfier. It's easy, cheap, fun and a wonderful way of keeping in touch with family who may be living long distances away or overseas, if it's saved on a computer, the newsletter could be emailed. It can be handwritten using brightly coloured pencils or pens, or produced on a computer using funky font sizes and colours. It really doesn't matter how, all that does matter is that you make sure that every family member contributes. Children could draw pictures or write a short poem, teenagers could write articles, parents could write something about the family history or the choices of what to eat for dinner! The list of possibilities is endless. Be creative and create something unique and special.

Keeping a dream journal

Keeping a dream journal is an easy and compelling way of finding out what is worrying us. All you need is a pad of paper and a pen placed by your bed. Every morning as soon as you wake up, jot down what you can remember from your dream. If you cannot remember anything then put down the first thought that came into your head. Alternatively, you could set your alarm for a few hours after you lie down to sleep, and, when you wake up to switch off your alarm, write down what you had been dreaming about and then go back to sleep. It is important that you keep the journal for at least a month before attempting to make some sense of what's been written. There are many books available on reading your dreams. Search them out and look up what has been happening in yours. It is a possibility that you might be able to find solutions, if so, you will be able to take steps towards dealing with the underlying problems.

Better breathing

I struggle greatly with my breathing at times of stress, and Mum taught me some important methods of 'controlling my breathing'. When we are stressed we breathe fast, which makes us feel stressed, which makes us breathe fast and so continues the stressed-out cycle. Take a few minutes and try some deep breathing. Below are two tips to use, which will help to calm your nervous system and decrease your stress. Do these whenever you find that you are starting to feel tense, fidgety or stressed.

Exhale for a count of six, inhale for a count of three and repeat for about three minutes.

Breathe in through your nose, for a count of five, and out through your mouth for a count of ten. Repeat this ten times.

Getting a good night's sleep

Believe it or not getting a good night's sleep is a fantastic stress-buster. Below are some tips on how to achieve a good night's sleep.

• Eat foods which contain carbohydrates before going to bed, such as peanut butter on wholemeal toast.

• Drink a milky drink such as Horlicks, Ovaltine, or hot chocolate, which are perfect for inducing sleep as they contain both milk and malt.

• Play a relaxing CD, sometimes after a hectic day it can be difficult to sleep in a quiet room.

• Keep a 'sleep book'. This is a notebook in which you write down all your worries before you go to sleep and don't open it again until the morning when you are fresh and awake, ready to face the day ahead.

Handling And Expressing Your Emotions

It's a well-known fact that every one of us feels anger at some point, but do you handle it well, or bottle it up inside? Below are some tips, which may help you to express how you are feeling when you are angry, down or just plain miserable.

• If someone has irritated, hurt or upset you, try to say so to them directly (there is no need to be rude), something along the lines of: what you said/did hurt my feelings/annoyed me. Try to be direct and express your feelings when you very first feel them.

- Don't try to blame other people for how you feel, and remember that it is OK to feel anger and frustration.
- When you feel like releasing your anger in a physical way, do not hit anyone! It's perfectly fine to hit a cushion or punch bag, but not another person.
- Try not to feel guilty about feeling angry or upset. Remember, it is human nature to have these feelings.

Anger is not constructive if:
- You bottle it up.
- You continually deny that it exists.
- You don't direct it at the right person.
- You turn it against yourself i.e. under-eating, over-exercising.

Chapter 46

Useful Contacts, How To Find Help, And Recommended Books

Listed in this chapter are telephone numbers and contact addresses for associations, which can provide you with help, support and guidance. These people know their business, and will provide you with information and reassurance, whether you are anorexic, a member of family or a friend.

There are also a number of highly recommended books about anorexia.

- Eating Disorders Association (EDA)

The EDA is a nationwide organisation, aiming to offer help, advice and support to sufferers and their families. They offer a telephone helpline, website, run self-help groups, send newsletters, reply to letters and provide information, advice and resources. Write, email or phone them for further details.

Website: www.edauk.com
Email: helpmail@edauk.com talkback@edauk.com
Address:
> Sackville Place
> 44 Magdalen Street
> Norwich
> Norfolk NR3 1JE

Youthline Up To 18:
0845 6341414 Monday–Friday 8.30am–8.30pm Saturday 1pm–4.30pm

- Childline

Childline is a confidential, sympathetic helpline for young people, and is active 24 hours a day, so whenever you feel the need to vent, pick up the phone. They are there to help you.
Helpline: 0181-514 1177

- MIND Redcar And Cleveland

MIND are a team based in the north-east of England, and help with all sorts of mental health issues from anorexia to depression.
Helpline:
01642-2996054
Leaflet:
Understanding Eating Distress

Contact Details

Website: www.lifeafteranorexia.com

My website offers guidance on anorexia and how to help yourself on the road to recovery, as well as providing an opportunity to see your work published on the site. It offers support with weight gain, and good eating. There are details from articles featuring me and my work, a guest book where you can leave your own thoughts about the site and much, much more.

Rosemary and Tony's contact details –

Email: parents@lifeafteranorexia.com

Books

- **Anorexia And Bulimia: How to help**
By Marilyn Duker and Rodger Slade
Published by the Open University Press

This is a very straightforward, to the point book, explaining everything that you need to know about anorexia from the first symptoms, right through to recovery, using easy to understand language. It is the book that has assisted me more than any other on the road to recovery.

- **Anorexia Nervosa : Finding The Life Line**
By Patricia M. Stein RD, MS, MA. and Barbra C. Unell
Published by Comp Care Publishers

This book provides insights into the worlds of recovering anorexics and has a large emphasis on anorexia in males which is more often than not forgotten about. It also offers clear and vital information and lists of practical prevention guidelines for parents.

- **Anorexia And Obesity : A Sense Of Proportion**
By Peter Dally and Joan Gomez
Published by Faber and Faber

The authors of this book have both had vast experience in the treatment of eating disorders and combine acute psychological analysis with much needed advice and information. It is a must-read for both parents and sufferers.

A family is an extremely important part of life. Don't lose touch with yours, whatever happens. And the same applies to your friends too. Losing touch is possible even when you are together in the same house. You can become completely detached from one another when you have an unwanted guest to stay.

Spend time with your family, share jokes and laughs, share your love and affection with each other, and enjoy life together. Grit your teeth when the going gets tough, and plough through your problems to come through triumphant and happy. Your family is valuable. Your family is irreplaceable. Remember this.

The same applies to your life. You only live *this* life once. You only have one family to live it with. Make the most of every day, every minute, every moment that you have together and every moment that *you*, as a person, have on this planet. There isn't time to worry about eating an ice cream or sleeping longer than usual. Enjoy your ice cream and enjoy your sleep. Live for the moment. Live for *you*.

Don't let an anorexia demon dictate how you live your life. Live this one life as you. It's your body, your mind, your spirit, your soul, and your life and you have to make your own decisions about how you live it.

We sincerely hope that this book, which has shown you visions of our daily lives as a family travelling the road to recovery together, will help you whether you are a sufferer, a carer, a sibling or a friend and help you on your journey and to success.

Remember, help is all around you. Reach out and someone will take your hand to guide you and to guide the ones you love.

Rosemary, Tony, Katie, Penny, Anthony and Sam Metcalfe

Help! I'm being bullied
by Dr Emily Lovegrove

An empowering workbook for the families of bullied children

Dr Emily Lovegrove, an expert on the psychology of bullying, has written this book to help both the children who are being bullied, and their parents. It is based on her research and work with many hundreds of young people and their families.

Whilst there are books aimed at teachers on this topic, this is the first book on the subject written especially for the parents of bullied children. It features a new approach to bullies and bullying that has been enormously successful.

DR. EMILY LOVEGROVE specialises in anti-bullying techniques. Working with parents, children, hospitals and schools, she lectures worldwide. Emily's work has been internationally reported and she has appeared extensively on TV - including BBC Newsround, GMTV and Sky - and BBC radio.

ISBN 1905170343   **Price £7.99**